Austria in the Age of

the French Revolution

1789-1815

AUSTRIA IN THE AGE OF THE FRENCH REVOLUTION

1789-1815

Edited by

Kinley Brauer

and

William E. Wright

Center for Austrian Studies

University of Minnesota

Minneapolis, Minnesota

1990

Copyright © by the Center for Austrian Studies
University of Minnesota.
309 Social Science Bldg.
Minneapolis, Minnesota 55455
All rights reserved.
Printed in the United States of America

The Center for Austrian Studies was founded in 1977 with a gift from the Austrian people to the University of Minnesota on the occasion of America's bicentennial. Its mandate is to serve as the focal point in North America for the study of Austria across disciplines: in the humanities, the social sciences, the applied sciences, and the fine arts. It pursues its mission by encouraging research on Austrian-related themes, by sponsoring symposia and conferences, by promoting student and faculty exchanges, and by publishing the *Austrian History Yearbook* and the fruits of its symposia.

Library of Congress Cataloging-in-Publication Data

Austria in the age of the French Revolution, 1789-1815 / edited by Kinley Brauer and William E. Wright
  p.   cm.
ISBN 0-9626990-0-4
1. Austria—History—1789-1815—Congresses. 2. Austria—Civilization—Congresses. 3. France—History—Revolution, 1789-1799—Influence—Congresses. I. Brauer, Kinley J. II. Wright, William E. (William Edward), 1926-   . III. University of Minnesota. Center for Austrian Studies.
DB76.A96   1990
943.6'03—dc20   90-40654
                                                            CIP

Cover: Photo by Susan Wood, courtesy of Charlotte Stokes
Design by Lois Stanfield

CONTENTS

CONTRIBUTORS ix

PREFACE xiii

INTRODUCTION xvii

THE AUSTRIAN ENLIGHTENMENT AND THE
FRENCH REVOLUTION 1
Ernst Wangermann

AUSTRIA'S ROAD TO AUSTERLITZ 11
Karl A. Roider, Jr.

THE PROUD ADVERSARIES: MASSÉNA AND THE
ARCHDUKE CHARLES 25
Donald D. Horward

THE PAPACY, AUSTRIA, AND THE ANTI-FRENCH
STRUGGLE IN ITALY, 1792-1797 47
Alan J. Reinerman

TAMING THE EAGLES: THE HABSBURG
MONARCHY'S POLITICAL USE OF THE
"REVOLUTIONARY" NEOCLASSICAL STYLE 69
Charlotte Stokes

ANTONIO CANOVA AND AUSTRIAN ART POLICY .. 83
Christopher M.S. Johns

THE CALL TO REVOLUTION IN THE BOUDOIR:
A NEW LOOK AT MOZART'S SUSANNA IN
THE MARRIAGE OF FIGARO 91
Doris P. Tishkoff

BEETHOVEN, THE REVOLUTION IN MUSIC AND THE
FRENCH REVOLUTION: MUSIC AND POLITICS IN
AUSTRIA, 1790-1815 107
John J. Haag

POLITICAL THEATER IN THE AGE OF REVOLUTION:
MOZART'S *LA CLEMENZA DI TITO* 125
John A. Rice

FEMALE SELF-DETERMINATION IN THE EARLY
DRAMAS OF FRANUL VON WEISSENTHURN 151
George W. Reinhardt

THE ORIGIN OF THE AUSTRIAN NATIONAL ANTHEM
AND AUSTRIA'S LITERARY WAR EFFORT 163
Hugo Schmidt

THE *WIENER ZEITUNG* REPORTS ON THE FRENCH
REVOLUTION 185
Alex Balisch

ILLUSTRATIONS

Schönbrunn palace 70

Franz Anton Zauner, The *Monument to Emperor Josef II* .. 76

Antonio Canova, *Theseus and the Centaur* 77

Peter von Nobile, Temple of Theseus 79

Antonio Canova, *Hercules and Lichas* 84

Antonio Canova, Tomb of the Archduchess Maria Christina of Austria 85

Title page of a piano-vocal score of Mozart's *La clemenza di Tito* 140

MAPS

Italian Campaign of 1797: Masséna's Pursuit of the Archduke Charles 31

Ulm Campaign 36

Campaign of 1809: Ratisbon Phase 39

Campaign of 1809: Wagram Phase (First Day) 41

Campaign of 1809: Wagram Phase (Second Day) 43

CONTRIBUTORS

ERNST WANGERMANN, professor of Austrian history at the University of Salzburg, studied at and graduated from Balliol College, Oxford, and was lecturer, senior lecturer, and reader at Leeds University from 1962 to 1984. He has published *From Joseph II to the Jacobin Trials* (1959; 2nd ed., 1969), *The Austrian Achievement, 1700-1800* (1973), and *Aufklärung u. staatsbürgerliche Erziehung. Gottfried van Swieten als Reformator des österreichischen Unterrichtswesens 1781-1791* (1978). He is currently researching the popular political and religious literature under Joseph II and Leopold II.

KARL F. ROIDER, JR. is currently professor and chair of the History Department at Louisiana State University, Baton Rouge. His most recent publications include *Austria's Eastern Question, 1700-1790* (1982) and *Baron Thugut and Austria's Response to the French Revolution* (1987).

DONALD D. HORWARD, professor of history at Florida State University, is a specialist in Napoleonic history. His publications include nine volumes, the latest being *Napoleon in Iberia: The Twin Sieges of Ciudad Rodrigo and Almeida, 1810* (1984), *Napoleonic Military History, A Bibliography* (1987), and *Napoleon in America* (with Robert Holtman, 1988), and thirty-five articles and chapters in edited works. He has held both the Chair of Military History at the United States Military Academy at West Point and the Conquest Chair of Humanities at Virginia Military Institute. His program in Napoleonic studies at Florida State University is among the most active such programs in the United States.

ALAN J. REINERMAN, associate professor of history at Boston College, is completing a study of *Austria and the Papacy in the*

Age of Metternich, 1809-1848, two volumes of which have appeared: *Between Conflict and Cooperation, 1809-1830* (1979), and *Revolution and Reaction, 1830-1838* (1989). He is now at work on a third volume covering the years 1838-1848.

CHARLOTTE STOKES is chair of the Department of Art and Art History at Oakland University, Michigan. She has published extensively on the surrealist artist Max Ernst and is currently writing a book about his collages, "From the Edges of Floating Worlds." She researched neoclassicism while academic director for the Midwest Consortium for Study Abroad in Vienna in 1987.

CHRISTOPHER M.S. JOHNS, assistant professor of art history in the McIntire Department of Art of the University of Virginia, has published articles on various aspects of eighteenth- and nineteenth-century art in both American and European journals. In residence at the American Academy in Rome in 1990, he is completing a book-length study on "Papal Art Patronage and Cultural Politics in Early Eighteenth-Century Rome."

DORIS P. TISHKOFF, assistant professor in the Social Sciences Department at Springfield College, Massachusetts, is a cultural historian of the eighteenth century whose special interest is the intersections of music, literature, social change, and the emerging role of women in the arts. Her publications include articles on Nancy Storace, literature and social change, the Enlightenment, and numerous music critiques and reviews. She is presently completing a book-length study entitled, "Mozart, Nancy Storace, and the 'Language of the Heart'," concerning the collaboration of Mozart with the singer who created the role of Susanna in *The Marriage of Figaro*.

JOHN HAAG, associate professor of history at the University of Georgia, received his doctorate from Rice University in 1969. He has published in the *Austrian History Yearbook*, *The Journal of Contemporary History*, *Central European History*, and other journals and is presently writing biographies of Egon Erwin Kisch, Max Hoelz, and Othmar Spann. He is especially interested in the interrelationship between music and politics in Central Europe between 1870 and 1950.

JOHN A. RICE, visiting assistant professor in the Department of Music at Colby College, studied classics and history at Harvard University and music history at the University of California. His book on Mozart's *La clemenza di Tito* is scheduled for publication in 1991 by Cambridge University Press as part of their Opera Handbook series.

GEORGE REINHARDT, late associate professor in the German section of the Department of Modern and Classical Languages at the University of Connecticut, was a specialist in German literature of the nineteenth century. He published widely in a number of edited works and professional journals. Professor Reinhardt died suddenly in January 1990 after a brief illness.

HUGO SCHMIDT, professor of German at the University of Colorado at Boulder, is the editor of Hofmannsthal's *Arabella* (1963), co-editor of a bilingual edition of Brecht's *Hauspostille* (1966, 1967), author of *Nikolaus Lenau* (1971) and of numerous articles on nineteenth- and twentieth-century Austrian and German literature, especially Grillparzer, Lenau, Hofmannsthal, Hauptmann, Stifter, Brecht, and Canetti. He has also made several translations and has a special interest in literary history and history as reflected in literature.

ALEX BALISCH, associate professor of history *emeritus* at the Memorial University of Newfoundland, has published "Die Entstehung des Exerzierreglements von 1749" in *Mitteilungen des österreichischen Staatsarchivs*, 27 (1974) and "Infantry Battlefield Tactics in the Seventeenth and Eighteenth Centuries in the European and Turkish Theatres of War" in *Studies in History and Politics*, III (1983/84). He is presently researching the officer corps of Maria Theresa.

PREFACE

In 1977 in commemoration of the bicentennial of American independence, the people and government of Austria presented the University of Minnesota a gift of one million dollars for the purpose of establishing a Center for Austrian Studies. The objective of the Center was to promote Austrian studies in the United States and to facilitate connections between Austrian and American scholars.

Under the directorship of William E. Wright, the Center quickly became involved in a wide variety of activities aimed at fulfilling its mandate. One such activity has been the holding of annual symposia. During its first decade, participants from Austria and other countries have joined American scholars to present papers on a variety of historical, cultural, and contemporary issues. With but one exception, a symposium on the Revolutions of 1848, all of the previous symposia have dealt with issues in late nineteenth- and twentieth-century Austria.

As the Center began its second decade last year, Professor Wright stepped down as director, and I became interim director until the university appointed a new permanent director. Among my first tasks was the selection of a symposium topic for the following year. It seemed to me that a changing of the guard at the Center, coinciding as it did with the international commemoration of the French Revolution provided a unique opportunity for widening the range of the Center symposia. After discussions with several colleagues at the University of Minnesota and the former director, we decided to examine Austria during the age of the French Revolution. And to open up participation to young scholars and those who had not been involved with (or in some cases had not even been aware of) the Center for Austrian Studies, we decided to invite only a few established authorities to participate and to solicit proposals for papers openly and widely from specialists in all disciplines.

The response to the Center's decision to move into the late eighteenth and early nineteenth centuries was uniformly enthusiastic both in the United States and in Austria. Although the Center was competing with a large number of societies and institutions around the world for papers, proposals and suggestions for presentations and sessions poured into Center's office. Most heartening was the eagerness with which younger scholars in fields under-represented in previous Center activities submitted titles for our consideration. Clearly, the study of Austrian history, music, art, and literature in this period is flourishing in North America. The essays published in this collection represent those selected by a special committee of the Center for the symposium.

The symposium, held at the University of Minnesota on 11-13 May 1989, brought together individuals from Austria, England, Canada, and the United States, specializing in the disciplines of history, art history, music, theater, journalism, and literature. The meetings were remarkable both for the congeniality of the participants and the easy and fruitful way in which the participants in quite distinct and discrete specialties discussed common topics and themes from different but complementary perspectives. There was an excellent willingness to share ideas and insights and to argue in constructive ways.

While it has always been the intention of the Center to publish the papers of its symposia, such has rarely been possible. The press of time, the nature of the papers, and a variety of other considerations have resulted in the publication of only one previous symposium, the first offered by the Center in 1978, entitled *Austria Since 1945* (1982). This publication signifies a renewed determination by the Center to publish the papers of future symposia. In the present case, all but two of the papers presented at the 1989 symposium are included in this volume.

Many individuals were involved in both the symposium and the publication of its papers. We are is deeply indebted to Professor Stanley Engebretson of the University of Minnesota School of Music, who chaired the symposium paper selection committee, and the members of his committee, Charles Haxthausen (Art History), and Frank Hirschbach (German). Their deliberations were superbly aided by the participation of Emeritus Professor R. John Rath, whose many and important contributions to the study of Austrian history over the past thirty years are most highly regarded. We extend our special thanks to Professor Rath.

The symposium, itself, was highly successful, not the least due to the financial support provided by the Austrian Cultural Institute in New York and the Austrian government. We especially wish to thank Dr. Wolfgang Waldner of the Cultural Institute for his aid and encouragement. Similarly, we are grateful to Professor J. Kim Munholland, director of the University of Minnesota Center for West European Area Studies, who also helped underwrite the costs of the meeting. In addition to those colleagues at the University of Minnesota mentioned above, we also thank Paul Bamford, Stanford Lehmberg, and Helga Leitner, each of whom participated in the symposium and helped make it a success.

In preparing this volume, we thank Dr. Barbara Brauer for her aid in editing and translation, and James Brown, editor of the Center for Austrian Studies *Newsletter* for making available his computer expertise.

Finally, we are especially grateful to Professor David F. Good, the new permanent director of the Center for Austrian Studies. Professor Good has provided enthusiastic support and encouragement throughout for the publication of this edition. The Center has assumed the entire costs of publication.

Kinley Brauer

Minneapolis, Minnesota
April, 1990

INTRODUCTION

The thoughts and deeds of our eighteenth-century forbears proved to be powerful forces in shaping the course of subsequent developments in European and American history. The American Declaration of Independence, the United States Constitution, the Declaration of the Rights of Man and the Citizen, and, in general, the ideas and principles of the Enlightenment produced most of the standards by which we measure the validity and justice of our practices today. Much of the turmoil of the nineteenth and twentieth centuries was engendered by our having failed to measure up to those ideals or by the several challenges to the righteousness of those ideals. The challenges, both from the Right and from the Left, to the precepts of the eighteenth century have been unsuccessful, but overcoming the challenges has sometimes been very costly in both blood and treasure.

Americans are inclined to think that their war for independence, the American Revolution, was the focal event of the century and should rightly be the focal point of contemporary attention to the eighteenth century. Indeed, the American Revolution, and the attendant documents of American notions about the people and their society enjoy a great deal of attention and respect. But the North American colonies, soon to be the new United States, were far from central to the main body of European society, and the unfolding of the history of that society, until the middle of the twentieth century. Whatever took place in North America, no matter how intriguing or useful in arguing principles, was not necessarily to be held as determining for Europe or the larger world. Furthermore, the Americans had not wrought a true revolution; they had conducted a war for independence to gain the right to shape their society as seemed appropriate to them, but the shaping would be done evolutionarily—not revolutionarily—and that evolution would unfold in a set of circumstances that were in many ways quite different from those of Europe. The American experience could not be as influential in the great scheme of things as would an event such as the French Revolution.

The great French Revolution of the eighteenth century was the most profoundly wrenching experience in modern European history and the most far-reaching and influential phenomenon of our times. If the Revolution was not as efficacious in remolding society as its protagonists wished and expected it to be, it was not for want of their trying. The revolutionaries intended to work a fundamental change in the social and political fabric. Certainly, their efforts brought extraordinary upheaval before society settled back into conditions that were neither what the revolutionaries envisioned nor a restoration of the *status quo ante* revolution. But if the revolutionaries had not made over France and Europe in the image of their vision, they did change for all time, for good or for ill, the way in which Western society looks at itself and the way in which social issues are stated and treated. The nineteenth and twentieth centuries have been laced with convulsions—the most salient of which were the revolutions of 1848 and the Russian Revolution—that trace their ancestry to the French Revolution of 1789.

It is not only in spectacular eruptions, however, that influences of the French Revolution are to be found. As the authors in this volume make known, there were many more ways in which the Revolution exerted influence on Europeans or prompted from them response to its ideas or acts. One finds the spoor of the French Revolution in the military, in the arts, in journalism, in public policy.

When one examines the radiation of the effects of the French Revolution into other reaches of Europe, Austria makes an especially interesting case study for a couple of reasons. First, since the Protestant Reformation and the Catholic Counter-Reformation, the House of Habsburg had been the champion of the resurgent Church and of a conservative social and political order. Their Austrian lands were the bastion of conservatism in Central Europe, opposing heresy in every quarter, forbidding new-fangled thought from the West to enter into Austria, cultivating a feudal aristocracy, maintaining the stilted Spanish etiquette at court, and, symbolically as well as practically, reaffirming the old order of things.

Another reason why a study of the influence of the French Revolution in Austria is interesting is that Austria was subjected to a kind of revolution from above in the second half of the eighteenth century, the experience being especially traumatic during the decade of Joseph II, on the eve of the revolution in France. The lands of the Habsburg monarchy seemed to be a most unlikely place for a great reform-program to be executed in the eighteenth century, especially if the reforms were to be of the kind that cured some of the ills that the *philosophes* railed so about. But Empress Maria Theresa, during her long reign from 1740 to 1780, conducted a program of reforms that would change the nature of the constitution and administration of the Habsburg empire. One should be quick to point out that, although her reforms anticipated, in many respects, the program of the revolutionaries in France, she was nowise inspired by the preachments of the *philosophes*. The empress was moved, rather, by most practical needs and carried out her reforms despite her distaste for all things that had the odor of the Enlightenment upon them.

The defeats of her armies on the field of battle and, emphatically, the loss of Silesia to Frederick II in the Wars of the Austrian Succession, made Maria Theresa painfully aware of the woeful state of the organization and administration of the Habsburg lands. The loss of Silesia not only wounded her pride—losing *anything* to "that wicked man" in Prussia wounded her pride—but it also diminished the wealth of her realm by a very great amount. She deemed it to be necessary, then, to recover Silesia. To do that, however, she would have to have a bigger and better-trained army. Such an army would cost substantially more than the imperial coffers contained or than could be raised in taxes, given the existing fiscal machinery at her government's disposal. She would have to find efficient ways to collect taxes; to do that she would have to rationalize her outmoded, uncoordinated administration, still largely in the hands of provincial estates, where there was much less concern for the prosperity of the dynasty than there was for the preservation of local aristocratic privilege. The taxes that were being collected were finding their way, more often than not, to other destinations than the imperial treasury.

Therefore, in order to get the money to build the army to recover the wealth of Silesia, Maria Theresa had to take the reins of administration, especially those of the fiscal system, closer into hand. That would entail a fundamental alteration in the relation of the crown to the estates of the various *Länder*, the diets of which were interposed between the government of the crown and the *Land*. It would be necessary to circumvent the estates and govern—and tax—directly from Vienna, no mean undertaking! The kind of people whom the empress needed to accomplish a task of such magnitude were not in abundant supply in Austria, for there was no numerous, sophisticated, politically able bourgeoisie as there was in the West. But there were some men, most of them noblemen, who were capable and willing to do her work; they were people who were conversant with enlightened thought. Thus when Maria Theresa took them into her service to achieve her practical objectives, she also put them into position to bring enlightened rationalism to bear on Austrian affairs.

Once Maria Theresa was embarked on a course of reform, she found that each element touched on others, and one change demanded others. It was of little advantage to tax directly if the peasants were too poor to pay taxes. This led her to take measures to improve the lot of the peasant serfs on private estates and to initiate abolition of *robota* on her cameral estates. Further, she began a reform of the law codes (but was reluctant to abolish judicial torture), rationalized the system of courts, and established a system of appellate courts, even to a supreme court in Vienna. She required that judges be trained and competent. She revised the system of taxation in order to make the burden of taxes fall more equitably; the nobility were called upon to shoulder some of the burden along with the commoners. If the lower classes were to profit fully from their bettered condition and prosper enough to pay taxes, they would need to be educated; so she established secular, state-supported, compulsory schools for elementary education. And, although she was a most pious Catholic, the Church did not escape her reforming attention. She asserted the *Placetum Regium*, intervened in the financial management of some of the orders, reduced the number of holidays and pilgrimages, and generally reminded the Church of its secular as well as its spiritual duties.

Maria Theresa's whole program of reforms was too elaborate

to be detailed here, but, taken altogether, the reforms of the empress launched Austria onto a course toward the development of a modern state with centrally focussed power and bureaucratic machinery to exercise that power in control of all public affairs.

It is no surprise that the prelates of the Church and the *Länder* were much discommoded and grumbled in opposition to the empress' changes. But if they chafed at the reforms of Maria Theresa, worse was yet to come after 1780, when the empress died and was succeeded by her son Joseph II. What Joseph would do in the decade of his reign would make the old order of Austria positively boil, for Joseph, as if he had a presentiment of the brevity of his time, took reforms farther and more swiftly than his mother had done.

Joseph quickly declared the abolition of censorship, the toleration of the principal religions in addition to Roman Catholicism (which remained the religion of state), further reduced the number of holidays, forbade pilgrimages, raised the age at which men could take holy orders, set out to abolish contemplative ("unproductive") orders, took over the training of clergy and the delineation of episcopal sees, extended the emancipation of peasants to private estates as well as to cameral, revised the land tax to equalize the incidence of taxation on peasants and noble lords, abolished judicial torture, equalized persons before the law, furthered the rationalization of the law codes, increased support to public education, made known his contempt for the privileged and unproductive, whether they were aristocrats or churchmen, and had declared that everyone and everything must be bent to serve the common weal or suffer disqualification to enjoy the benefits of the community.

To the old order, already under pressure for the forty years of Maria Theresa's reign, Joseph's ten years posed an intolerable provocation and threat. And, when in Joseph's final year the French Revolution erupted, it confirmed all the worst fears of the privileged and gave new life to their foreboding convictions that reform such as they had experienced at the hands of their monarchs led inevitably to revolution just as the agitation of the enlightened *philosophes* had led to revolution in France. One could expect only catastrophe and destruction of all civility and proper order in society if one permitted reformers to have their way.

The beneficiaries of the old order in Austria understood, as

Professor Wangermann points out in his essay in these pages, that enlightened reform did not diminish the zeal for change and afford immunity against revolution, but rather tended to sweep society along toward more, even revolutionary change. For this reason, when Joseph's brother, Leopold II, a man at least as enlightened and even more able than Joseph, succeeded to the Austrian throne, the powers of the old order clamored unceasingly for restoration of their world and insisted on revocation of the reforms that seemed to them to be simply the prelude to a revolution like the one that gripped France.

The first great influence of the French Revolution in Austria, then, was the stiffening of the opposition of the stalwarts of the established order against all reforms. The excesses of the Revolution gave them a means of embarrassing reformers and discrediting their programs of reform. Although the conservative forces of Austrian society could successfully campaign to compel Leopold to turn back the tide of reforms set in flood by his predecessor, they could not prevent influence of other kinds streaming from Revolutionary and Napoleonic France and coming to play in Austrian life, as the authors in this book attest.

In the first essay, Professor Wangermann, agreeing with de Tocqueville about the relationship between reform and revolution, sees the period of reform in Austria before the French Revolution not as a kind of immunization against revolution but rather as an inducement to revolution. Austrian officialdom and those sympathetic to the Enlightenment both saw the situation in the same light. As elsewhere in Europe, the government tried to stifle support for the French Revolution, or praise of it, in Austria; but, despite the Jacobin Trials and the Metternichian suppressions, it became evident with the outbreak of the revolution in 1848 that the spirit of the Enlightenment and of the French Revolution had survived.

Professors Horward and Roider look to the period of the Napoleonic wars to find a confrontation with the most striking early product of the French Revolution—Napoleon Bonaparte. Horward delineates the careers of Masséna and Archduke Charles, both of whom came to be successful commanders in the military but from markedly different origins and by quite different routes. They were symbolic of their two societies: Masséna climbed from the lowest rungs of the social ladder to the upper reaches;

Introduction xxiii

Archduke Charles stood at the very pinnacle of the Austrian social order because he was born to it. But they gained parallel successes in their profession of arms. Roider is concerned with Archduke Charles too, but he is primarily interested in the manner in which Austrian diplomacy and administration responded to the challenge of Bonaparte. Whereas Charles seemed to understand the nature of Napoleon and his threat, others responsible for Austrian affairs did not and therefore led Austria to defeat.

The papacy and Austria, the ecclesiastical and secular citadels, respectively, of the old order, are the subject of Professor Reinerman's discourse. They were both challenged at the same time and the same place when Napoleon's armies campaigned in northern Italy beginning in 1796. One might imagine that the Habsburg and the Vatican would be so sensible of their common interests in opposing Napoleon and the French that they would cooperate swiftly and efficiently to repel the threat. That was not the case, however; Austria and the papacy exemplified the fecklessness which so often marked the attempts of the *ancien régime* to resist the incursions of the Revolution and its offspring, Napoleon.

At the turn of the century, as Napoleon came to power in the world of politics, so did Ludwig van Beethoven begin to demonstrate his genius and come to dominate the world of music. Professor Haag finds in the man and in his music statements of belief in the ideals of the French Revolution, but he also finds some ambivalence about Napoleon as the propagator of those ideals. However, there was no ambivalence in Beethoven's espousal of the republican notions of freedom and equality that were being broadcast from France. For his sentiments in that regard, Beethoven was held in suspicion by Austrian officials, and he might have been harassed by the police had he not been protected by his close friendship with the Archduke Rudolf. Professor Haag accounts Beethoven to be one of those ". . . titanic forces in Western civilization that have made the world since 1789 uniquely creative and at times explosively unstable."

Where music and drama meet, in opera, Professor Rice and Professor Tishkoff deal with another kind of reflection of Revolutionary influence in Wolfgang Amadeus Mozart's *La clemenza di Tito* and *The Marriage of Figaro*. In the former, the librettist, Caterino Mazzolà, thoroughly rewrote the earlier version by Pietro Metastasio in order to make a pointed defense of enlightened monarchy, exemplified by Leopold II, and to caution against the excesses and evils of revolution as the French practiced it. The production in 1791 of *La clemenza di Tito* reveals a change of humor from the pre-revolutionary production of *The Marriage of Figaro*. In 1786, as Professor Tishkoff shows, Mozart and his librettist, Lorenzo da Ponte, were indulging in the rather common practice of chiding the aristocracy and allowing lackeys to outwit and bring down their noble masters. The theme of *Figaro*, taken from Pierre de Beaumarchais, was one regularly found in the literature of protest against the *ancien régime*, a literature which, it could be urged, helped to bring on the French Revolution. Mozart was not a political radical, his displays of irreverence and his affiliation with Freemasonry notwithstanding; but after the Revolution began to unfold, Mozart's irreverence gives way to a defense of the good in the Old Regime.

Professor Reinhardt recounts how Franul von Weissenthurn, especially in her comedy *Beschämte Eifersucht*, held the bourgeoise qualities and values emanating from France up to those of the Old Regime in such a way as to validate the new at the expense of the old. At the same time, with near-republican fervor, she used her talent as a dramatist to assert the worth and abilities of women and to persuade men that their relations with women would be more comforting and profitable if they recognized their women's worth. It was an argument based on rational considerations, the kind of reasoning in fashion in the eighteenth century and borne across Europe by its advocates during the Revolution.

The Revolution was a phenomenon that engendered great popular enthusiasm which could be marshalled to serve the purposes of the leaders. Revolutionary and patriotic verses and songs soon proved to be an effective device in directing the people's enthusiasm. Professor Schmidt recounts how Joseph Haydn, familiar with the British experience with the anthem "God Save the King," composed the Austrian anthem to inspire and capture popular support for the monarchy just as "La Marseillaise" had galvanized revolutionary fervor in France. Schmidt also cites other essays in literature which were designed to stir up patriotic passions. But precisely because these endeavors stirred passions, they smacked too much of revolution to suit Austrian officials and they were darkly suspicious of patriotic songs.

Introduction   xxv

It is to be expected that the Habsburgs would react to the French Revolution and Napoleon with regard to matters of art. States and dynasties have always done so. Professor Johns relates why Emperor Franz rejected Antonio Canova's *Hercules and Lichas* while accepting his Tomb of Archduchess Maria Christina. Professor Stokes discusses how the Habsburgs turned Revolutionary and Napoleonic art to their own purposes and, in the process, imported into Austria a French neoclassical art in which the French had imbued a bourgeois morality.

In the final essay, Professor Balisch reports that the *Wiener Zeitung*, the principal purveyor of news in Austria, brought information on the events in Revolutionary France swiftly and accurately. The reporting was factual and dispassionate, qualities not to be take for granted at that place and in the heat of those times—or, indeed, in any time!

The essays appearing here do not by any means present a compendium of the influences of the French Revolution on Austria, but they do offer the reader a wide, rather representative appreciation of some particular ways—some subtle, others not so subtle—in which the developments in Revolutionary and Napoleonic France were felt in Austria and how Austrians reacted to the influence of those developments.

William E. Wright

Minneapolis, Minnesota
April, 1990

THE AUSTRIAN ENLIGHTENMENT AND THE FRENCH REVOLUTION

by

Ernst Wangermann

Certainly everyone is aware of the standard view of the question raised in the title of this essay. It can be put like this: the enlightened reforms of Maria Theresa and Joseph II brought about many necessary changes in the Habsburg Monarchy by means of a "revolution from above," changes which in France were brought about by the violent upheaval of mass revolution. In this way, the reforms saved Austria from the blood and violence of the French Revolution.

Though it is possible to find this argument in the contemporary political literature, I find it unconvincing, particularly in the unqualified form in which it is often stated. Rather than considering reforms as an alternative to revolution, as something which makes revolution unnecessary, I am more persuaded by the Tocquevillian view that reforms may open up the way to revolution. The reforms of Maria Theresa and Joseph II, and the reaction to these reforms—both among conservatives and among the adherents of the Enlightenment—bear this out, and do so not only in the case of the Austrian Netherlands.

The conservative opposition to the reforms, the opposition of the traditionalist and curialist Churchmen and of the vested interests articulated through the Estates, brought the men of the Enlightenment onto the political battlefield to defend and justify the reforms with arguments taken from the well-stocked armory of the Enlightenment.

Now, whatever one may think of the merits of the arguments, the especially interesting aspect is that some of these champions of enlightened reform did not long confine themselves to defense and justification, but became critics themselves. They did not criticize the reforms as such, but rather criticized the manner of their execution. One striking example is Johann Friedel. He had made his name as a *Wiener Author* with a panegyric of the ecclesiastical reforms, typical in its uncritical praise of the reforming emperor. By 1786, he had become a critic, and wrote:

> To introduce a decree . . . bringing about a reform merely with the words: We decree this, because We who rule by the grace of God consider it conducive to the welfare of our subjects, has the one slight disadvantage . . . that the subject most humbly takes the liberty of doubting, whether it really is conducive to his welfare.[1]

With this wittily formulated thought, Friedel threw out a challenge to a fundamental thesis of Joseph II that only the Prince and his chosen advisers had a sufficiently broad view of public affairs to know what was in the general interest.[2] In the tract quoted, Friedel put forward a different thesis: "Ministers cannot by themselves discover everything that is relevant to the welfare of the country. The people must be able and be allowed to think about this themselves, and to make relevant proposals."[3] Thinking about the welfare of the country and making relevant proposals presupposes access to the necessary information, and Friedel, quite logically, included in the same tract the demand for freedom of information. He pointed to England as a country which enjoyed the "publicity of public affairs" which he was demanding, and referred to Necker's *Compte rendu au Roi* (1781) as a first step in this direction in France.[4]

Although nearly every publication advancing serious criticism of

---

[1]J. Friedel, *Historisch-philosophische u. statistische Fragmente, mehrentheils die österreichische Monarchie betreffend* (Leipzig, 1786), p. 33.
[2]Derek Beales, "Joseph II's Rêveries," *Mitteilungen des österreichischen Staatsarchivs*, XXXIII (1980), 155-160, esp. lines 15-17, 98-101.
[3]Friedel, *Historisch-philosophische . . . Fragmente*, p. 38.
[4]*Ibid.*, p. 37.

Joseph II's policies provoked a response in defense of these policies, research into the political publications appearing between 1785 and 1790 leads one to conclude that Friedel's tract was representative of a general trend in enlightened opinion in Austria. It was a trend which encouraged pamphleteers to explore political horizons beyond the limits of enlightened absolutism of the Josephinian variety. It was a trend towards some skepticism concerning absolutism as the best proposition in the long term for attaining enlightened reform; and, in proportion to the growth of this skepticism, grew a sense of the political maturity of the subject, entitling him (and it was still in the main a question of *him*) to share responsibility for his own and the general welfare.[5] The prevailing political vision was moving on from that of the enlightened absolute ruler philosophically promoting the welfare of his subjects, to that of an enlightened man of courage and honesty persuading the absolute ruler to give up some of his power and endow his subjects with political rights which would make them citizens. This trend was not confined to the Habsburg territories. There is, in fact, no better representation of it that the scene in the third act of Schiller's *Don Carlos*, published and first performed in 1787, in which the Marquis de Posa tries to persuade Philip II to restore political rights, to let flourish the sublime and proud virtues of freedom, and to make his kingdom a model of happiness which the rest of the world would have to imitate.[6]

If one bears in mind this trend and the vision arising from it, one will the better understand the intense interest and the great hopes which the news of the convocation of the Estates General in France aroused among the Austrian partisans of the Enlightenment. It was tempting to interpret what was happening in France as the process of this vision being turned into reality—with Necker playing the role of the Marquis de Posa and succeeding with Louis XVI where Posa had failed with Philip II: "In France

---

[5]See also Ernst Wangermann, "L'Idée de citoyenneté dans le cadre des Lumières autrichiennes," in *Actes du Colloque international de Belfort (October, 1988)* (Belfort, 1989), pp. 390-393.
[6]Friedrich Schiller, *Don Carlos, Infant von Spanien* (Stuttgart, 1979), pp. 108-110.

a light is being lit which will benefit the whole of humanity. Necker has persuaded the king to step down from the throne of despotism and to set an *exemplum sine exemplo* which sooner or later the whole world will have to follow. For this he deserves a golden monument."[7]

The person who saw the opening stages of the French Revolution in this optimistic light—as *Don Carlos* with a happy end—was Conrad Dominik Bartsch, editor of the *Wiener Zeitung*. His reporting of the subsequent developments in France was profoundly marked by the vision of humanity's progress into the realm of political maturity and freedom; and the same applies to most of the newspapers available in the Habsburg territories at this time.[8] Moreover, Austrians could not fail to be aware of the similarities between many of the decrees of the National Assembly and the reforms of Joseph II, especially with regard to ecclesiastical policy. But the greatest enthusiasm of the enlightened journalists was reserved for the fact that the French decrees were not issued on the basis of the arbitrary power of an absolute monarch, but adopted by a majority of the representatives of a sovereign people. All Louis XVI's actions symbolizing his willingness to accept a constitutional role, were reported prominently and with strong emotional undertones.[9] Louis himself was presented as deeply moved on these occasions, moved even to tears, and was thus made to conform to another cherished Enlightenment vision—that of the man who acts morally under the impulse of his tender emotions, sentimentally following the dictates of his heart. That these were the qualities the Enlightenment still *expected* from a ruler was the message conveyed to Leopold II in the Mazzolà-Mozart revival of *La*

---

[7]Bartsch to Hajnoczy 12 May 1789, quoted in Ernst Wangermann, *From Joseph II to the Jacobin Trials* (2nd ed., Oxford, 1969), p. 24.
[8]See *Wiener Zeitung* 60, 29 July 1789; *Wiener Zeitung* 62, 5 August 1789; for some provincial papers cf. D. Zwitter-Tehovnik, *Wirkungen der Französischen Revolution in Krain*, in *Veröffentlichungen des Historischen Instituts der Universitäts Salzburg*, XII (Vienna and Salzburg, 1975) p. 17.
[9]See, for example, *Wiener Blättchen*, 29 July 1790, pp. 458-459.

clemenza di Tito on the occasion of his coronation in Prague.[10] The story of Louis XVI's stepping down from the throne of despotism was reported in a way which clearly implied that this example would now have to be followed by other monarchs. Enlightened tracts in the years 1790 to 1792, especially those of Adolph Freiherr von Knigge, argued that monarchs who refused to go the way shown by or to Louis XVI would face revolutionary upheavals. The assertion which one can frequently find in the German and Austrian pamphlets of these years, that a revolution like that in France was not necessary east of the Rhine because in the *Reich* lived free subjects of enlightened rulers, could plausibly be interpreted as the same argument in a cautious and tactful guise.

It is therefore hardly surprising that the government in Vienna should quickly take alarm at the way events in France were being reported and should launch an ideological counteroffensive. In the summer of 1790, a book of modest dimensions appeared under the title *Betrachtungen über die Revolution und das sogenannte demokratische System in Frankreich. Herausgegeben von Friedrich Schilling, k.k. wirklichem Hofsekretär.*[11] Schilling was *Hofsekretär* and *éminence grise* at the Ministry of Police under Pergen. His name therefore gave the publication a semi-official character. It attempts a bold, though hardly profound, argument against the French Revolution, and rejects the Enlightenment assumptions which provided the basis for the hopes and enthusiasm which it had aroused. Inequality was natural, according to the author of the *Betrachtungen*, and therefore in the interests of all, also of the lower classes, who have no time to concern themselves with public affairs. Public affairs have to be managed by a directing class, and the subordination of the majority to the directing class is most conveniently secured by investing the latter with hereditary distinctions and privileges. These instill a "beneficent habit" of

---

[10] See esp. Act II, Sc 12, Tito's aria No. 20, Reclam Universal—Bibliothek 9926, Stuttgart 1986, p. 84:
   Se all'imperio, amici Dei,
   necessario è un cor severo;
   O togliete a me l'imperio,
   O a me date un altro cor.
[11] Wiener Stadt- u. Landesbibliothek, A 70688.

obedience and a "happy prejudice" of deference in the majority. An old order which had so much going for it would not have disintegrated, if it had not been intentionally destroyed by the "democratic sect," described by Schilling as a group of paid agitators and hotheads intent not on remedying genuine abuses but on furthering their own private interests. Now that their "poison" had done its deadly work in France, they were intent on disseminating it throughout the rest of the world. It was therefore high time to apply an antidote.[12]

It was soon to become clear that this was the official view of the French Revolution in Leopold II's Austria and that it was to be propagated energetically until it replaced the view disseminated by the enlightened journalists.[13] Schilling himself, in his capacity as *Hofsekretär* at the Ministry of Police, made proposals on how to handle the newspapers. Because of their great popularity, he advised against total suppression. But he suggested a press policy in which negative censorship—the "ruthless suppression of everything which might make a harmful impression on the minds of the readers"—was supplemented by positive manipulation. The censors should see to it that the papers featured prominently such news from France as ". . . highlighted the disorders provoked by the democratic system, and thus demonstrated the beneficence of a monarchical system of government, and showed in all its sharpness the contrast between a good prince and a few hundred despots risen from the common people."[14] It would be difficult to find a clearer demonstration of the relationship between the Austrian Enlightenment and the French Revolution than this proposal, which Leopold II fully sanctioned. Reports from France would be manipulated to create an aversion against political self-determination, for which the Enlightenment had just begun to give Austrians a taste, and for which the French Revolution, as reported by enlightened journalists, had whetted the appetite even

---

[12]*Ibid.*, *Betrachtungen*, pp. 68-88, 122-128, 131-134.

[13]For the organization of Leopold II's counter-revolutionary propaganda, see G. Lettner, *Das Rückzusgefecht der Aufklärung in Wien 1790-1792* (Frankfurt, 1988), pp. 33-115.

[14]Quoted by Ernst Wangermann, *Von Joseph II. zu den Jakobinerprozessen* (Vienna, 1966), p. 74.

more.

How would the ideological battle have progressed under the conditions of more or less peaceful coexistence between monarchical Austria and revolutionary France beyond the spring of 1792? Schilling himself seems not to have been overconfident. At least one may conclude this from the fact that the *Betrachtungen* ended with an argument in favor of a war of intervention against revolutionary France. The ideological counteroffensive would provide an effective curtain-raiser to the war. The argument was that, even if one could silence the enlightened authors and persuade well-disposed authors to unmask the revolutionary conspiracy and even if all genuine causes of popular discontent were removed, the mere existence of revolutionary France would constitute a danger to monarchical Europe. The book therefore concluded with a call for an alliance of Princes "for the defense of public truth and faith."[15]

Though Leopold II put all his energy and ingenuity behind the effort to launch the ideological counteroffensive against the French Revolution and its glorification by the partisans of the Enlightenment, he seems to have rejected the argument for a war of intervention. Until his death in March 1792, an uneasy peace was maintained. His death almost exactly coincided with the appointment by Louis XVI of a "popular" ministry, led by politicians who saw in war the means of solving the growing political problems and social tensions brought about by the great upheaval in France. The policy of Leopold's son and successor, Francis II, can best be described as a complacent readiness to be involved in a war against France. The root of this complacency was an excessive faith in the effectiveness of the alliance with Prussia, which he inherited from Leopold, and a greatly exaggerated notion of the "anarchy" prevailing in France as a result of the destruction of absolute monarchy.

Among the partisans of the Enlightenment the outbreak of the war in April/May 1792 aroused shock and horror such as had already been articulated at the time of the Declaration of Pillnitz (August 1791), when war had first seemed imminent. This shock and horror was rooted in a much more realistic assessment of the

---

[15]*Betrachtungen*, pp. 163-171.

prospects of the war than that made in the Austrian and Prussian cabinets. Most of the Austrian *Aufklärer* had been students of Sonnenfels, from whom they had learned that agrarian reforms which emancipated the peasants and gave them full security of tenure would turn an agrarian people into a nation of patriots.[16] Lieutenant Hebenstreit of the Vienna garrison, who was arrested in July 1794 and charged with high treason, told his investigating commission that he had always predicted an unsuccessful course of the war for Austria because he could not convince himself that "armies could prevail against an entire people."[17] Hebenstreit's friend, Andreas Riedel, who had been mathematics tutor to Francis and his brothers at the Florentine court, went personally to an audience with his former students to urge them to attempt a speedy conclusion of the war, only to be told that "the French business was of little importance and would be over in a few months."[18]

This staggering complacency provoked Riedel, Hebenstreit and their circle of enlightened supporters of the French Revolution to embark on the dangerous course of systematic political opposition in wartime. Their tactics appear at first sight absurd, but they do make sense, if one bears in mind the impossibility of legal opposition and the almost paranoic fear of the spread of revolution in governmental circles. They produced and distributed revolutionary material such as calls to insurrection, seditious poems, satirical and irreverent prayers for victory, and the like, in order to create the impression of widespread discontent and opposition to the war and thus to conjure up a danger of revolution. They reckoned that this would undermine governmental complacency about the war and frighten the ministry into a conclusion of peace, perhaps even into a resumption of enlightened reforms.

Early in 1793, this agitation came up against a different shock and horror, namely that aroused by the execution of Louis XVI. This momentarily transformed the widespread sympathy for the

---

[16]Ernst Wangermann, "Joseph von Sonnenfels und die Vaterlandsliebe der Aufklärung," in H. Reinalter, ed., *Joseph v. Sonnenfels* (Vienna, 1988), pp. 158-159.
[17]Wangermann, *From Joseph II*, p. 120.
[18]*Ibid.*, pp. 120-121.

revolutionary changes in France into a general anti-French hysteria. Hence the most interesting product of the opposition to the war, the *Eipeldauerlied*, begins by addressing itself to this sudden wave of anti-French sentiment:

> Was denkt's enk denn, daß gar so schreits
> Und alles auf d'Franzosen?
> Den Ludwig haben's köpft—na und, mi freut's
> Er war schlect bis in d'Hosen.
>
> (What are you thinking then, that you shriek so
> And everything at the French?
> Louis they've guillotined—and I'm glad.
> He was bad down to his drawers.)[19]

However, as the war dragged on unsuccessfully through the campaigns of 1793 and 1794, the public mood changed once again to one of widespread war weariness. Under these circumstances, the government began to consider the opposition and their seditious products a serious danger. In a way, therefore, the opposition may be said to have attained its immediate objective. But it was the irony and the tragedy of the Austrian "Jacobins," as the government's opponents came to be called, that Francis II and his advisers decided not to end the war, but to destroy the opposition.

In the Jacobin Trials, which followed numerous arrests of suspects in July, August and September 1794, these opponents of the war against revolutionary France were represented as the hotheaded conspirators and hardened disseminators of revolutionary poison to whose activities the French Revolution was ascribed in Schilling's *Betrachtungen*. Schilling, as *Hofsekretär* at the Ministry of Police, was himself in charge of the preliminary investigations. After the convictions and the brutality of the sentences imposed, as well as the amendment of the criminal law making all "insolent criticism" of governmental policies a felony, open expression of Enlightenment political attitudes became impossible in the

---

[19]H.W. Engels, ed., *Lieder und Gedichte deutscher Jakobiner* in W. Grab, ed., *Deutsche Revolutionäre Demokraten*, 1 (Stuttgart, 1971), 127-128.

Habsburg territories.[20] The partisans of the Enlightenment had to learn the art of indirect expression, which they did. Under the surface, the political tradition of the Enlightenment was kept alive, quickly coming to the surface every time the Francisco-Metternichian system was relaxed or momentarily cracked, as in 1807-1809, 1830-1831, and in 1848. In the latter year, the close historical relationship between the Austrian Enlightenment and the revolutionary tradition was again demonstrated, when almost the first publication to appear after the abolition of the censorship in March was the *Josephinische Curiosa*.

---

[20]For the trials and their consequences, see Wangermann, *From Joseph II*, chapters V, VI.

AUSTRIA'S ROAD TO AUSTERLITZ

by

Karl A. Roider, Jr.

On 13 August 1805, Napoleon, as was his custom, dictated a number of letters to his waiting secretaries. One was to his arch-chancellor that warned, "The fact is that this power [Austria] is arming itself; I wish it to disarm; if it does not, I will go there with 200,000 men to pay it a nice visit that it will remember for a long time." Another was to his foreign minister, the celebrated Talleyrand, instructing him to notify the French envoys in Europe that France was being compelled to go to war by Austrian aggression "so that the general feeling of disgust and danger may seize that skeleton Francis II, who was placed on the throne by the merit of his ancestors." Then, turning back to the secretary transcribing the letter to the arch-chancellor, Napoleon remarked almost as an aside, "Anyone would have to be totally mad to make war against me."[1]

Given the result of the campaign of 1805, "mad" in its nonclinical sense seems an appropriate adjective for the Austrian ministers and their decisions in that fateful year. Austria's armed resistance to Napoleon barely exceeded three months and was demonstrably ineffectual. On 29 August the emperor and his council of ministers decided in favor of war against France; on 20 October the bulk of the Habsburg forces in Germany surrendered at Ulm; on 11 November the first units of the French army entered Vienna; on 2 December Napoleon crushed a remnant of the Austrian army

---

[1] Napoleon to Cambacérès and Napoleon to Talleyrand, 13 August 1805, in Napoleon Bonaparte, *Correspondence* (Paris, 1863), XI, 79-81.

and its Russian allies at Austerlitz; and on 6 December the emperor agreed to an armistice that closely resembled simple surrender.

Given the swiftness of Austria's defeat, one wonders what possessed the ministers to challenge Napoleon at the height of his powers. Indeed, an examination of Austria's internal affairs makes the decision seem utter folly, for much militated against the monarchy's risking war at this time. First of all, the government's financial condition was not only shaky but was causing distress among the people at large. From 1793 to 1801 the monarchy had paid for the wars of the first and second coalitions not primarily by British subsidies—as British historians would have us believe—but by issuing paper currency. At the beginning of the campaign of 1799, the first year of the War of the Second Coalition, paper notes amounting to approximately 92,000,000 gulden were circulating, a figure that rose to 141,000,000 by early 1800, to 201,000,000 by 1801, and, despite efforts after the war to curtail the abundance of paper, to 339,000,000 by the beginning of 1804.[2] Soldiers and bureaucrats received their wages and salaries in paper currency and represented the chief source of its distribution throughout the monarchy, which caused significant resentment toward these people since they were perceived as the source of the ubiquitous devalued money and its accompanying inflation. Even violence occurred from time to time, such as a free-for-all that erupted in Lublin in Galicia when local merchants instantly doubled the prices of their wares when soldiers arrived at their market place.[3]

Besides the inflation caused by the excess of paper currency, the government was strapped by staggering debt. From the outbreak of the War of the First Coalition in 1793 to 1801, the debt increased from 390,130,000 gulden to 613,195,000, an increase of 76 percent in eight years. This leap in the debt, along with inflation, caused considerable anxiety in the upper ranks of Habsburg officialdom, and from 1801 to 1805 many proposals were

---

[2]Adolf Beer, *Die Finanzen Österreichs im XIX Jahrhundert* (Prague, 1877), p. 8.

[3]August Fournier, *Gentz und Cobenzl: Geschichte des österreichischen Diplomatie in den Jahren 1801-1805* (Vienna, 1880), p. 116.

offered and discussed to confront a financial situation "worse" according to one minister "than even the finances of Spain."[4] Actually, this official was being overly pessimistic. By 1803 revenues exceeded expenditures, mainly because of severe budget-cutting, most notably in military matters where appropriations fell from 87,731,000 in the peacetime year of 1801 to 35,902,000 in 1803, a drop of 59 percent that boded well for the deficit but ill for the army's preparedness in the campaign of 1805.[5] As impressive as these figures were, both the official and popular perception of the state of the monarchy's financial health inspired little confidence in its ability to sustain a significant military effort.

Besides the financial trouble, in the very year of the campaign, 1805, internal troubles offered impressive evidence that the monarchy was ill-prepared psychologically for war. In May food shortages and their accompanying civil unrest became so acute in Bohemia that Francis himself journeyed to the stricken areas to discuss the situation with local officials. In Vienna the senior ministers speculated as to the causes of the shortages, one suggestion being that there had been excessive exports and another that the administration was faulty, while the war ministry noted that, if Russian troops were to come to Austria's aid in an emergency, they would find no supplies if they passed through Galicia and Bohemia and so would either have to bring their own food or find an alternate route to Germany via Hungary and Austria itself.[6]

In early July trouble erupted in Vienna proper. Shortages prompted riots in the suburbs where people stormed bakeries and butcher-shops. General pillaging continued for four days until it was finally quelled by the military. Whereas some interpreted the riots as being the work of hotheads and French agents, the foreign minister argued that the roots were neither food shortages nor the wish for democracy ("the times of general penchant for democracy being over") but by the "deranged state of our finances" which was

---

[4]Franz von Colloredo to Louis Cobenzl, 24 December 1802, Vienna, Haus-Hof- und Staatsarchiv, Grosse Korrespondenz, Karton 452. Hereafter cited as HHStA, GK.
[5]Beer, *Finanzen*, p. 390.
[6]L. Cobenzl to Colloredo, 2 and 7 June 1805, HHStA, GK, 467.

the cause for inflation and the general disruption of exchange.[7] Whatever the cause, the government transferred significant armed forces to Vienna and its environs in case of further unrest.[8]

Internal instability and financial weakness certainly argued against Austria entering a war in 1805, and other reasons existed as well. The government itself seemed to be suffering from a form of gridlock, to use a modern term. The years 1801-1805 witnessed numerous complaints about Austrian officialdom from both inside and outside its ranks and from the administration's top to its bottom. In his "Serious Observations concerning the Present State of the Austrian Monarchy in comparison to France before the Outbreak of the French Revolution," Archduke Charles, the emperor's brother and Austria's military hero, declared simply that "Austria has no more dangerous enemy than its own government." Nothing, he argued, was working as it should. The leading internal advisory body, the *Staatsrat*, spent its time not on great issues but on "who will be the head of custom station x or if n should have a writing desk." Likewise, the judicial system was a shambles, as local customary practices intermixed with Roman principles to the point that people were forced "to turn themselves over to the pleasure or displeasure of lawyers." And bureaucrats at all levels were venal, incompetent and ignorant, some even bragging that they "had not read a book in thirty years."[9]

Although the archduke's observations are the most famous of the criticisms of the Austrian government at this time, they were by no means alone, and a common complaint, uttered more often privately than publicly, was that the emperor himself contributed as much to the problems as anyone. One of his chief critics was his cabinet minister and closest adviser, Franz von Colloredo, who wrote in June 1802: "Not a day goes by that I do not make strong recommendations to His Majesty that the actual state of affairs

---

[7]L. Cobenzl to Colloredo, 13 July 1805, *ibid*.

[8]"Given the number of troops patrolling the city," wrote the British ambassador, "one would suppose that we were on the eve of some dreadful Explosion. As far as a spectator can judge, nothing can be quieter than the People appear to be." Paget to Mulgrave, 24 July 1805, London, Public Record Office, FO7, 74.

[9]Archduke Charles to Francis II, October 1802, in Archduke Charles, *Ausgewählte Schriften* (Vienna and Leipzig, 1894), V, 549-604.

requires serious amelioration and that he must make without delay the necessary decisions so that nothing will be neglected that is essential to the maintenance of the Monarchy. I am vigorous, but nothing changes and that which must be done today is postponed until tomorrow or the next day and in the end nothing happens."[10] As late as July 1805, Colloredo's opinion of his master had scarcely moderated, for he complained of all the time Francis spent at work while accomplishing so little. "He is always indecisive and full of doubts so that affairs are dealt with quite slowly and a great deal of precious time is lost."[11]

Financial troubles, civil unrest, and governmental inefficiency each might have persuaded the Austrian statesmen to avoid war, but these reasons were compounded by yet a more compelling one: a crisis in military leadership. After the defeat in the War of the Second Coalition, complete control of the military establishment was placed in the hands of Archduke Charles with the understanding that he would introduce the reforms that would make the Habsburg armed forces far more effective at a considerably reduced cost. Despite his substantial authority and a popularity unrivalled among the citizenry and enlisted men, the archduke possessed a few traits that limited his effectiveness and stimulated doubts about his judgment among the emperor's major advisers. One of these traits was his poor health. Archduke Charles suffered from epilepsy, whose attacks were often quite severe and on occasion incapacitated him for days. Not infrequently his bouts with the illness led to speculation that he would soon die. That speculation led in turn to questions of whether so much authority should be left in the hands of an unwell man and whether in fact his advisers and confidants were running the war ministry with insufficient oversight from the archduke himself.

These questions were aggravated by another of his qualities, a tendency to rely on officials who were competent but arrogant and insulting. Chief among them was Matthias Fassbender, a Rhinelander by birth and professor of law by occupation who in 1799 became a councillor in the war ministry and associate of the archduke. Described by one historian as "conceited, boastful,

---

[10]Colloredo to L. Cobenzl, 25 June 1802, HHStA, GK, 451.
[11]Colloredo to L. Cobenzl, 25 July 1805, *ibid.*, 455.

incautious, and intriguing," Colloredo wrote of him, "I swear that I do not like this man who has never inspired confidence in me; I have no good opinion of his character or morals."[12] The archduke's second trusted officer, Lieutenant Field Marshal Peter Duka von Kadar, inspired as little confidence among the ministers as did Fassbender. Colloredo and the foreign minister, Louis Cobenzl, regarded Duka as essentially incompetent, an individual who they believed constantly opposed any resort to arms out of fear that it would expose his own inadequacies.

Making these matters worse was the archduke's inveterate pessimism. He always saw foreign and domestic matters in their worst light and did not hesitate to share his dark views with his brother and fellow ministers. Of course his interpretation was often the right one—especially in 1805—but it became hard for the other ministers to distinguish when the archduke was being realistic and when he was overly despairing. In Habsburg governmental circles Archduke Charles became something of a Cassandra, offering gloomy prophecies that often came true to officials who, while not necessarily putting affairs in their rosiest light, were searching for measures that would lead to less than the total submission to Napoleon that the archduke seemed always to recommend as the only possible course of action.

Because of the archduke's pessimism, ill-health, and reliance on dubious associates, Cobenzl and Colloredo began searching for military men upon whom they could rely at least for other opinions, and this led to their placing confidence in the hapless and ill-fated General Karl Mack. Mack's career before 1805 had been spotty. While he had defeated the French revolutionary armies in 1794, he had suffered defeat, humiliation, and capture when he led the Neapolitan forces against the French in 1799. Mack was generally recognized as a good organizer, having learned his trade with Field Marshal Franz Moritz Lacy, the distinguished military reformer of the reigns of Maria Theresa and Joseph II (the old foreign minister Baron Thugut described Mack as a "brouillon," who "could be used to create an army, to get it moving, but never should one let him command one or draw up

---

[12]Fournier, *Gentz and Cobenzl*, p. 111; Colloredo to L. Cobenzl, 21 February 1803, HHStA, GK, 452.

strategy for one. . . ."[13]). But Cobenzl and Colloredo appreciated him more as a foil for Archduke Charles's pessimism. In early 1804, after receiving the archduke's views on a possible war with France as an ally of Russia, Cobenzl suggested asking for the opinions of two other generals, one being Heinrich Josef Bellegarde and the other Mack, "the first because he is more cautious and the second because he is more determined and eager." In fact, Cobenzl suggested that the cautious view of Bellegarde might be more reliable "were the assessment of the ministry of war not so discouraging."[14]

From that time on, Mack became increasingly the foreign minister's favorite, not so much because Cobenzl thought him a genius but because he exuded the "can-do" spirit that civilians appreciate in military men and that many military men take great pains to cultivate. The distinction between the confidence displayed by Mack and the pessimism of Archduke Charles and his associates reached its sharpest in April 1805, when the ministers, having just learned of Napoleon's plans to become king of Italy, inquired of the ministry of war when the army could be ready for military action should it become necessary. The answer was six months, a time that came as quite a surprise since, even if finances and administration remained a muddle, the prevailing assumption had been that Archduke Charles was effectively reforming the military. Instead, it sounded as if the army were in worse shape than ever. "That's like saying we have no army at all because what enemy would allow us six months [to get ready]?"[15] In response to the war ministry's projection, Cobenzl and Colloredo pushed ever harder for Mack to take charge of military preparations, especially since he contended that he could mobilize the army in significantly less time than six months. They succeeded in winning the approval of the emperor, who on 12 April recommended Mack to the archduke for the office of quartermaster-general. But the archduke rejected his brother's recommendation, which caused considerable agitation among the other ministers and

---

[13]Colloredo to Francis II, 18 May 1805, HHStA, Kaiser-Franz Akten, Karton 78b.
[14]L. Cobenzl to Colloredo, 9 March 1804, *ibid.*, GK, 463.
[15]L. Cobenzl to Colloredo, 4 April 1805, *ibid.*, 457.

which launched a series of tension-filled meetings among the emperor and his senior advisers. Finally, on 22 April the archduke accepted Mack's appointment and agreed to the transfer of Duka far into the Balkans and to Fassbender's removal from service. Needless to say, Mack's elevation by no means ended the squabbling in the high command. Mack proceeded with plans essentially modeled after Napoleon's logistical practice of living off other people's resources, while Archduke Charles wrote memorandum after memorandum on why those plans would not work. Neither one set of proposals nor another but the wrangling itself became Austria's essential military weakness. Wrote Cobenzl, "In order to arrive at a state of respectable defense, we must follow the plans of clear-thinking men and not let ourselves be hamstrung by cabals and not lose entire months in debate, especially when facing a man like Napoleon who makes decisions on the field and whose orders are followed with the greatest speed."[16]

To summarize, Austria was thoroughly ill-prepared for war with Napoleon in 1805. And yet go to war it did. The question is why did it do so, when every consideration argued against it? In the general historiography of this campaign, the focus has been on assigning blame. Some scholars, especially those attracted to the famous publicist Friedrich von Gentz, have argued for the triumph of a war party in Austria; some have blamed the Russians for bending Austrian policy to fit Russian needs and the Austrians for not resisting them; some have blamed Mack's ego; and one has defended Mack while placing the blame on a rather malicious Louis Cobenzl.[17]

The documents related to these matters reveal that those ministers with the most influence in determining Habsburg policy—Cobenzl and Colloredo—were not only aware of all of the monarchy's limitations but had created a long-term policy, the intent of which was to avoid utterly any war with Napoleonic France. This policy was first articulated in May 1803 in response

---

[16]L. Cobenzl to Colloredo, 1 May 1805, *ibid.*
[17]Oskar Regele, "Karl Freiherr von Mack und Johann Ludwig Graf Cobenzl. Ihre Rolle im Kriegsjahr 1805." *Mitteilungen des österreichischen Staatsarchivs*, XXI (1969), 142-164.

to the news that Britain and France had resumed their struggle against one another. Cobenzl believed that the only position Austria could adopt regarding the two belligerents was one of "perfect neutrality," positive assurances of which "had to be given to both powers." In Cobenzl's eyes, however, the danger of the Franco-British conflict lay in the certainty that it would be a naval struggle and as such that Napoleon would lose it (Cobenzl never believed that Napoleon would invade England). Owing to his ego, his status as a parvenu in European politics, his reputation for invincibility, and his concern about maintaining his authority in France itself, Napoleon would have to find some compensation for such a defeat, and so "he will eventually think of undertaking a campaign against us to make up for all the losses he will suffer in that naval war." The policy for the monarch, Cobenzl went on, was not so much one of simply proclaiming perfect neutrality but proclaiming it while doing all it could to discourage Napoleon from attacking. After all, "if Bonaparte feels certain that he can cross our territory and impose his law upon us without running any great risk, how could he resist the temptation to do so?" For now Cobenzl recommended reforms, especially military reforms that would increase the army's efficiency and speed, two improvements that he thought would cost no additional funds. Then, he concluded, "we will approach the state of being able to guarantee the defense of the monarchy and, without clamor, without sensation, we will find Bonaparte less tempted to strike a blow against us."[18]

Discouraging Bonaparte from attacking Austria remained the essence of Cobenzl's policy to the end, but its implementation clearly did not achieve its corollary of keeping the peace, and the question now becomes: how did it go wrong? An important step on the road to the policy's ruination was the alliance with Russia, concluded in December 1804. Russia had supported Bonaparte's actions in the transformation of Germany that had occurred between 1801 and April 1803, but, with the French occupation of Naples, Brindisi, and Otranto at the beginning of the war with Britain, he seemed to be threatening the Russian position on the island of Corfu—and by extension Russian influence in the

---

[18]L. Cobenzl to Colloredo, 22 May 1803, HHStA, GK, 461.

Balkans—and Saint Petersburg began to have second thoughts about conceding to French wishes. On 1 September 1803, Prince Dolgoruky, on a mission to Vienna to purchase supplies for the Russian army, inquired of Cobenzl "when the two imperial courts would finally make an end to the French usurpers." Cobenzl was quite pleased with this inquiry, not at all because he intended to make an end to French usurpers but because he believed that a restoration of Austro-Russian friendship would quite nicely underscore his policy of discouraging a French attack. "I thought that if Bonaparte sees the two principal continental courts as tightly united as they must be for their mutual advantage, that alone would stop him from many things."[19] Moreover, by having the added weight of Russia as a guarantor of peace, Cobenzl could concentrate more on what he believed were the truly important issues in the monarchy: financial, administrative and military reform.

Cobenzl's positive response to Dolgoruky's inquiry inspired the Russians to offer a formal alliance, something a bit more binding than Cobenzl had in mind. Nonetheless, Cobenzl did not want to reject the offer because he feared the monarchy's being exposed to Bonapartist adventurism with insufficient protection. To Colloredo he wrote,"We want peace and we need it. But we also want good relations with Russia and we need them no less. If we cannot depend on Russia, France will soon stop respecting us, and where then can we find help if this power has in mind a continental war?"[20] But it was precisely this association with Russia that raised doubts that Cobenzl's policy was as safe as he made it sound. As early as November 1803 Colloredo, while expressing agreement that closer Austro-Russian relations were desirable, warned, "We must be very much on our guard not to be compromised by our part in it."[21]

From this time—late 1803—to the beginning of the war itself in late August 1805, the question of the Russian alliance dominated the debates about policy in the Habsburg Monarchy.

---

[19]L. Cobenzl to Colloredo, 1 September 1803, in Fournier, *Gentz und Cobenzl*, pp. 81-82.
[20]L. Cobenzl to Colloredo, 21 January 1804, *ibid.*, p. 86.
[21]Colloredo to L. Cobenzl, 20 November 1803, HHStA, GK, 453.

All of the other issues relating to foreign affairs that figure so prominently in this time—the capture and execution of the Duc d'Enghien, the question of imperial titles, and the proclamation of Napoleon as ruler of Italy—were peripheral to this one. And the sides did not reflect those of war parties or peace parties, but whether or not the alliance with Russia would discourage Napoleon from attacking Austria. As initiator of that view, Cobenzl believed that it would and argued that point practically to the bitter end. As late as 30 July 1805, one month before war erupted, the foreign minister was assuring his associates that Austrian and Russian steadfastness was doing what it should precisely because Napoleon was making threats and provocative moves. "When Bonaparte wants to make war, he makes his preparations in order to hit as hard and accurately as possible. Here, however, he threatens before having armed; he retires from the scene believing that such a show is sufficient to stop us totally and to render the wrath of Russia meaningless."[22] In Cobenzl's rather self-deluding view, Napoleon was *not* dangerous when he was making threats and *was* dangerous when he was not making threats.

The figure who considered this policy utter folly was Archduke Charles. Over and over he contended that an Austro-Russian alliance would inspire Napoleon to attack Austria rather than discourage him from doing so, that he would more likely strike before the Austrian and Russian armies could unite and thus defeat them separately, and, for good measure, that Russia posed as great a threat to Austrian interests as France did. In the middle were Colloredo and the emperor, who did not know what to do but feared the worst. In late March 1805 Colloredo wrote, "The more I think about it, the more I find that our affairs are in a terrible state and they threaten to become even worse. I continue to do all that is necessary to achieve the desired result, but I fear that all of our efforts will be for naught, that Napoleon will change none of his projects that he has resolved to carry out . . . . We must avoid war as long as we can and not let ourselves be dragged into it either by the promise of aid from Russia or the

---

[22]Colloredo to L. Cobenzl, 30 July 1805, *ibid.*, 467.

hope of subsidies from England."[23] Because of his influence with Colloredo and the emperor, and not least because of his office as foreign minister, Cobenzl's views became policy. After a year of negotiation, debate, and hand-wringing, Austria and Russia concluded their alliance in December 1804, but one which Cobenzl insisted be kept secret. The internal contradictions of his policy were no better revealed than in this condition. The alliance's purpose was to deter Napoleon's aggression and at the same time be kept secret from him in case it should prompt him to attack; in other words, even Cobenzl realized that it could prompt the very action it was supposed to deter. In the end Napoleon did trigger the war against Austria in the sense that he issued an ultimatum that the monarch's policy-makers believed that they could not accept.

The essential problem that Cobenzl and the others faced in determining their policy was that Napoleon represented a challenge that seemed to fit none of the traditional great-power rivalries, a challenge not unlike the one that faced the statesmen of the democratic powers in the 1920s and 1930s. While not at all equating Napoleon with Hitler or Mussolini, one could argue that Cobenzl at this time was unwilling to follow a policy of appeasement, preferring to risk the very existence of the monarchy rather than to conform to the whims of what he perceived to be an enigmatic but possibly insatiable conqueror. But that interpretation might give Cobenzl too much credit, because it attributes to him a sense of honor that he might not deserve and assumes a certain foresight that he probably did not possess. His choices, as he saw them, were either to continue the policy of resistance to—one might even say containment of—Napoleon through international alliances, as his predecessor had done, or to appease Napoleon while examining the political and social structure of the Habsburg Monarchy for those resources which, after proper nurturing, would provide the monarchy with the strength to resist Napoleon without relying on the other anti-French powers.

While recognizing that the latter was the necessary long-term policy, Cobenzl lobbied for the former as the short-term policy. But in promoting that short-term policy, he could not come to

---

[23]Colloredo to L. Cobenzl, 27 March 1805, *ibid.*, 455.

grips with the differential between France's strength and Napoleon's genius on the one hand and Austria's vulnerability and Russia's and Britain's strategic advantages for withdrawal on the other. Consequently, Cobenzl came to base his policy on wishful thinking, and that led him to put his faith in Mack's optimism and Russian assurances. That faith was misplaced, and the result was defeat for Austria and humiliation and disgrace for him, Colloredo, and Mack. The lone survivor was Cassandra, Archduke Charles himself, who went on to the next interwar period warning of the futility of resisting Napoleon and ultimately taking part in another futile effort to do so.

THE PROUD ADVERSARIES:

MASSÉNA AND THE ARCHDUKE CHARLES

by

Donald D. Horward

During the Napoleonic Wars there was a remarkable number of extremely talented generals. Their names are legion and for a brief time their activities determined the fate of Europe. Among this select group were two men who came from contrasting cultures; they had nothing in common except that they possessed an unusual talent or genius to motivate and lead men in battle. Indeed, both possessed the abilities, the courage, and the charisma to be numbered among the greatest soldiers in an age of great warriors. They have left a legacy of sacrifice and dedication that is still recognized in their own countries and throughout Europe. These men are André Masséna of Republican France and the Archduke Charles von Habsburg of the Habsburg Empire.

Although these two men met as equals on the battlefield, Masséna, nurtured on the ideals of the French Revolution, had little in his heritage to recommend him for command, while Charles grew to manhood as a privileged member of the royal house of Austria. Masséna gained recognition through his own merit, while Charles, who might have done likewise, often received his awards as a matter of privilege. Both achieved brilliant success and tasted the bitter fruits of defeat, only to be retired and ignored; yet today statues and monuments to their victories grace the squares and museums of their homelands where they are still honored.

The early childhood educations of Masséna and Archduke

Charles were hardly comparable. Masséna, born in the Italian county of Nice in 1758, received no formal education whatsoever. Orphaned at the age of six, he lived with an uncle who set him to work as a soapmaker. His free time was spent in the streets where he led a neighborhood gang of street urchins. Hyperactive and rebellious, he ran away to sea for three years before enlisting in the Royal Italian regiment of the French army. Thanks to an uncle serving in the regiment, he learned to read and write French as well as master the basic duties and responsibilities of a soldier. Within two years he was a corporal, but his promotion to sergeant took twelve more years of dedication and effort. As an experienced drill-instructor, he looked forward to a commission that had been promised but never came. Disgusted, he retired from the service in 1789 and married the daughter of a surgeon, hoping for financial security, but to his dismay, he was soon the proprietor of a grocery store.[1]

The education of Archduke Charles reflected the inequities of the age. He was born in 1771, the third son of Leopold, the grand elector of Tuscany. His early years were spent at court where the royal tutors catered to his father's instructions to ignore topics concerning the military. Nevertheless, young Charles quickly became fascinated by the military profession. In 1790, when Leopold became Holy Roman Emperor, Charles, then almost twenty, was sent to the Austrian Netherlands to live with his aunt and her husband, Duke Albert Saxe-Teschen, who fancied himself an accomplished warrior. Contrary to Leopold's wishes, they appointed an elderly Prussian tactician, Colonel Carl Lindenau, to serve as his military tutor. It was not long before Charles felt the grime of battle.[2]

With the outbreak of the revolution in France in 1789, the futures of both Masséna and Charles were altered permanently.

---

[1] Pierre Sabor, *Masséna et sa famille* (Aix-en-Provence, 1926), pp. 224-254; Archives de Masséna, MSS, I. These documents are in the possession of the Seventh Prince d'Essling, Victor André Masséna who permitted the author to work in his family archives.

[2] Gunther E. Rothenberg, *Napoleon's Great Adversaries: The Archduke Charles and the Austrian Army, 1792-1814* (Bloomington, 1982), pp. 42-43; Richard M. Long, "The Relations of the Grand Duchy of Tuscany with Revolutionary France, 1790-1799," doctoral dissertation, Florida State University, 1972, pp. 4-11.

Within eight month after Masséna's resignation from the army, the French National Assembly opened the commissioned ranks to non-nobles on the basis of ability. Joining a civic guard as captain-instructor, Masséna transformed his irregular troops into a well trained unit, proficient in the use of arms and drill. Within the year he was elected colonel of his battalion. When war broke out in 1792 with Austria and Sardinia, he led his troops in the bloodless occupation of Nice. As a result of his leadership, when the Army of Italy was created, his battalion was included in its composition.[3]

Conversely, the early years of the revolution had little direct impact upon Charles until the safety of his aunt, Marie Antoinette, queen of France, was threatened. When war erupted between Austria and revolutionary France, the commander of Austrian forces in the Netherlands, Prince Josias Coburg, planned an invasion. In this operation, Charles had his first opportunity to observe the mechanics of war. As a general by right of birth, his first battle experience was gained in 1793 at Neerwinden, where he commanded the left flank of the army. In this Austrian victory, Charles, much to the surprise of the other generals, exhibited a remarkable aptitude for war and a personality that appealed to his troops. Although appointed governor-general of the Austrian Netherlands, he anxiously returned to the army in May 1794 in time to take part in the battle of Tourcoing. During the two-day struggle he suffered an epileptic seizure which inhibited his activities and led to indecision and ineffectiveness on the battlefield. A month later he directed two columns against the French positions at Fleurus only to be repulsed twice in this crucial French victory.[4]

Apparently Fleurus had considerable effect on Charles, both physically and psychologically. He retired from the army to study and write about warfare. His labors produced a treatise which considered the inability of experienced and well-equipped Aus-

---

[3] Sabor, *Masséna*, pp. 250-281; Philip J. G. Bouchez, *Histoire de l'assemblée constituante* (5 vols., Paris, 1846), II, 451-461.
[4] Ramsay W. Phipps, *The Armies of the First French Republic and the Rise of the Marshals of Napoleon* (5 vols., London, 1926-1939), I, 155, 297-302, II, 158-164.

trian forces to turn back the untrained French hordes.[5]

While Charles was pouring over his manuscript, Masséna, serving in the Alps against the Sardinians, was promoted to general and given command of a brigade because of his "valor, experience . . . zeal, and fidelity" to France.[6] Posted high in the snowcapped mountain camp of Fougasse, he was constantly under attack by well-supplied enemy troops while his own men endured starvation and deprivation. In December of 1793, he was sent to Toulon where a young captain named Napoleon Bonaparte was besieging the city. Arriving in time to take part in the final assault, he captured Fort St. Catherine. For his efforts he was named general of division, the highest rank in the army.[7] Through 1794 and 1795 he continued to perfect his understanding of mountain warfare, and to develop self-confidence, composure, and a charisma that inspired his men to do what seemed impossible. These qualities were demonstrated in a brilliant operation in November of 1795 when he led the bulk of the army in a complex maneuver that resulted in the capture of the vital town of Loano—his first major victory. As a result, he was placed in temporary command of the entire army in February 1796. He naturally assumed that he would become its commander, but he was disappointed to learn that Napoleon Bonaparte had received the appointment.[8]

While Masséna commanded the Army of Italy, Charles was named field marshal of the empire and commander of the Habsburg armies in Germany. The Emperor Franz, however, limited Charles's authority by appointing a deputy and several aides to oversee his operations, and if necessary, to veto any of his decisions. Charles introduced some minor reforms in the army, but his views were based on eighteenth-century tactics so he ignored the innovations that had made the French army so effective.[9]

---

[5]Rothenberg, *Adversaries*, p. 43.
[6]Archives de Masséna, I.
[7]Jean-Baptiste Koch, ed., *Mémoires de Masséna rédigés d'aprés les documens* . . . (7 vols., Paris, 1848-1850), I, xvi-xix, lxxxiv-lxxxv.
[8]Auguste Amic, *Histoire de Masséna* (Paris, 1864), pp. 38-44; Phipps, *Armies*, III, 264-271.
[9]Rothenberg, *Adversaries*, pp. 43-44.

When the campaign began in June 1796, the French armies crossed the Rhine and advanced through Germany. Despite the bickering of his generals and the political maneuvering among the members of the *Hofkriegsrat*, or council of war, in Vienna, Charles split the French forces. He assumed the offensive and, through a series of adroit maneuvers, coupled with French errors, he inflicted heavy losses on General Jean-Baptiste Jourdan at Amberg and Würzburg before driving him across the Rhine. By 1797 Charles had completed the reconquest of Germany, a splendid achievement that marked him as one of the foremost commanders in Europe.[10]

Meanwhile, Masséna became a divisional commander in Bonaparte's Army of Italy. He was resentful at first, but his attitude changed quickly. Indeed, during the next year he would see more action under Bonaparte than he had in his entire career and he would learn more about the art of war than in any other period in his life.[11]

Although facing an acute lack of both resources and manpower, Bonaparte launched his campaign against the Austro-Sardinian forces in April 1796. Aware of Masséna's talents from earlier campaigns, Napoleon placed his division on the vital right wing of the army, always in a position to outflank the enemy. Operations began on 12 April and Bonaparte's first victory, Montenotte, was actually fought and won by Masséna. In each succeeding operation, Masséna's division played a vital part in the victory. At Lodi in June, he demonstrated his leadership and courage by leading a French column across a 170-yard bridge into the muzzles of the enemy cannon. The defeated Austrian army retreated to the fortress of Mantua to await reinforcements. In a series of operations that can only be described as brilliant, Bonaparte defeated four Austrians relief armies sent into northern Italy. Masséna played a crucial role in crushing each of them—at Castiglione, Bassano, Arcola, and especially Rivoli. Without doubt, Bonaparte owed more to Masséna than to any other man in the army, since Masséna's division had carried the brunt of the

---

[10]Phipps, *Armies*, II, 325-382.
[11]Donald D. Horward, "André Masséna, Marshal of France," in Henry Bausum, ed., *Lectures in Military Leadership and Command, 1986* (Lexington, VA, 1987), p. 60.

fighting. Clearly, the strategy was Bonaparte's major contribution to the campaign, but the implementation of that strategy was, to a large degree, achieved through Masséna's abilities and superb leadership.[12]

With the conquest of northern Italy almost completed, the French army advanced across Venetia toward Austria (see map, p. 31). Charles, fresh from his victories in Germany and regarded as the hope of the empire, was quickly transferred with units from the Rhine to halt Bonaparte's movements. Instead of facing the unimaginative old Austrian generals who had commanded in Italy, the French would now have to contend with the Emperor Franz's most successful commander, his brother, the Archduke Charles. Moving swiftly before Charles could deploy his forces on the Tagliamento, Bonaparte marched with the main army along the coast while Masséna struck off into the mountains with his division. Discouraged by the condition of his troops, Charles fell back towards the frontier with Masséna in hot pursuit. Masséna caught his rear guard several times, capturing thousands of prisoners. After passing through the snow-capped peaks of the Julian Alps, he reached the breathtaking pass above Tarvisio where he met Charles on the field of battle for the first time. There an unforgettable struggle took place between these two gifted generals amid the icy peaks, high above the clouds. Charles's rear guard was dislodged and he lost some two thousand men. The next day 1,540 more prisoners were taken despite his appeals to the demoralized men to stand and fight.[13]

Masséna led his division into Austrian territory, pressing Charles relentlessly, as Bonaparte raced to support him. In this operation his decisiveness, intuitive insights, and skillful daring discouraged Charles who was, for the first time, in the presence of a truly great general. Indeed, Charles would not forget this experience, yet he failed to recognize that the primary reason for his defeat was his unwillingness to replace outmoded tactics and strategy with the new system employed by the French. By 7 April, Masséna was

---

[12]Koch, *Mémoires de Masséna*, II, 1-320; W. G. F. Jackson, *Attack in the West* (London, 1953), 78-222; Phipps, *Armies*, IV, 5-157.
[13]Paul Charles Thiébault, *The Memoirs of Baron Thiébault*, trans. and ed. Arthur J. Butler (2 vols., London, 1896), I, 318.

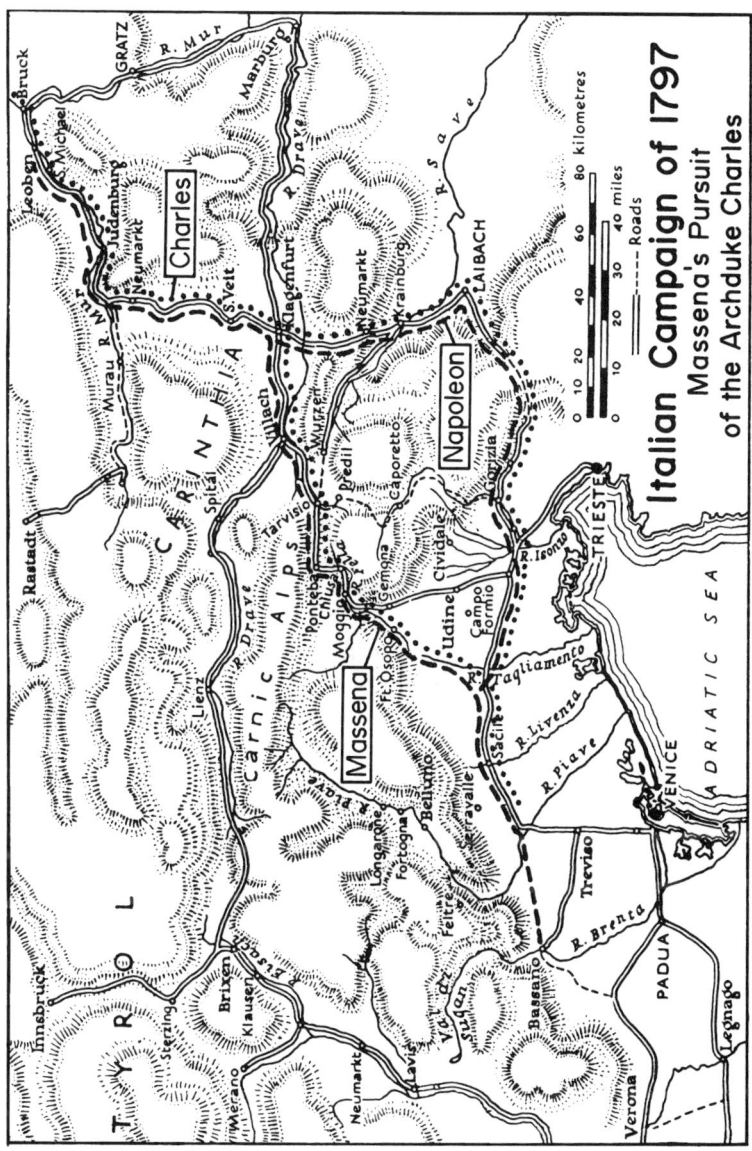

All maps used in this essay are based on the *Atlas to Accompany Napoleon as a General* (West Point, 1958), modified by cartographer Peter A. Krafft of Florida State University.

within a hundred miles of Vienna, and Charles, after appealing to the emperor for weeks to make peace, finally received permission to open negotiations with the French. The armistice was signed at Leoben and later confirmed by the Treaty of Campo Formio in October 1797.[14]

While Masséna returned to Paris with the trophies of victory, Charles was ordered back to his former army on the Rhine. Peace had been restored, but it was short-lived. In 1798 while Bonaparte was leading an expedition to Egypt, the government of the Directory pushed its expansionist policies into Holland, Switzerland, Germany, and Italy. It was only a matter of time until the Second Coalition would be organized against France. During the interim, minor reforms were introduced into the Austrian army, but Charles's proposals were largely ignored.[15]

War erupted in March 1799 when General Jourdan led his Army of Mayence, forty thousand strong, across the Rhine. With sixty thousand men, Charles advanced to Stockach where he met and defeated the French in a bloody encounter. Meanwhile, Masséna had been given command of the Armée d'Helvétie, posted at Zürich. With thirty-four thousand men, he formed the link between the French armies in Italy and Germany. He was depressed by the results of Stockach, and when the French armies in Italy were crushed in August by Marshal Alexandre Suvorov's Russians, he realized that he would have to face two powerful enemy armies alone.[16]

Charles, recognizing the threat that Masséna's army posed in Switzerland, defied his orders and advanced on Zürich. During the first week of June, the two adversaries were again locked in combat. With fifty-five thousand men, Charles attempted to storm Masséna's entrenched positions around Zürich, which was defended by forty-five thousand troops. His attacks were repulsed, but after the battle, Masséna withdrew to an even more formidable

---

[14]Phipps, *Armies*, IV, 158-78; Koch, *Mémoires de Masséna*, II, 320-385; James Marshall-Cornwall, *Marshal Massena* (London, 1965), pp. 50-55.
[15]Rothenberg, *Adversaries*, pp. 50-51.
[16]Edouard Gachot, *Le campagnes de 1799, Jourdan en Allemagne et Brune en Hollande* (Paris, 1906), pp. 65-130; Steven T. Ross, *Quest for Victory, French Military Strategy, 1792-1799* (New York, 1973), pp. 231-232.

position at Utliberg, two miles south of Zürich. Masséna remained in Utliberg for four months, confident that Charles could not force this position. However, some in Paris complained of his inactivity, prompting him to offer his resignation—it was rejected.[17]

By the end of August one Russian army had reached Zürich and the second army under Suvorov had driven the French out of most of northern Italy. Facing the combined forces of Russia and Austria, Masséna's position seemed hopeless. Yet with the arrival of the Russians, Austrian strategy was modified, and Charles, despite his strong opposition, was ordered up the Rhine toward Mainz.[18] An Austro-Russian army of sixty thousand men was left near Zürich to confront Masséna's force of less than fifty-five thousand men. Suvorov's army of twenty-five thousand men was expected to march from Italy through St. Gothard to unite with forces at Zürich and complete the destruction of Masséna's army.[19]

On 25 September, after Charles had moved toward Mainz, Masséna launched a series of coordinated attacks around Zürich. Within two days the Austro-Russian force had been destroyed as an effective fighting force. When Suvorov finally reached St. Gothard Pass, unaware of the fate of the armies at Zürich, he was set upon by Masséna's forces. Struggling through Pregel Pass to Glarus, Suvorov found each route blocked by French troops. By abandoning his baggage and wounded, he escaped by mule-track across Panixer Pass with the loss of five thousand more troops. This battle, known collectively as Zürich, was the crowning achievement of Masséna's career. Considering the strengths of his enemies, his own dangerous position, and the consequences of failure, he had carefully planned a series of decisive attacks which destroyed each of his enemies. As a consummate tactician and a master strategist, Masséna had driven the allies out of Switzerland, saved France from invasion, preserved the revolution, and marked the beginning of the collapse of the Second Coalition. When Charles heard of the defeat at Zürich he was stunned, but he could do nothing to reverse the outcome which he had predicted.

---

[17]Edouard Gachot, *La Campagne d'Helvétie (1799)* (Paris, 1904), pp. 96-113.
[18]Karl A. Roider, *Baron Thugut and Austria's Response to the French Revolution* (Princeton, 1987), pp. 312-324.
[19]Gachot, *Campagne d'Helvétie*, pp. 247-261.

Consequently, a disgusted Charles, claiming poor health, requested to be relieved of his command.[20]

Masséna, in the meantime, had returned to Paris where Bonaparte, now First Consul, ordered him to take command of the remains of the Army of Italy, threatened by two Austrian armies in the vicinity of Genoa. Although promised supplies and necessary manpower, Masséna found his army in miserable condition, without clothing, food, or pay, and vastly under strength, numbering only thirty thousand men. The siege of Genoa was begun on 4 April by sixty thousand Austrians. For the next two months, the city was defended with a tenacity seldom seen in European warfare. Although Bonaparte had promised to relieve the city, after he crossed Great St. Bernard Pass in mid-May, he turned to pursue the Austrian field army. Masséna held out until 6 June, forcing the Austrians to maintain an army around Genoa, thereby preventing them from uniting all their forces against Bonaparte at Marengo. Although Bonaparte won a decisive victory at Marengo, he complained about what he called Masséna's "faulty strategy" at Genoa; however, the Austrian chief of staff more accurately observed, "You won the battle, not in front of Alessandria [Marengo] but in front of Genoa."[21]

Following the defeats at Zürich, Marengo, and finally Hohenlinden in December 1800, Austria signed the Treaty of Lunéville, again accepting a humiliating treaty. However, this disaster served to restore Charles's credibility and influence at court. The emperor gave him vast powers as minister of war to reorganize the army. The *Hofkriegsrat* was restructured and the military bureaucracy streamlined; funds were sought to improve the armaments and supplies of the army. Formal military training was emphasized and professionalism was introduced into the officer corps; yet Charles clung to the military trivia symptomatic of Austrian armies. He did make an attempt to copy some French reforms, but he could not appeal to the nationalistic spirit of the

---

[20]Koch, *Mémoires de Masséna*, III, 293-407; Ross, *Quest for Victory*, pp. 261-289; Gachot, *Campagne d'Helvétie*, 171-473; Louis Hennequin, *Zürich, Masséna en Suisse* . . . (Paris, 1911); Phipps, *Armies*, V, 130-193.

[21]Paul-Charles Thiébault, *Journal des opérations militaires du siège et du blocus de Genes (an 9)* (Paris, 1801); Edouard Gachot, *Le siège de Genes* (Paris, 1908); Koch, *Mémoires de Masséna*, IV; Marshal-Cornwall, *Massena*, p. 115.

soldiers, fearful that it might lead to disturbances within the army.[22]

While Charles introduced military reforms, the war party at court clamored for a new war against France. Austria joined the Third Coalition, but a cautious Charles opposed renewed hostilities, not only because the army was unprepared, but also because he was convinced that Russia could not counterbalance the numerical superiority of the French army. As a result of court intrigues, Charles was replaced by General Karl Mack who pushed his own army reforms and promised success in a new war.[23]

War broke out in September 1805, and Mack invaded Bavaria, while Charles was sent to Italy with an army of almost ninety thousand men. Depressed by the condition of his army, apprehensive about the vulnerable position of Mack's forces in Bavaria, and fearful that he would be facing over one hundred thousand Frenchmen, Charles was not anxious to engage the enemy. His adversary was again Masséna, who commanded an army of just over forty thousand men (see map, p. 36). Awaiting news from the German theater of the war, Charles and Masséna established an armistice that could only be broken with a six-day notice. The truce held until Napoleon was ready to confront Mack at Ulm; Masséna then gave notice and six days later French troops drove the Austrian pickets off the bridge over the Adige and occupied eastern Verona. Charles fell back to his entrenched positions at Caldiero where he awaited Masséna. Upon hearing of Mack's debacle at Ulm, he decided to defend Caldiero and inflict enough casualties on the French so they would be unable to pursue him. Simultaneously, Masséna had been ordered to attack Charles and press him so that he could not disengage.

Between 29 and 31 October the two armies were engaged in battle. The French, unable to capture Charles's positions, suffered almost seven thousand casualties, while the Austrians acknowledged six thousand losses. Nevertheless, within a day Charles was in retreat. Masséna caught his rear guard and inflicted

---

[22]Christopher Duffy, *Austerlitz 1805* (London, 1977), pp. 24-29; Rothenberg, *Adversaries*, pp. 69-71.
[23]*Ibid.*, pp. 35-39; Rothenberg, *Adversaries*, p. 76.

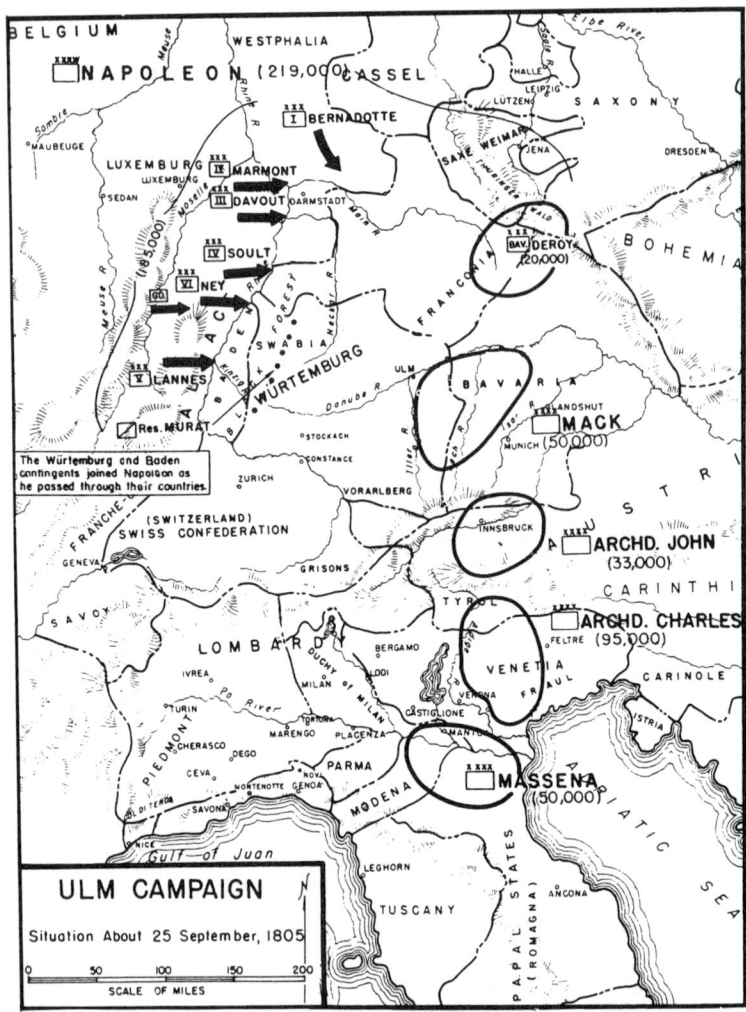

over five thousand more casualties before Charles was finally able to slip away on 5 November. An anxious Napoleon ordered him to pursue the enemy relentlessly so Charles could not attack him while he was facing the entire Russian army. By the end of November Masséna was in Liabach and the Austrian army was eighty miles away at Marburg. Charles, deeply discouraged by the turn of events, remained along the Mur River with his army of eighty-five thousand men. On 2 December he resumed his march eastward and a few days later he learned of the decisive Austro-Russian defeat at Austerlitz. The Treaty of Pressburg followed three weeks later and Austria again had been humiliated in defeat.[24]

In the Caldiero campaign, Charles proved to be a capable commander against Napoleon's finest general, but he also demonstrated a lack of initiative, confidence, and audacity. Masséna was less effective than usual, perhaps because he was heavily outnumbered and on the offensive, so Napoleon expressed his displeasure.[25]

After the disastrous defeat at Austerlitz, Emperor Franz turned to Charles who had emerged from the war with his military reputation intact and his political wisdom recognized. Once again, Charles began to reorganize the Austrian army. Reforms related to enlistment, training, and tactics were implemented in each branch of the army. In the area of strategy, he collaborated on a book analyzing the fundamentals of the art of war, but he refused to modify his views on tactics, strategy, or leadership.[26]

During 1808, the military situation changed radically in Europe when Napoleon's armies tasted defeat for the first time in Spain. Before the end of the year, Napoleon and several hundred thousand troops were deep in Spain, giving rise to a war party at the Austrian court, and, surprisingly, a conservative Charles embraced the movement. Political alliances were forged and soon the Fifth Coalition was preparing for war. Charles planned to march up the Danube, hoping German nationalism would spark support from Bavaria and other German states.

Although Charles was given supreme command of all the Austrian armies, bickering and dissension continued at headquarters. Last-minute changes were made in strategy just as the invasion was to begin, which required shifting two corps south

---

[24]Jean-Jacques Pelet, "Bataille de Caldiero," *Le spectateur militaire* (Paris, 1830), IX, 1-26; Edouard Gachot, *La troisième campagne d'Italie (1805-1806)* (Paris, 1911), pp. 24-256; Koch, *Mémories de Masséna*, V, 41-251.
[25]Berthier to Masséna, 22 November 1805, Napoléon I, *Correspondance de Napoléon Ier publiée par ordre de l'empereur Napoléon III* (Paris, 1858-69), No. 9518, XI, 525-526; Napoléon to Joseph, 15 November 1805, Napoléon I, *Lettres inédites de Napoléon premier (an VII-1815), publiées par Léon Lecestre* (Paris, 1897), I, 62-63.
[26]Rothenberg, *Adversaries*, pp. 106-120.

of the Danube. Hostilities began on 10 April. Surprised by the speed of the Austrian advance, Napoleon struggled to concentrate his army. Charles marched north of the Danube and crossed the river at Ratisbon to confront Marshal Louis Davout; his two corps were beaten by Napoleon and chased to Landshut, where Masséna unsuccessfully tried to encircle them (see map, p. 39). On 22 April, as Charles attacked Davout's isolated corps, Napoleon, accompanied by Masséna, arrived with reinforcements at Eckmühl in time to defeat him.[27]

Charles retired down the north bank of the Danube while the French, with Masséna in the vanguard, advanced along the southern bank of the river toward Vienna, which fell on 12 May. Since Charles's army was safely on the north bank of the Danube, Napoleon ordered Masséna to throw up a series of bridges that would span the Danube via the island of Lobau. By 20 May the bridges, extending over two miles, had been completed, and Masséna marched his three divisions of some twenty-four thousand men across the Danube into the villages of Aspern and Essling. Napoleon planned to move the remainder of the army across the bridge the next day. That night, when Masséna met with Napoleon in a council of war, he was the only commander who expressed grave reservations about the precarious position of the army, then straddling the river.[28]

Charles, in the meantime, began preparations for a mighty assault on Masséna's enclave early on 21 May (see map, p. 41). Although slow in starting, the unexpected attack of almost one hundred thousand men broke around Masséna's bewildered troops. At the same time, the bridge was cut, halting the arrival of reinforcements. Napoleon had miscalculated and Charles took the opportunity to deliver a stunning blow against his enemy. Several

---

[27]Jean-Jacques Pelet, *Mémoires sur la guerre de 1809, en Allemagne* ... (Paris, 1824-1826), II, 1-147; Charles Saski, *Campagne de 1809 en Allemagne et en Autriche* (Paris, 1913), II, 247-360; Edouard Gachot, *1809, Napoléon en Allemagne* (Paris, 1913), pp. 60-109; Koch, *Mémoires de Masséna*, VI, 117-178.
[28]Gachot, *Campagne de 1809*, pp. 152-212; Pelet, *Mémoires*, III, 249-347; Saski, *Campagne de 1809*, III, 256-358, Donald D. Horward, "Le général Jean-Jacques Pelet: Homme de guerre, humaniste et homme d'État," *Revue historique des armées*, II (1988), 29-31; F. Loraine Petre, *Napoleon and the Archduke Charles* (London, 1907), pp. 261-298; Koch, *Mémoires de Masséna*, VI, 221-263.

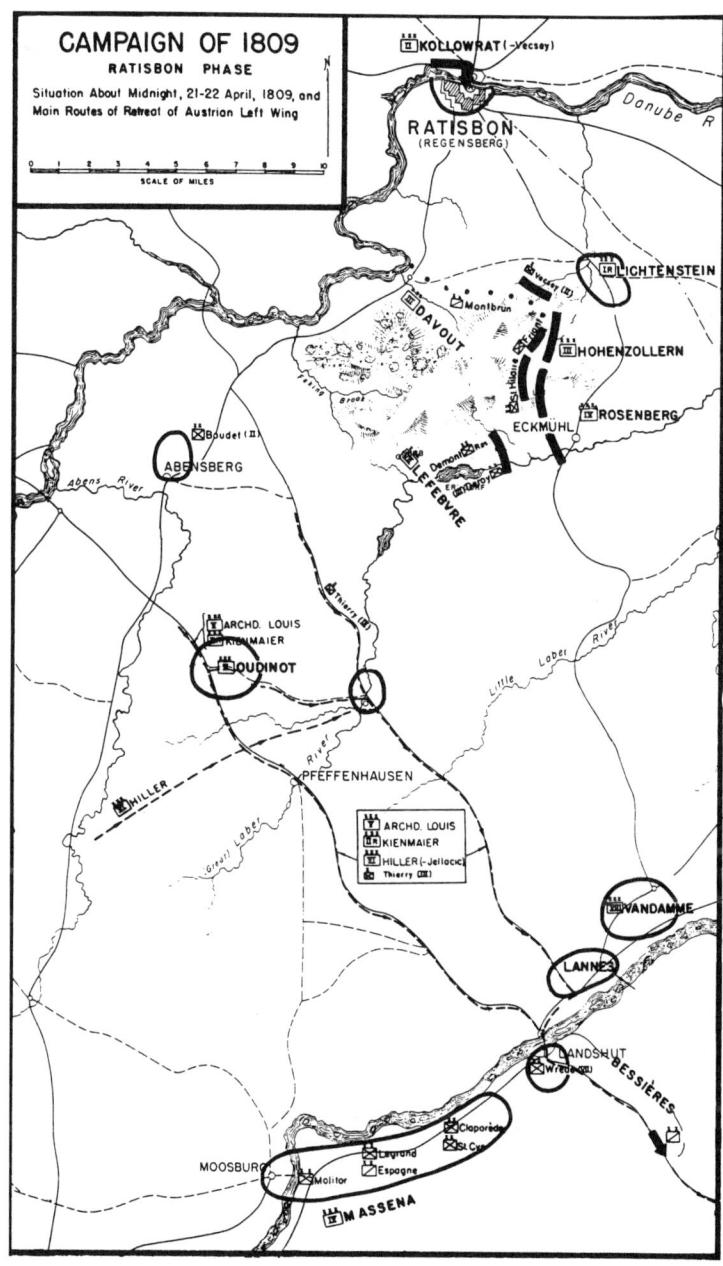

successive attacks were launched against Masséna's division at Aspern; each was repulsed in furious hand-to-hand fighting. Other unsuccessful attacks were directed against Essling where Marshal Jean Lannes commanded one of Masséna's divisions. Outnumbered almost four to one, Masséna's men were fighting for survival. Yet Napoleon was determined to hold on until reinforcements arrived. The bridge was restored during the night and twenty-five thousand reinforcements crossed the Danube.[29]

Before five o'clock the following morning, Charles, mounted several powerful attacks which drove the French troops out of Aspern; Masséna recaptured it two hours later. The Austrian attacks were also repulsed at Essling. Before 9:00 a.m. Napoleon noticed a gap in Charles's line and ordered Lannes to attack. The French advanced, carrying all before them. As the Austrian line appeared to be breaking, Charles rode into the midst of the Zach Regiment, rallied the troops, and led a counterattack. Meanwhile, a large segment of the bridge had been carried away, halting all French reinforcements. Ammunition was dangerously low and Austrian artillery was exacting a terrible toll. Although Charles's last attack was beaten back, Napoleon realized the battle had been lost. Masséna was ordered to disengage the enemy and evacuate the remainder of the army to the Island of Lobau. The losses were horrific; the French had at least twenty thousand casualties and the Austrians lost in excess of twenty-five thousand men. Napoleon was shocked by the results of the battle, but he had no one to blame but himself.[30] On the other hand, in the midst of the impending disaster, this was one of Masséna's finest hours; he had done what seemed impossible. Charles might have achieved decisive victory if he could have driven the French into the Danube or pursued them on to Lobau. But this was undoubtedly his greatest battle. He had done what no other commander had ever done; he had defeated an Imperial army under Napoleon's direct command.

To reverse the defeat at Aspern-Essling, Napoleon began to concentrate forces from all over the empire; he soon had 180,000 men on Lobau ready to cross the Danube. Charles was surprisingly

---

[29]*Ibid.*
[30]*Ibid.*

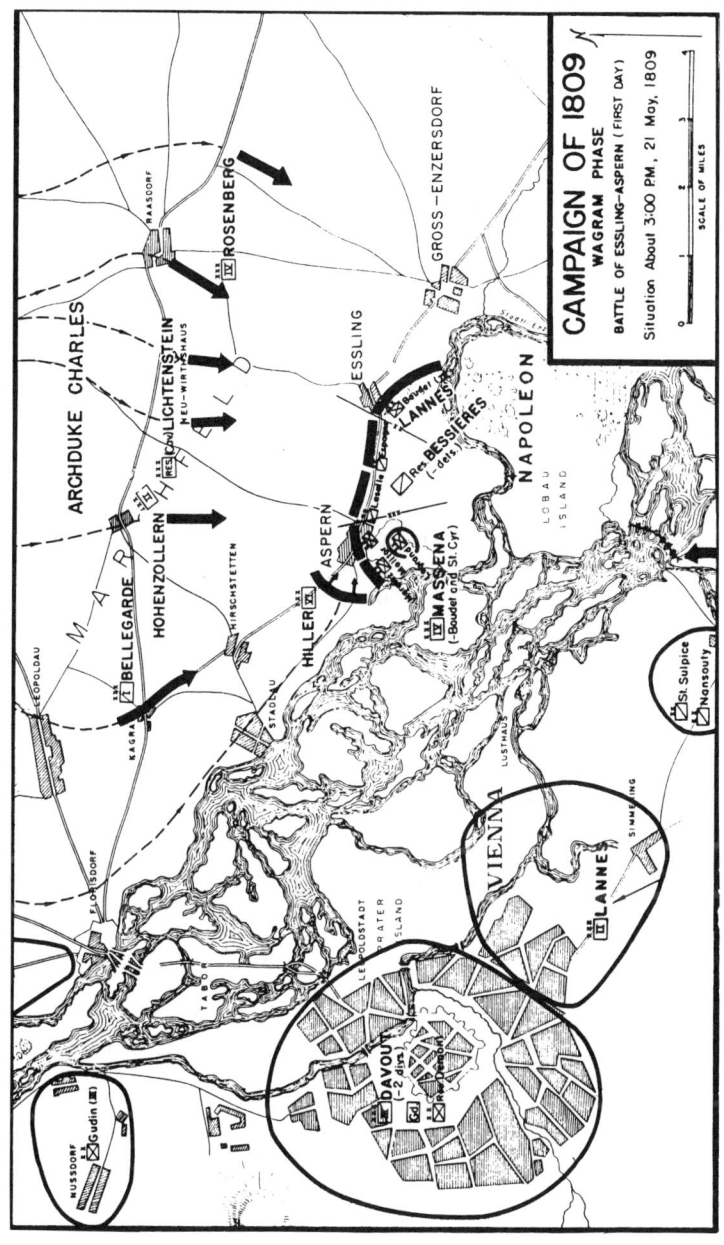

inactive during this period; he made little effort to strengthen his position or increase his manpower beyond an appeal to Archduke Johann for twenty thousand reinforcements. In fact, he was anxious to secure peace, fearful that Austria could still be crushed. Plans were drawn up to repulse a French attack, but no battle strategy was developed. On 5 July Napoleon launched his attack from Lobau. With Masséna's troops in the advance guard, the French army crossed the Danube and marched on Charles's positions behind the Russbach stream. The advance seemed destined to succeed until Charles intervened personally, rallying his troops to halt the French.[31]

Napoleon planned to turn the Austrian left flank the next morning, but curiously Charles had decided to employ the same maneuver against the French (see map, p. 43). Before Napoleon could begin his attack toward Wagram, Charles launched his offensive along a twelve-mile front. Although there was a lack of coordination among his corps, considerable progress was made at Aderklaa when Napoleon's Saxon troops panicked. Masséna quickly moved into the village to plug the gap. Charles's flanking movement, however, succeeded admirably in reaching Aspern to threaten Napoleon's rear. Masséna, although commanding from a carriage as the result of an injury, was ordered to march his corps parallel to the enemy, a very perilous maneuver, and reinforce the French left. This was completed as Davout began to turn the Austrian left. In the center a massive frontal attack was launched on Charles's position. The Austrian line began to collapse, forcing Charles to order a retreat, thereby ending the largest battle in European history to that date. The losses were staggering; each army suffered almost thirty thousand casualties.[32]

It was an exhausting battle for both armies, and the pursuit did not begin until late the next day. There were several bitter rearguard actions between Charles's troops and Masséna's pursuing advance guard, but at Znäim on 12 July, Charles proposed an armistice on his own authority. Ultimately this led to the Treaty

---

[31]Petre, *Napoleon and Archduke Charles*, pp. 331-379; Gachot, *1809, Napoléon en Allemagne*, pp. 224-287; Pelet, *Mémoires*, IV, 132-242; Koch, *Mémoires de Masséna*, VI, 264-333.

[32]*Ibid.*

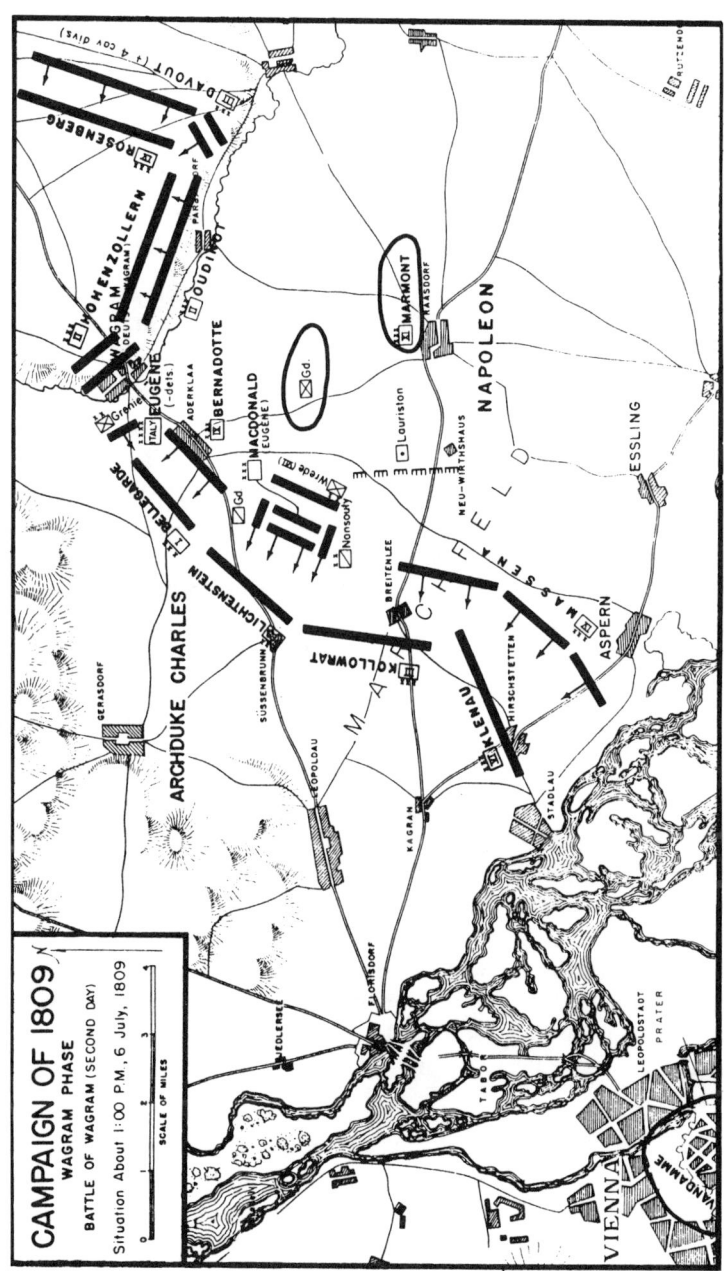

of Schönbrunn in October 1809, and the war of the Fifth Coalition had come to an end, as did the active military career of Charles. The Emperor Franz relieved him of all duties except those over his immediate army. On 23 July, Charles resigned his command and went into retirement at the age of 38; his services were later offered in 1813, but he would never again lead Austrian troops in battle. Although he lived until 1847, he was without influence in government and his contributions to Austria were all but forgotten.

Masséna's brilliant record of success also ended on the battlefield of Wagram. Napoleon honored him for his vital role in the campaign by naming him the Prince d'Essling. Masséna looked forward to retirement and a life of leisure, but Napoleon had other plans for him. In 1810 Masséna was forced to accept command of the Army of Portugal with orders to invade Portugal and drive the Duke of Wellington into the sea. Although initially successful, without adequate resources or manpower he was forced to withdraw from Portugal with his mission unfulfilled.[33] Masséna, who had been described by Napoleon as "the greatest name of my military Empire," returned to Paris, broken in health and largely ignored by Napoleon. He occupied administrative posts during the Bourbon restoration and the Hundred Days, but he never again commanded a French field army. He died in semi-disgrace in 1817 and was laid to rest without fanfare.

The similarities in the careers of Masséna and Charles did not end with their deaths. Recognition of their contributions came only generations later. Yet, to walk by the equestrian statue of Charles before the Neue Hofburg palace, to see his resting place in the crypt of the Capuchin church, or visit the 1809 Room in the Military Museum in Vienna, is to know that Charles's efforts were not in vain. He was the spark that kept Austria's hopes alive during a period of great adversity. Similarly, to visit Les Invalides in Paris, to walk through the art gallery at Versailles, or to examine the collections in the Musée Masséna at Nice is to

---

[33]Donald D. Horward, ed. and trans., *The French Campaign in Portugal, 1810-1811, An Account by Jean-Jacques Pelet* (Minneapolis, 1973); Donald D. Horward, "Napoleon and Masséna: Abandonment in Portugal," *Military Affairs*, XXXVII (1973), 84-88.

conjure up visions of a proud defiant Masséna who achieved glory in the wars fought to preserve the ideals of the French Revolution that we commemorated in 1989—the bicentennial year of that revolution.

THE PAPACY, AUSTRIA, AND THE
ANTI-FRENCH STRUGGLE IN ITALY, 1792-1797

by

Alan J. Reinerman

In October 1796, as the armies of revolutionary France advanced into Italy, Pope Pius VI sent a diplomatic mission to Vienna to seek cooperation against the approaching danger.[1] This move was a reversion to traditional concepts of Austro-papal relations, but a break with recent papal policy: despite bitter quarrels with France over both religious and political issues, Rome had in general sought to avoid involvement in the war.[2] True, in the first year of the war, when both its extent and its dangers had seemed small, there had been a certain degree of cooperation between Rome and Vienna. In May 1792, the Pope had asked Austria to use its influence to ensure that the Venetian fleet would defend the papal coast against possible French naval attack.[3] Austria had not only agreed, but had promised to win back for

---

[1] The standard works on Pius VI and his pontificate are still Jules Gendry, *Pie VI* (2 vols., Paris, 1906) and Ludwig von Pastor, *The History of the Popes from the End of the Middle Ages*, vol. XL, *Pius VI*, trans. E.F. Peeler (40 vols., St. Louis, 1953).

[2] For an introduction to the vast literature on the religious controversy in France and the subsequent break between France and the Papacy, see John McManners, *The French Revolution and the Church* (New York, 1969); André Latreille, *L'Église Catholique et la Révolution Française* (2 vols., Paris, 1946-1950), and Owen Chadwick, *The Popes and European Revolution* (Oxford, 1981).

[3] Caprara to Thugut, Vienna, 15 May 1792, Haus-, Hof- und Staatsarchiv, Vienna (hereafter: HHStA), Rom: Varia.

Rome its enclave of Avignon, lately annexed by France. In return, it asked the pope to use his moral influence to urge Portugal and Spain to join the war against France, and Pius VI had done so.[4] Rome had also asked for officers to help train its army and for various military supplies, and Austria had agreed to most such requests.[5] Such cooperation was in keeping with the traditional pattern of Austro-papal relations, the Union of Throne and Altar, in which the emperor lent his material protection to the pope, receiving in return the support of the latter's moral authority, a pattern which, however eroded by a changed political and intellectual climate and by bitter quarrels over Joseph II's religious policy, still survived in 1792.[6]

---

[4]Thugut to Caprara, Vienna, 18 May 1792; Caprara to Thugut, Vienna, 27 June 1792, Zelada to Caprara, Rome, 1 August 1792, *ibid.*

[5]Caprara to Thugut, Vienna, 13 November 1792; Zamperoli to Thugut, Vienna, 25 February, 23 October 1793; Thugut to Caprara, Vienna, 15 November, 22 December 1792; Caprara to Zamperoli, Vienna, 18 March, 23 October 1793, *ibid.*

[6]Little attention has been given to political, as distinct from religious, relations between Austria and the Papacy during the 1790s. That works written from the Austrian angle, most recently, Karl A. Roider, Jr., *Baron Thugut and Austria's Response to the French Revolution* (Princeton, 1987), give it only a passing reference is perhaps not surprising, since it was not a major element in Austrian policy; it is more surprising that works from the papal side, such as Pastor and Gendry, also pass over it rapidly, since the papal leaders of that time recognized relations with Vienna as of key importance, e.g. Busca to Albani, Rome, 15 October, 22 October, 29 October, 2 November 1796, Archivio Segreto Vaticano (hereafter: AV), Germania, or Zelada to Ruffo, Rome, 24 June, 18 October 1795, AV, Archivio della Nunziatura di Vienna (hereafter: ANV). The only useful study is Lajos Pasztor, "Un capitolo della Storia della Diplomazia Pontificia," *Archivum Historiae Pontificae*, I (1963), 195-338, which examines the mission to Vienna of 1796 on the basis of AV documents. Nor is there any comprehensive study of Austro-papal relations before the nineteenth century; the more important specialized studies are listed in the bibliography in Alan J. Reinerman, *Austria and the Papacy in the Age of Metternich, 1809-1848*, vol. I: *Between Conflict and Cooperation, 1809-1830* (2 vols. to date, Washington, 1979, 1989). On the religious policy of Joseph II and its impact on Austro-papal relations, see Eduard Winter, *Der Josefinismus* (2nd ed., Berlin, 1962), and Ferdinand Maass, *Der Josephinismus* (5 vols., Vienna, 1951-1961). The survival of the idea of Austro-papal relations as the Union of Throne and Altar in action can be observed in the examples of 1792-1793 described in the text, in the use of Austrian influence to defend papal interests during 1794, e.g., for the protection of Catholics in the Ottoman Empire or in support of Rome in a dispute with Venice, Ruffo to Zelada, Vienna, 7 April, 22 May 1794, AV, ANV,

During 1793, however, the war came to assume a wider and more dangerous aspect, and Rome became increasingly reluctant to be involved. To some extent, its reluctance only mirrored that of the other Italian states. Aside from Sardinia, none of them felt directly threatened by French attack. Strong Austrian forces held northern Italy against France and protected the rest of the peninsula; no one dreamed how quickly those defenses would collapse in 1796. There thus seemed no impelling reason for the Italian states to join in the war, but there was the prospect of expense and unnecessary provocation to France. They tended to regard the current war as merely one more round in the centuries-long struggle between France and Austria for predominance in Italy, a struggle in which the Italian states were mere pawns whose best course was to evade involvement as far as possible.[7] However, the pope's attitude was also conditioned by his distinctive status as a religious as well as a political leader. Papal attitudes towards war had long vacillated uneasily between the concept of the just war and that of Christian pacifism. In recent centuries the conviction had taken hold at Rome that, in wars between Christian states, neutrality was its moral obligation unless directly attacked; and even if Jacobin France could not be considered a Christian state, there were many at Rome who agreed with Cardinal Zelada, the Secretary of State, that "The Pope as Common Father of the Faithful must strive for the conversion, not the death, of the enemies of religion."[8] Neutrality was also Rome's most practical option, given its material weakness: its army was notoriously ineffective, and its treasury usually too impoverished to allow a strong military effort.[9]

---

and in the assurances of protection for papal interests in any peace talks with France given by Thugut and the emperor in 1795, described on page 4. The idea survived this period, to be revived under Metternich: see Reinerman, *Austria and the Papacy*, I, 1-49.

[7]On the reaction of the Italian states to the danger of invasion by revolutionary France and the Austrian attempt to rally them against it, see Giuseppi Nuzzo, *Italia e Rivoluzione Francese. La resistenza dei principi* (Naples, 1965).

[8]Promemoriale of Cardinal Zelada, 22 February 1794, AV, Germania.

[9]On the military problems of the Papal State, see A. Da Mosto, *Milizie dello Stato Romano dal 1600 al 1797* (Città del Castello, 1914); on its economic and financial problems and the efforts, generally unsuccessful, of Pius VI to deal with

The move of the Italian states away from involvement in the war came just as Austria decided to seek greater support from them. Even before the French invasion of Liguria in April 1794 made the danger to the peninsula clear, Austria had invited the Italian states to send representatives to Milan to discuss with the governor, the Archduke Ferdinand, the ways in which they could cooperate for the common defense.[10] The discussions went on in desultory fashion for several months; yet in the end Austria had little to show for its efforts. Naples and Modena agreed to send small bodies of troops to join the Austrians in Lombardy; the other states gave small contributions in money or supplies, or nothing at all.[11]

The papal response was typical. The pope sent to Milan Monsignor Giuseppi Albani, an experienced diplomat and member of an aristocratic family related to the Habsburgs and long the leaders of the pro-Austrian party in the Curia.[12] He had little chance to display Austrophile sympathies on this occasion, however, since his instructions ordered him to evade virtually every request the archduke was likely to make.[13] When the archduke requested men and money, Albani rejected the first on the ground that Rome lacked sufficient troops even for its own defense and the second because Rome's perennial financial problems made it

---

them, see Luigi Dal Pane, *Lo stato Pontificio e il movimento riformatore nel Settecento* (Milan, 1959).

[10]Thugut to Herzan, Vienna, 3 February, 13 March 1794; Herzan to Thugut, Rome, 1 March 1794, HHStA, Rom: Weisungen. Worth noting in Thugut's dispatches is his appeal to the Union of Throne and Altar to justify his request for papal aid in the war against revolutionary France, pictured as the same sort of common enemy of church and state as the Turks had once been.

[11]On the Austrian effort to win greater support from the Italian states in 1794, see Giuseppi Nuzzo, *Austria e governi d'Italia nel 1794* (Rome, 1940).

[12]Giuseppi Albani (1750-1834); his uncle was Cardinal Deacon and the leader of the pro-Austrian party in the Sacred College; his father had been majordomo of the Archduke Ferdinand, Governor of Milan. After his diplomatic missions of the 1790s, he became a cardinal in 1801 and was chosen by Austria to be Cardinal Protector of the German and Austrian Nation in 1803, a sinecure which made him in effect Austria's representative in the Sacred College. He played an important role in papal politics and Austro-papal relations until his death; see Reinerman, *Austria and the Papacy*, I: 116-124, 153-173; II: 4-10, 96-103, 134-42.

[13]Avvertenze ed istruzioni per mons. G. Albani, Rome, 1794, AV, Spogli Albani.

impossible. That last argument also served to justify rejection of a request for a loan of a million scudi, while a request that Austria be allowed to recruit in the Papal State was denied because, given popular hostility to military service, it would "alarm the people and lead to riots."[14] Also denied with a proposal that the galleys of the papal navy aid in cutting the flow of supplies to the French army in Liguria, though as some compensation Rome agreed to give, "absolutely without cost," two small coastguard boats, of dubious seaworthiness.[15] Particularly disconcerting was the papal refusal to use its moral authority to urge the Italian states to join wholeheartedly in the defense of Italy on the ground that it would be useless—Rome's voice was no longer "heard, respected, and obeyed" as in the past.[16] This had been the most important form of aid for which Austria had hoped, and its refusal was taken at Vienna to imply that Rome was no longer willing to play its former role in the Union of Throne and Altar.[17] In the end, Albani agreed only that Rome would make the very modest contribution of fifty thousand scudi to Austria.[18]

The conferences at Milan left the Austrian foreign minister, Thugut, utterly disgusted with "the inertia of the Italian princes."[19] Their "criminal indifference" might "one day bring disaster upon their land,"[20] and he warned that their refusal to cooperate for the defense of their own country might lead Austria to "abandon Italy

---

[14]Reports of Albani, Milan, 30 July, 1 October, 14 November 1794, *ibid.* Nuzzo, *Austria*, pp. 142-144, Memoria dell'Arciduca Ferdinando; pp. 148-151, Promemoria per Sua Altezza Reale.

[15]This request was also made directly to Rome and was rejected by the secretary of state: Ruffo to Thugut, Vienna, 28 October 1794, HHStA, Rom: Varia, with Memoria of the Secretary of State, 1 October 1794, on the sad state of the papal navy; also, Ruffo to Zelada, Vienna, 30 October, 22 December 1794, AV, ANV.

[16]"True, once the voice of the Roman pontiff was heard, respected, and obeyed; but now . . . [rulers] barely have the courtesy to listen, and no action at all is taken." Avvertenze ed istruzioni per mons. G. Albani, Rome, 1794, AV, Spogli Albani.

[17]Thugut to Herzan, Vienna, 13 March 1794, HHStA, Rom: Weisungen.

[18]Nuzzo, *Italia*, 268, Tableau des négociations, 1794.

[19]Ruffo to Zelada, Vienna, 22 December 1794, AV, ANV.

[20]Thugut to Herzan, Vienna, 17 December 1794, HHStA, Rom: Weisungen.

to its own resources."²¹ He was particularly annoyed with Rome for its refusal to use its moral authority, as it had in the past, for the "good cause" in what was truly a war of religion: "when it comes to bravely upholding the Cause of God, any sort of worldly political motive suffices to introduce into Papal policy a reluctance that must discourage its most ardent defender."²²

Thugut's complaints elicited no change in the papal stand, but only a lengthy memoir from Zelada, who after explaining the "disastrous state of the Papal finances" and its "total lack of military means," mentioned the "generous gifts" of fifty thousand scudi and two boats, and concluded that Rome had "contributed to the defense of Italy in the most vigorous way possible to it."²³ That Rome truly believed this claim, and failed to realize that its reluctance was perceived at Vienna as a betrayal of the Union of Throne and Altar, seems indicated by its reaction in 1795 to reports that Austria was about to make peace with France. Fearful that this might be a separate peace, similar to those made by Prussia and Spain, which would leave the Italian states defenseless, Rome promptly appealed to the emperor, as "the born Protector of the Church," to insist that in any peace the safety of the Papal State would be guaranteed.²⁴ Thugut, no doubt unwilling to alienate the papacy by a flat refusal of support which might never be necessary, agreed to do so;²⁵ but at heart he remained critical of Rome.²⁶

Such was the state of Austro-papal relations when Napoleon burst upon Italy in 1796. After forcing Sardinia to make peace in April and after defeating Austria in May, he invaded the Papal State in June, easily defeating the papal army and seizing the Legations of Bologna, Ferrara, and Ravenna, the richest part of the state. The Directory urged him to march on Rome and destroy that "center of fanaticism,"²⁷ but he refused to be diverted from

---

[21]Ruffo to Zelada, Vienna, 3 November 1794, AV, ANV.
[22]Thugut to Herzan, Vienna, 3 December 1794, HHStA, Rom: Weisungen.
[23]Memoir of Zelada, with Zelada to Ruffo, Rome, 24 June 1795, AV, ANV.
[24]Memoir of Zelada, with Zelada to Ruffo, Rome, 6 May 1795, *ibid.*
[25]Ruffo to Zelada, Vienna, 25 May, 11 June, 25 June 1795, *ibid.*
[26]Thugut to Herzan, Vienna, 25 May 1795, HHStA, Rom: Weisungen.
[27]Pastor, *Popes*, XL, 293; Gendry, *Pie VI*, II, 245-247.

defeating Austria. Instead, he signed an armistice with the papacy on 23 June, mediated by the Spanish ambassador, Azara, now the most influential diplomat at Rome; it provided that Napoleon would evacuate the Legation of Ravenna but continue to hold the others, and that the pope would pay a huge indemnity in cash and works of art. A final peace treaty would be negotiated at Paris.[28]

Worse was to come. When peace talks were held, France insisted on terms Rome could not accept: French officials should supervise the financial and military affairs of the papal government, payment of the indemnity should continue without limit as long as France remained at war, and—worst of all, from the papal viewpoint—the pope must retract all declarations since 1789 relating to France, implying admission that he had committed errors in matters of faith.[29]

Azara urged acceptance, and under his influence the peaceloving Zelada was inclined to agree; but these terms were too much for the pope. Zelada was dismissed and replaced by Cardinal Busca, a leader among those who favored resistance to France in alliance with the coalition.[30] On 13 September, the papacy decided to reject the French demands and accept the consequences, presumably another French invasion.[31]

To meet the threat, Rome organized a militia and expanded its regular army, but those forces were unlikely to be able to halt a serious French attack; both militia and army lacked training, arms, and officers.[32] This was not, however, a novel situation; for

---

[28]Pastor, *Popes*, 293; Gendry, *Pie VI*, II, 245-247.

[29]Gendry, *Pie VI*, pp. 250-261; Pastor, *Popes*, XL, 303-309; Latreille, *L'Église Catholique*, I, 233-236; Joseph Du Teil, *Rome, Naples, et le Directoire, armistices et traités, 1796-1797* (Paris, 1902), pp. 193-247, 340-368; B. Maresco, ed., "Memorie del Duca di Gallo," *Archivio storico per le Provincie Napoletane*, I (1888), 205-441.

[30]Ignatio Busca (1731-1803), cardinal in 1789. The official explanation for Zelada's resignation was ill health: Pastor, XL: 306; but the true reason, as Busca explained, was "the virtual subjection of my predecessor to the Spanish ambassador, on whose advice he relied and by whom he was intimidated, which is not the case with me. . . ," to Albani, Rome, 26 November 1796, AV, Germania 696.

[31]Pastor, *Popes*, XL, 307-309.

[32]"Time, money, weapons, leaders, supplies, everything is lacking." Consalvi to Litta, Rome, 30 August 1796, Paul Wittichen, "Brief Consalvi's aus den Jahren 1795/96 und 1798," *Quellen und Forschungen aus italienischen Archiven*, VII (1904), 139-170.

centuries Rome had relied for its defense upon the protection of the Catholic powers, and in 1796 its instinct was to turn to them again. An appeal was sent to Spain, under whose mediation Rome had signed the June armistice, denouncing the harsher terms now demanded by France and appealing for support against them.[33] Negotiations were opened with Naples for a defensive alliance against France.[34] However, Busca's great hope lay in Austria. Far stronger than Naples, unlike Spain still at war with France, it was also the power which had traditionally been regarded as the papacy's natural ally for the defense of Catholicism against Moslem Turks, Orthodox Russians, and Protestant Germans in the Union of Throne and Altar—a union which Busca now hoped to revive.[35]

Busca realized that Austria's protection might not be automatic, given its manifest unhappiness with Rome's meager contribution to the war. Thugut had shown no sympathy whatever with the misfortunes Rome had suffered in 1796, declaring them its just reward for failing to aid Austria's defense of Italy.[36] It would be necessary, Busca knew, to "justify our conduct to that court . . . and implore its protection."[37] However, he felt that the traditional role of the Holy Roman Emperor as protector of the papacy, reaffirmed as recently as 1795, their common hostility to the revolution, and the harm that a French annexation of the Legations would do to Austria's strategic interests should suffice

---

[33]Copy with Busca to Albani, Rome, 30 November, 1796, AV, Germania 696.
[34]Du Teil, *Rome, Naples*, pp. 343-347; Pastor, XL, 309-311.
[35]Busca to Albani, Rome, 22 October, 29 October, 2 November 1796, AV, Germania. Perhaps because of the assurances of support given Rome by Austria in 1795, as noted on page 4, Busca seems not to have realized how far Rome's refusal to aid Austria in 1794 had alienated that power. From the Austrian point of view, it had been the papacy that had first abandoned the tradition of the Union of Throne and Altar by refusing to use its moral authority on behalf of Austria, even though the latter was acting de facto as the protector of the Papal State and was fighting in what Vienna, with some reason, regarded as a war for religion.
[36]E.g., Ruffo to Zelada, Vienna, 20 August 1796, AV, ANV, 202A, reporting Thugut's sarcastic comments on the contrast between the huge indemnity which Rome now had to pay France and the meager sum which it had been willing to give Austria in 1794, when a larger measure of support might, he felt, have helped stave off the French victories.
[37]Busca to Caleppi, Rome, 16 October 1796, AV, Carte Caleppi.

to secure its aid. Both military and diplomatic aid was needed: the Austrian army should defend the Papal State, while its diplomats should ensure that in any peace treaty the harsh terms of the June armistice were abrogated. In return, the papacy would contribute what resources it had to the common struggle.[38]

This mission too was entrusted to Albani.[39] Although Busca urged him to haste, he took a month to reach Vienna, partly because of accidents along the way, partly because he had also been directed to gather information on the situation in northern Italy and to purchase guns at Trieste for the papal army.[40] Meanwhile, events took place that made his mission still more vital. By mid-October, the negotiations with Naples for a defensive alliance seemed close to success.[41] Confident of Neapolitan support, Busca bluntly refused a French demand to resume delivery of the indemnity.[42] But in late October he learned that Naples had signed a peace treaty with France, leaving Rome in the lurch.[43] A possible escape route opened when Napoleon, instead of reacting to the papal refusal with an invasion, offered to discuss more lenient peace terms. But most at Rome doubted his sincerity, correctly suspecting that his real aim was to play for time, avoiding distraction in the South while he was fully occupied with Austria.[44] Realizing that it would be unwise to reject his offer until certain of Austrian support, the papacy too decided to play for time, carrying out talks with the French but avoiding an agreement until

---

[38] Busca's instructions for Albani seem not to have survived in AV, but they can be deduced from the recapitulation given in Albani to Busca, Vienna, 28 December 1796, AV, Germania.

[39] Albani's letter of introduction of Francis II and Thugut from Pius VI, dated 8 October, are in AV, Epistulae ad Principes; they are general in nature and do not mention the aim of his mission. Albani does not give the date of his departure in his reports, but Thugut wrote Herzan, 30 October 1796, HHStA, ROM: Weisungen that it was 9 October.

[40] Busca to Albani, Rome, 15 October 1796; Albani to Busca, Vienna, 30 October 1796, AV, Germania.

[41] Busca to Albani, Rome, 15 October, 22 October 1796, *ibid.*

[42] Busca to Albani, Rome, 15 October 1796, *ibid.*

[43] *Busca to Albani, Rome,* 29 October 1796, *ibid.*

[44] Du Teil, *Rome, Naples,* pp. 381-383.

the outcome of Albani's mission was known.[45]

Albani finally reached Vienna on 10 November, and had his first meeting with Thugut two days later.[46] Thugut was not in an accommodating mood. The distrust created by Rome's refusal to aid Austria in the past had been increased by the long delay in Albani's arrival: "this slowness of movement surely shows an intention to procrastinate rather than a determined resolve to join in the struggle . . . ; it is irritating to have to deal with governments so vacillating."[47] Consequently, Albani received an unsympathetic hearing when he presented the papal request for aid, using Busca's arguments to justify it and promising that the pope in turn would cooperate "with all the means at his disposal" and would be forever grateful. Thugut "began by shrugging his shoulders and remarking that what had befallen us served us right, for had it not been for us, all Italy would not have been lost." He repeated his complaints of the past two years at Rome's failure to "contribute even what its limited means permitted to the good cause." Albani sought to rise above these charges, declaring that the past was past, and "now was the time to unite for our common interests." Thugut, however, denied that "this was the time, for we must wait to see how matters turn out at Mantua," where Austria was about to make a major effort to break the siege. As Albani realized, a victory at Mantua would place Austria in a better position to impose its will upon Rome as well as upon France. The only satisfaction Thugut would give Rome was to agree to its request to send an Austrian general and officers to train and lead the papal army.[48]

If this first meeting left Albani discouraged, their second, on 18 November, left him decidedly alarmed. This meeting made clear that the talks involved two very different perspectives on international relations. Papal policy was still based fundamentally upon a medieval world view, the old concept of the two swords, the secular and the spiritual powers, each with its own set of rights and duties—a view in which it was the duty of the emperor, by

---

[45]Busca to Albani, Rome, 2 November 1796, AV, Germania.
[46]Albani to Busca, Vienna, 13 November 1796, *ibid.*
[47]Thugut to Herzan, Vienna, 30 October 1796, HHStA, Rom: Weisungen.
[48]Albani to Busca, Vienna, 13 November 1796, AV, Germania.

virtue of his office, to protect the papacy with the material power which it lacked.⁴⁹ This ideal, never fully realized in practice, was now far gone in decline outside of Rome. Thugut stood for another and very different concept, formed in an age of iron power politics, of a Darwinian struggle between powers whose rivalries, ruthless enough before 1789, had become yet more bitter under the impact of the revolution and the changes in the international order which it unleashed, an age when the very survival of the Habsburg Empire was in question. The incompatibility between these views was revealed on 18 November when Thugut made clear that, in contrast to the papal assumption that the emperor was Rome's protector by the nature of his office, he would assume that role only in consequence of a formal treaty and only at a price. Negotiations were now underway between France and England in which the latter acted for its Austrian ally. By promising to defend the Papal State, Austria would exclude itself from any peace that might result, and might find itself at war only to defend papal interests; "this commitment surely deserves some sacrifice in compensation for the danger and expense to which we would be exposed." The compensation desired was not the money or supplies that Rome was ready to give, but rather territory.⁵⁰ Since Rome could not recover Bologna and Ferrara by its own efforts, it had lost them in any case, and might as well cede them to Austria. When Albani pointed out that if Rome were prepared to abandon its provinces it could have peace with France without the risks of a war at Austria's side, Thugut declared that in Austrian hands they would at least not become a center for radical agitation or further French attacks on the Papal State, but would provide Rome with a friendly neighbor to guard its northern frontier.⁵¹

Albani was "shocked to the core" by this "completely unexpected

---

⁴⁹This view appears frequently in the correspondence between Busca and Albani, e.g., Busca to Albani, Rome, 26 November, 3 December (dictated by the Pope), 21 December 1796, 25 February 1797; Albani to Busca, Vienna, 24 November, 30 December 1796.
⁵⁰Albani to Busca, Vienna, 19 November 1796, *ibid.*
⁵¹Albani to Busca, Vienna, 24 November 1796, *ibid.*

demand;"[52] indeed, so little had the papacy foreseen the Austrian stand that his instructions had contained no mention of territorial cessions or even of a formal treaty—all that he would need to do, it had been assumed, was explain Rome's desperate need for help and its willingness to cooperate with Austria against France.

Thugut's demand sent shock waves through the backward-looking world of Rome, where their memory reverberated for half a century, hindering good Austro-papal relations and making Thugut's name a byword for unscrupulous ambition;[53] but what it in truth revealed was less a personal lack of moral principle than a realization that Austria must adapt to an increasingly ruthless and unfavorable international system if it wished to survive. And it was indeed Austria's survival, at least as a great power and perhaps in any sense, that lay behind Thugut's demand. Austria had lost ground steadily in the international balance of power over the last decade. In the second and third partitions of Poland, Austria had suffered relative to her rivals Russia and Prussia, which had made greater gains. Austria had also suffered the greatest losses thus far from the advance of revolutionary France: Belgium seemed surely lost, Lombardy hung in the balance, losses seemed possible in Germany. If Austria was not to fall irrevocably behind the other powers—which would mean in the long run its decline from great-power status and leave it prey to the ambitions of its neighbors, as Poland and Turkey had become—it must find compensation somewhere for its losses and its rivals' gains. The Legations were among the few areas where such compensation seemed possible. Traditional concepts of Austro-papal relations must not be allowed to stand in the way of satisfying this imperative need. In any case,. the papal failure to aid Austria over the past two years had convinced him that Vienna had no moral obligation to help Rome now; quite the contrary. "Albani is not too happy with me," he wrote on 10 November; "these gentlemen, the Italian princes, would all prefer that His Majesty fight for

---

[52] Albani to Busca, Vienna, 19 November 1796, *ibid*.

[53] On the lasting impact made on Austro-papal relations by Thugut's attempt to annex the Legations, which he renewed in 1799-1800, see Reinerman, *Austria and the Papacy*, I, 1-2, 8-9, 120, 172. On the hostile attitude towards Thugut at Rome, which lasted until at least 1818, see Mémoires sur Rome par Altieri, 1818, HHStA, Rom: Varia.

everyone, that he defend everyone, without it costing them anything except a few cajoleries and a certain submission, when by their imprudence and cowardice they have not only ruined their own position, but that of others as well." He concluded happily that "if Alvinitzy continues to have some success, I confidently hope for some good gains in Italy."[54]

His views were not appreciated at Rome. By its nature, the papacy at all times tended to view political questions from a moral perspective; and from that perspective, the Austrian demand for lands legally Rome's for centuries was totally unjustifiable, doubly shocking in that it came from the power that Rome felt had a particular duty to protect it. With unanimous support from the cardinals, Pius VI dictated a firm refusal even to discuss surrendering territory.[55] There was, however, no change in papal policy. Not only was the traditional tendency to look to the empire hard to abandon for a court so wedded to tradition as Rome, but the hard truth of the international scene was that Austria was its only hope. France continued to offer to discuss peace on more lenient terms,[56] but few believed it sincere. Naples still refused to consider resuming the war or defending the Papal State. As for Spain, the appeal for help sent there received a reply as disconcerting as that from Vienna. In late November came a letter from Godoy, the all-powerful Prince of the Peace, which not merely rejected the appeal, but advised Rome that its temporal power was now only a source of danger and distraction, which it ought to abandon so as to concentrate on its spiritual mission.[57] Though this advice was in a sense far-sighted, in 1796 the thought of abandoning

---

[54]Thugut to Colloredo, Vienna, 20 November 1796, in Alfred von Vivenot, ed., *Vertrauliche Briefe des Freiherrn von Thugut* (2 vols., Vienna, 1872), I, 355. On the difficult Austrian position and Thugut's efforts to improve it, by annexing the Legations among other plans, see Roider.

[55]Busca to Albani, Rome, 3 December 1796, AV, Germania, which had been dictated by the pope.

[56]By early December Napoleon was so eager not to be distracted from the war in Lombardy that he proposed that in a peace treaty France would "entirely abandon" its demands of the previous summer, and "would not even insist that the armistice be carried out in full." Instead of the huge indemnity, "perhaps a million in cash and a few statues would settle everything." Consalvi to Albani, Rome, 10 December 1796, *ibid*.

[57]Copy with Busca to Albani, Rome, 30 November 1796, *ibid*.

rights held for a thousand years "caused consternation,"[58] and was seen as simply a cover for the wish to gain part of the Papal State for the Spanish Duke of Parma.[59]

Under these circumstances, it is not surprising that the pope continued to look to Austria; but he would not buy its help at the price of the Legations. The pontiff continued to act on the assumption that aiding Rome was a duty which the emperor must eventually recognize and fulfill; the pope need only wait until his categorical refusal of concessions had brought Austria to its senses and led to a change in its stand. If necessary, a personal appeal to the emperor would be made. For the present, Albani was to continue to press for Austrian aid, but use only the same arguments as before.[60]

The pope might have had a long wait if the Austrian army had had the success for which Thugut hoped; but instead it was again defeated near Verona. The fall of Mantua seemed increasingly likely.[61] Thugut did not despair, but realized that nothing that might strengthen the Austrian position in Lombardy should be overlooked.[62] His priorities in dealing with Rome now changed; he aimed not at gaining territory, but at securing whatever help Rome could provide. When he saw Albani on 24 November, he no longer demanded sacrifices but spoke the traditional language of the Union of Throne and Altar which he had brushed aside when used by Albani. "A close unity of action becomes ever more essential," he declared. The war was "of as great an interest to the papacy as to Austria, for it is in essence a war for religion." Therefore, Rome, spurning the deceitful peace offers of France, should join with all its resources in the struggle. Though "the pope can do little by military means," he could do much by "putting to work all his spiritual powers," above all, "declaring a war of

---

[58]Busca to Albani, Rome, 30 November 1796, *ibid*.
[59]Albani to Busca, Vienna, 12 December 1796, *ibid*.
[60]Albani to Busca, Vienna, 3 December 1796, *ibid*.
[61]"We have everything to fear for Mantua, barring a miracle or some unforeseen event," he wrote on 1 December 1796. Vivenot, *Vertrauliche Briefe*, I, 361.
[62]*Ibid*., 3 December 1796, I, 363. Albani to Busca, Vienna, 24 November 1796, AV, Germania. On the deterioration of the Austrian position in Italy during 1796-1797, see Roider, pp. 225-230.

religion" that would inspire popular resistance to France not only in Italy but throughout the Catholic world. As a first move, the pope should "send exhortations to the princes to defend religion against France." Thugut had in mind the rulers of Portugal, Sardinia, Saxony, and especially Spain. Thugut did not mention the Legations; when Albani raised the question, Thugut assured him that there would be no mention of sacrifices in the treaty they should sign—that point could be settled at the general peace. This was not entirely reassuring, but it did at least mean that Rome could secure Austrian protection in a treaty without first committing itself to yield the Legations. Albani reflected that the papacy could, if necessary, probably mount a successful defense of its territory at the final peace by appealing to the emperor, to Catholic opinion, or to the other powers. What was important now, he advised Busca, was to act before this favorable moment was lost.[63]

Yet, though the moment for which Rome had been waiting had apparently arrived, the Vatican hesitated, despite Albani's repeated pleas for quick action.[64] Busca's cautious and indecisive character and the age and ill health of the pope played some part in this, no doubt. More fundamental, however, was the shock which Thugut's territorial demands had given the Roman ruling class, undermining their traditional faith in the empire. Busca became virtually obsessed with those demands, and, ignoring Thugut's partial retreat, gave them far more attention than reaching an agreement to assure Austrian protection.[65]

However, Rome also hesitated because it had reservations about a war of religion. This was not a matter of principle, since it felt it had "just and well-founded motives to declare a war of religion against the French, who have turned against God, destroyed the Church in their country, maltreated and killed its ministers, and try by propaganda and arms to spread their errors."[66] Unfortunate-

---

[63]Albani to Busca, Vienna, 24 November 1796, AV, Germania.
[64]Albani to Busca, Vienna, 14, 21, 28 December 1796, *ibid.*
[65]Busca's instructions to Albani during December stress the need to avert Austrian designs on the Legations while virtually ignoring the need to secure Austrian protection.
[66]Busca to Albani, Rome, 31 December 1796, *ibid.*

ly, there were practical problems. Most Catholic states had by now made peace with France; to declare a war of religion would be "to stir up disobedience in those states, whose governments wish them to be at peace, while the Church urges them to go to war." To cause such turmoil was distasteful in principle, and might also provoke retaliation against the Church by many rulers.[67] Moreover, the proclamation of the war would no doubt provoke the French invasion that Rome wanted to avoid.[68]

The Austrian proposals therefore led to long debate within the papal government. Busca's first comment, on 10 December, was only that the matter was being discussed, but the pope, "eager to gratify the Emperor," would write a letter of exhortation to Saxony. This was unlikely to satisfy Thugut, since there was no mention of the other rulers to whom he wished the pope to write; and even the brief to Saxony was not sent until 13 January.[69] Busca did not refer to the question again for three weeks, nor did he send Albani plenipotentiary powers. Albani had not been given such powers at the outset since neither he nor Busca had foreseen the need to negotiate a treaty. He had therefore to request them on 19 November and repeatedly over the next six weeks,[70] but no reply came. Busca feared that, if given these powers, Albani might agree to yield the Legations—a fear that reflected not any real weakness on Albani's part, but rather Busca's obsession with the Legations, which paralyzed Albani for six crucial weeks.[71]

Albani saw Thugut frequently during December, but without plenipotentiary powers, with no word from Rome on the war of religion, he could undertake no serious negotiation. Thugut showed growing irritation;[72] the Austrian position in Italy was deteriorating while Rome delayed action that might help to shore

---

[67]Also 17 December 1796, and Consalvi to Albani, Rome, 10 December 1796, *ibid.*
[68]Busca to Albani, Rome, 31 December 1796, *ibid.*
[69]Busca to Albani, Rome, 10 December 1796, 13 January 1797, *ibid.*
[70]Albani to Busca, Vienna, 19, 24 November, 14, 24, 28, 30 December 1796, *ibid.*
[71]Busca to Albani, Rome, 17 January 1797, *ibid.* Nothing in Albani's reports indicates that he was any more willing to cede the Legations than was Busca.
[72]Albani to Busca, Vienna, 18, 24, 28, 30 December 1796, *ibid.*

it up. His comments became increasingly suspicious and bitter. If Rome truly wanted an alliance, why did the Vatican not send Albani plenipotentiary powers? Austria was willing to defend the papacy, but the Holy See must sign a formal treaty, and must first show its sincerity by proclaiming the war of religion. Albani sought to restrict the extent of the war of religion to those areas where Catholics were under attack by the French, but Thugut insisted it must be general, and especially that it apply to Spain, which he hoped might be forced by Catholic pressure to break with France.[73]

In late December Thugut found another way in which Rome might be useful. Albani had mentioned that Rome had an army of fifteen thousand, but lack of officers, arms, and training made it of little use. Thugut saw that, properly led and armed, this force could be of value by attacking the French from the south while the Austrian army attacked from the north. He promised to hasten the departure of General Colli and a staff of officers to train the papal troops, and to send as many weapons as he could.[74]

Albani was encouraged by this promise, and also by an audience with Francis II on 17 December, which convinced him that the emperor "could not be better disposed towards us." Most of the Emperor's remarks, however, were general in nature; his only specific promise was to include the papacy in any armistice with France. Albani tactfully brought up the Legations, not in the context of Thugut's demands, but only of Spanish and French interest in them. Francis II agreed that their loss would undermine the papal economy and declared he would "do all he could to save them."[75] His remarks aroused great hopes at Rome, where they were interpreted as proving that he did not support Thugut's demands, though this was only an argument from silence.[76]

Albani was nonetheless pessimistic, foreseeing a breakdown of the talks unless Rome acted soon. On 28 December he warned that Rome "must come to a decision now," or it would lose any hope of Austrian protection. Either "we trust in the general

---

[73]Albani to Busca, Vienna, 18 December 1796, *ibid.*
[74]Albani to Busca, Vienna, 21 December 1796, *ibid.*
[75]Albani to Busca, Vienna, 18 December 1796, *ibid.*
[76]Busca to Albani, Rome, 7 January 1796, *ibid.*

assurances given us and decide on that basis to break with France . . . and ally with the emperor, . . . or we decide that those assurances do not suffice, and . . . negotiate with France."[77]

And indeed, the next day Thugut told him bluntly that the emperor, his patience exhausted, demanded that Rome end its procrastination. With bitterness he reviewed the talks to date, condemning Rome's failure to send plenipotentiary powers or declare a war of religion, and accusing it of "trying to gain time to see if Mantua falls, so it can join the winning side." Rome had wasted six vital weeks; "now the time for a treaty is past . . . ; if you want to go to war, do so, we will give you what help we can."[78]

Albani's report of this conversation arrived just after Rome had finally reached a decision. On 31 December, Albani was sent powers to sign "a most secret treaty" in which the emperor should "promise to preserve the integrity of the Papal State, including the Legations . . . ; and to save the Pope from his obligations under the armistice." In return, the pope would unite his army with Austria's, send all the supplies and money he could, and declare of war of religion—but the latter must not be mentioned in the treaty. As Busca explained:

> Since the declaration of a war of religion must be independent of any worldly consideration . . . you must not put this promise into writing, . . . so that no document will appear that would allow anyone to say the Pope used the cloak of religion to cover a war in defense of his temporal domain . . . . Later, the Pope will solemnly proclaim a war of religion, inviting all Catholic princes to take part. . . .[79]

This proviso followed from the principle that papal spiritual powers must not be used for temporal ends. However, it posed an obstacle to a treaty, for while Rome insisted that a war of religion be proclaimed only after the signing of a treaty, Thugut demanded that its proclamation must precede a treaty. Moreover, papal

---

[77]Albani to Busca, Vienna, 28 December 1796, *ibid.*
[78]Albani to Busca, Vienna, 30 December 1796, *ibid.*
[79]Busca to Albani, Rome, 31 December 1796, *ibid.*

insistence that the emperor promise to defend the integrity of the Papal State conflicted with Thugut's interest in the Legations. It would thus have been difficult for Albani and Thugut to come to terms under the best of circumstances; but as it was, time had run out. When Albani showed Thugut his powers to negotiate a treaty, the minister replied only "this is all very well, but it is too late."[80]

It was indeed too late for Austria, whose position in Lombardy was on the verge of collapse—Mantua fell on 2 February—and which had then to concentrate on defending its core lands, with nothing to spare for the Papal State. Busca, under attack for his handling of the negotiations, then declared the failure to sign a treaty an "act of Providence," for otherwise Rome would have been tied to the losing side.[81] But Rome was not to escape unscathed; time had also run out for its hope of escaping another French attack, ironically, as a result of its attempt to secure Austrian protection against that contingency. Busca, encouraged by the Emperor's benevolent words, wrote Albani on 7 January to express enthusiasm for the alliance and promise that Rome would do all it could to help Austria.[82] Unfortunately, "the courier was arrested by order of General Bonaparte, and his letters seized. . . ."[83] On 2 February he invaded the Papal State and again defeated the papal army. The papacy at first refused to seek peace, preferring another appeal to Francis II.[84] Thugut replied that Austria had no aid to send; the most he could offer the pope was a refuge at Vienna if he were driven from Rome, adding, in one

---

[80]Albani to Busca, Vienna, 14 January 1796., *ibid.*
[81]Busca to Albani, Rome, 4 February 1797, *ibid.*
[82]Busca to Albani, 7 January 1797, *ibid.*
[83]Busca to Albani, 18 January 1797, *ibid.* Napoleon's proclamation of 1 February 1797, in his *Correspondence* (32 vols., 1858-1870), II, 371-372. Busca was not at first much alarmed by the interception, for a new Austrian army was advancing from the north, while General Colli believed that he would need only six weeks to whip the papal army into fighting shape, and he could then attack the French from the south, but on 13 January Napoleon defeated the Austrians at Rivoli and drove them northward again; the fall of Mantua was now inevitable: Busca to Albani, Rome, 4 February 1797. The contrast between the views of Napoleon and those of the Directory towards Rome at this time are brought out in Giustino Filippone, *Le relazioni tra lo Stato Pontificio e la Francia Rivoluzionaria: storia diplomatica del Trattato di Tolentino* (2 vols., Milan, 1961-1979), II, 623-628.
[84]Busca to Albani, Rome, 4 February 1797, AV, Germania.

last effort to salvage something, that in that case "it would greatly please the Emperor," if Pius first proclaimed the war of religion.[85] But Napoleon's inexorable advance had driven the papacy to realize at last how futile were its hopes of Austrian protection; when he suggested peace talks, the papacy agreed, and on 19 February signed the Treaty of Tolentino.[86] The terms were still harsher than those of the armistice: all three Legations were ceded, papal claims to Avignon abandoned, and a larger indemnity imposed. However, Napoleon did not attempt to impose conditions infringing papal religious authority; it was this "one true and essential advantage" that allowed Rome to accept the treaty.[87]

Busca was universally criticized for this disastrous outcome,[88] with some justice. His failure was owing in part to the defects of his character—indecisive, overly cautious, lacking in the successful diplomat's pragmatic grasp of reality, of the art of the possible; but it was also owing to an anachronistic view of international affairs in general and Austro-papal relations in particular, and this he shared with most of the Roman ruling class. As Albani pointed out, Busca had in essence two options. He could put his trust in Austria, sign a treaty as Thugut insisted, trusting in Rome's ability to evade any later demand for the Legations, and throw all Rome's moral and material resources into the struggle against France. Then, if Austria won, Rome could hope to escape without loss from the crisis of 1796. Alternatively, Busca might have explored the French offers to discuss a more lenient peace and so, perhaps, have freed Rome from some conditions of the armistice.

---

[85] Albani to Busca, Vienna, 15 February 1797, *ibid.*

[86] On the negotiation of the Treaty of Tolentino, see the exhaustive account in Filipponi, *Le relazioni.*

[87] "The conditions are hard, but since the Catholic religion remains intact, all the rest can be endured in return for this one true and essential advantage." Busca to Albani, Rome, 28 February 1797, AV, Germania.

[88] "I am now a target for everyone's criticism," he lamented to Albani on 11 March 1797. He was forced to resign on 18 March 1797. Albani's career may also have suffered as a result of the failure of his mission, though he had in reality done as well as anyone could have under these difficult circumstances. His promotion to cardinal had been generally expected in 1796, but did not in fact take place until 1801, a delay for which the failure of the 1796 negotiations with Vienna seems a plausible explanation. Consalvi to Litta, Rome, 16 April 1796 in Wittichen, "Brief Consalvi's," p. 157.

Busca did neither. He ignored the French offers, but delayed a treaty with Austria until too late. In the end, Rome was left alone to face another French invasion.

Still, if Busca's diplomacy left much to be desired, it must be admitted that even a far better diplomat would have been hard pressed to achieve a satisfactory outcome. The position of the Papal State in 1796-1797 was difficult indeed, perhaps hopeless. It is far from certain that either of the options suggested by Albani would have led to results truly better. Busca's assertion that it was providential that Rome had not signed a treaty with Austria was self-serving, but it held an element of truth. In retrospect, it seems clear that Austria had little hope of defeating Napoleon in 1796-1797, and so was not in a position to protect Rome, treaty or no treaty. One may ask: Might the war of religion have altered the balance, arousing resistance that would have tied down enough of Napoleon's strength to allow Austria to defeat him? Certainly, the potential for resistance existed.[89] There was much popular hostility to the French in Italy, and, even without papal encouragement, there were numerous uprisings. Scattered and uncoordinated, they achieved nothing, but perhaps, given direction and leadership by Rome and Vienna, they would have been more effective. After all, in 1799 the *Sanfedisti*, the peasant Army of the Holy Faith led by Cardinal Ruffo, did drive the French from southern Italy. But this potential must not be exaggerated; the *Sanfedisti* won their victories mainly in rugged terrain well-suited to their irregular style of warfare, not in the flat Lombard plain, and they did not have to face Napoleon, but only lesser commanders and demoralized troops. Napoleon might have been capable of neutralizing a war of religion. When he invaded the Papal State in 1797, he carried out a skillful propaganda, stressing that he was not fighting religion, but only the papacy as a political power; this propaganda, accompanied by elaborate displays of respect for churches and clergy, was effective—he met no popular resistance.[90] Thus it is

---

[89]On the popular uprisings against the French, see G. Lumbroso, *I moti populari contro i Francesi (1796-1800)* (Florence, 1932).

[90]See Filipponi, *Le relazione*, II, 626-648, on the care Napoleon took to convince the people of the Papal State that he was not fighting against religion or the Church, and his success in preventing a popular uprising out of religious motives, a danger which he took very seriously.

not at all clear that a war of religion would have given Austria the edge over Napoleon; what is clear, is that an unsuccessful war of religion would have made Rome's position far worse.

As for the second alternative, it seems doubtful that Rome would have gained much by responding to French offers to discuss a more lenient peace. Those offers were made, not from a sincere wish for peace, but only to buy time. It is unlikely that France would have given Rome better terms once Austria had been defeated, and still more unlikely that, even had such a peace been signed, it would have lasted. On that score, the events following the Treaty of Tolentino are instructive. Busca was replaced in March 1797 by Cardinal Doria, who was well regarded at Madrid and Paris; his appointment signified a swing away from the policy of resistance to France and back to that of attempted conciliation of France in reliance upon Spain.[91] This policy was no more successful than under Zelada. Partly because of bad luck—the death of another French dignitary in a Roman riot—but primarily because of the Directory's policy of expansion in Italy and its essential hostility to the papacy, the French again invaded the Papal State in 1798, this time carrying off Pius VI to die in captivity and replacing the Temporal Power with a transitory Roman Republic.[92]

During 1796-1799, then, circumstances were so unfavorable to the papacy that all its options were likely to end badly. In this it only exemplified the situation of all the Italian states during these years. Those that tried to follow a peaceful policy and to conciliate France, like Tuscany, fared no better than those that fought, like Sardinia. All in the end fell victim to the dynamic, imperialistic, and messianic drive of revolutionary France.[93]

---

[91] Jean Leflon, *Pie VII* (Paris, 1957), p. 155.
[92] Pastor, XL, 324-390. Gendry, II, 280-445.
[93] On the efforts of Tuscany to stay out of the war, conciliate France and preserve its independence, all ultimately unsuccessful, see Franz Pesendorfer, *Ein Kampf um die Toskana. Großherzog Ferdinand III* (Vienna, 1984).

TAMING THE EAGLES: THE HABSBURG MONARCHY'S POLITICAL USE OF THE "REVOLUTIONARY" NEOCLASSICAL STYLE[1]

by

Charlotte Stokes

When Napoleon lived in Schönbrunn palace during the French occupation of Vienna, he had two eagles, his personal symbols, mounted on obelisks on either side of the royal palace's main gate. (Figure 1) Historians later remarked in bemused tones that upon the restoration of full Habsburg power, Franz I refused to remove the eagles. But these historians should not have been so surprised; the Habsburgs had been turning revolutionary art to their own purposes since the beginning of the French Revolution and would continue to do so through the Biedermeier period and into the building of the Ringstrasse in the last half of the nineteenth century.

The symbolism of Napoleon's imperial eagles[2] originally came from the ancient Romans. The eagles were only a small aspect of the Neoclassical style that swept Europe in the late eighteenth

---

[1]The author wishes to thank her colleague, Professor Susan Wood, for taking the photographs used in this essay.

[2]The importance of the eagle as Napoleon's personal symbol is evident, long after his death, in Antoine-Louis Barye's *Napoleon I Crowned by History and the Fine Arts*, the 1857 pediment for the New Louvre. See Glenn F. Benge, "*Napoleon I Crowned by History and the Fine Arts:* The Drawings for Barye's Apotheosis Pediment for the New Louvre," *Art Journal*, XXXVIII (Spring 1979), 164-170.

Figure 1. Schönbrunn palace, main gate flanked by obelisks topped with Napoleon's eagles, Vienna.

century. However, the self-conscious use of antique motifs had begun during the Renaissance when Neoplatonic artists combined Classical mythology and Christianity. For example, in *The Birth of Venus*, Botticelli combined the Virgin Mary and Venus in one personage who symbolized a high moral state in which passion has been calmed and controlled by spiritual contemplation. However controlled, the crusading Savonarola had burned similar paintings because of their potential corruption of Christian belief. Clearly, the blending of the Classical and the contemporary had its dangers.

In their architecture, Renaissance masters not only employed such forms as Classical columns with a good understanding of the various orders, but also organized these forms into repeated patterns by using a rigorous modular geometry. In general, architects who looked to the Classical past have found that the rational, understandable, and predictable rules underlying the forms are as useful as the forms themselves.

Beginning with the first tries at real archeology at Pompeii and Herculaneum on the slopes of Mt. Vesuvius, the relationship between the eighteenth century and the Classical is much more complex than in the preceding periods. Indeed, by the end of the century, the height of Neoclassical style in France coincided with the French occupation of Italy, especially that area around Mt. Vesuvius. In their visits to Pompeii itself, the artists and their educated patrons had seen the *real* Classical past. In 1740 Horace Walpole wrote to a friend:

> There is nothing of the kind known in the world; I mean a Roman city entire of that age, and that has not been corrupted with modern repairs. . . . Most of the discoveries in Rome were made in a barbarous age, where they only ransacked the ruins in quest of treasure, and had no regard to the form and being of the building; or to any circumstances that might give light into its use and history.[3]

If the artists and their patrons could not travel to see the originals at Pompeii or other ancient sites, they could see engraved reproductions in such publications as *Le Antichità di Ercolano esposti* and Stuart and Revett's *The Antiquities of Athens*.[4] During the middle years of the eighteenth century the use of Classical art was mild and decorative, as seen in the works of Raphael Mengs, giving little hint of the astringent style that was to follow. Often contemporary paintings seemed only popular dressing to promote the sale of copies of antiquities or the actual plunder from the digs at Pompeii and Herculaneum.[5]

---

[3]University of Michigan Museum of Art, *Pompeii, As Source and Inspiration: Reflections in Eighteenth- and Nineteenth-Century Art*. ([Exhibition organized in 1976-1977 by graduate students in the Museum Practice Program] Ann Arbor, 1977): p. 14.

[4]Accadèmia ercolanese di archeologia, *Le Antichità di Ercolano esposti* (8 vols., Naples, 1757-1792) and James Stuart and Nicholas Revett, *The Antiquities of Athens: Measured and Delineated by James Stuart and Nicholas Revett* (5 vols., London, 1762-1830).

[5]Albert Boime, *Art in an Age of Revolution: 1750-1800* (Chicago, 1987), pp. 60-62.

Throughout the last half of the eighteenth century the Habsburgs incorporated many Classical subjects into their palaces, churches, and gardens. Johann Christian Wilhelm Beyer's group *Olympia and her Son Alexander* was among many he tucked into the shrubbery of the Schönbrunn palace gardens from 1771 until 1781. But in these gardens the serious rectitude of Classical subjects was overshadowed by the opulence of the setting. Images taken from Greece and Rome were also made to speak of a sensual life that reinforced the sumptuousness of the royal Rococo. Such sculptures as Beyer's nymph, *Egeria* (c. 1779) the bearer of the beautiful fountain's waters in the grotto of Schönbrunn garden had its source in the lighter, more sensuous antiquities. Thus the artists and the nobility, who were concerned only with Rococo adornment, could find what they wanted in the rich mines on the flanks of Mt. Vesuvius.

The ideas on which the French Revolution was based began to imbue the Classical themes with moral weight. The first sign of this shift was the introduction of a middle-class morality. These values are present in Angelika Kauffmann's *Cornelia, Mother of the Gracchi* (1785), which told the moralistic story of a virtuous Roman matron: when a friend boasted of her jewels, Cornelia responded by saying that her children were *her* jewels. In Classical terms Kauffmann's painting recast the domestic bliss found in royal group portraits in which Empress Maria Theresa is surrounded by her many children.

Although the serious use of Classical themes had begun before the French Revolution, during and just after the Revolution the Neoclassical style in art and architecture became the outward and visible sign of the new political structure. Simple, columned buildings were seen as purifying the tradition of highly ornamented Baroque buildings that had served the European monarchies. In 1808, during Napoleon's most successful years, Pierre Vignon's grand and severe La Madeleine was begun in Paris as the Temple of Glory. Like such recreations of ancient temples the stoic draped or nude figures carved of plain white marble established a rigorous morality beyond that of the histrionic gestures of Baroque art. Paintings, such as Jacques-Louis David's *Oath of the Horatii* (1784), told stories of the strictest republican virtue. David's equally strict flat image, which was based on ancient reliefs, was in sharp contrast to the three-dimensional indulgence of Rococo decorative painting.

The Neoclassical usually meant a direct—sometimes slavish—use of antique motifs and an architecture governed by a geometric regularity. In those times of great chaotic change, it seemed that Neoclassical rules gave to art a traditional structure that was lacking in society. During the French Revolution the Neoclassical style provided not only strict moral and patriotic models from the past, but also indicated that the past—albeit the distant and foreign past—could provide some rules for the future. By taking the ancient arts of Greece and Rome as their models, the revolutionaries could maintain that they were not completely cut adrift from all moorings; the tighter the rules the more comforting the result. But artists and architects had to be exact in their applications to make the moral implications of their choices understood.

Above all, Neoclassicism was a political tool. Distinct from earlier uses of similar themes and forms, the eighteenth-century revolutionaries used Neoclassicism as propaganda—not just as an aesthetic device or even a general philosophy. Their art was marked by a reverence for the values of the Classical past and a high moral tone that manifested itself in Classical symbolism for contemporary issues. Indeed, they reinterpreted the past in order to meet contemporary needs. The ancient pagan subjects had been flexible enough to become handmaidens of Christian thought, but, of more use to those who wanted to rid themselves of all recent institutions, Classical subjects had a long tradition and an ethical structure that could substitute for Christian thought, morality, and belief. According to Levey, the ethical systems of Neoclassicism did replace religion during the late eighteenth century.[6] Of this new ethos Praz wrote:

> It was in the spirit of Plutarch that the men of the Revolution interpreted the history, the art and the character of the ancients. In the eyes of Claude-Nicolas Ledoux and of Friedrich Gilly, the Doric order was radiant with revolutionary spirit: they seemed to feel geometrical shapes to be imbued with a human character, animated by an energetic will. In Plutarch, and in the Doric manner, they discovered a lesson in virility, in firmness, in heroic spirit. . . . In [portraits] classicism was no longer the material

---

[6]Michael Levey, *Rococo to Revolution* (New York, 1969), p. 166.

of dreams; rather, it permeated a living material with its own quality.[7]

The change that Praz described is quite evident in the ways political leaders were portrayed. In the years before the French Revolution, Beyer placed *Cincinnatus* (1771-1881) among the sculptures of Greek and Roman gods, heroes, and allegorical figures that decorated the Schönbrunn gardens. Cincinnatus was the Roman general who fought successfully for the state and modestly returned to civilian life afterwards. His presence in the royal gardens hints at the acceptance of a modern definition of patriotism reflecting the revolutionary ideas that were being formed elsewhere.

When the ideas associated with Cincinnatus were included in the portrait sculpture *George Washington* (1788-92), by French sculptor Jean Antoine Houdon, the symbols of the Classical past were fully integrated into revolutionary political life. (Cincinnatus was a commonly understood reference to Washington, especially after he declined a kingship and voluntarily returned to private life at the end of his Presidency.) In Houdon's sculpture Washington, who wears the uniform of a general, holds a walking stick, indicating his return to the life of a gentleman farmer, while his sword, his military duty, hangs inactive on fasces, the bound rods that symbolize the union.

Although Washington is shown as very much a gentleman of his own time, the sculpture has a strong Classical flavor. The American Cincinnatus stands in a Classical *contrapposto* pose, or as close to such a position as can be expected of an eighteenth-century gentleman in heeled boots and knee breeches. The details of fabric and fashion are meticulous, but the pose and the monumentality of the figure seem derived from such works as the *Apollo Belvedere*, a first-century Hellenistic sculpture, much admired in the eighteenth century. Houdon's *Washington* is a work of art that effectively integrates the values of the past into the present. In it contemporary political issues are given a depth of meaning from the Classical past, while Classical ideas gain relevance in contemporary events.

---

[7]Mario Praz, *On Neoclassicism*, trans., Angus Davidson (London, 1969), p. 99.

The *Apollo Belvedere* may have been a less happy influence on *Napoleon as Jupiter* (1806) by the Italian sculptor Antonio Canova. In this larger-than-life-size nude portrait of Napoleon, the balance between contemporary political issues and symbolism from the past has been tipped to the past—to a very stylized past. To viewers today, the sculpture does not speak as much to Napoleon's greatness as to the irony of the great general standing stark naked in the stairwell of the London house of his victorious nemesis, the Duke of Wellington.

With their long traditional reign, the Habsburgs had only rare need for Neoclassicism's moral authority and strict forms. One such instance is the commission by Franz I to Franz Anton Zauner to cast a monument to honor his uncle and mentor, Josef II, to be placed in the Josefsplatz in the Hofburg. The *Monument to Emperor Josef II* (1795-1806) (Figure 2), which is closely based on the second-century Roman statue *Marcus Aurelius*, firmly put the Austrian Emperor in the line of the Classical caesars.[8] Begun in 1795, three years after Franz I ascended the throne, the monument was erected in 1807, between Napoleon's two occupations of Vienna.

Although it is a very correct example of Neoclassicism, the *Monument to Emperor Josef II* neither speaks the moving rhetoric of the Revolution, nor argues the more controversial aspects of the reign of Josef II. The bronze reliefs on the base show the emperor dressed as he is in the equestrian monument, as a Roman general, among Classical allegorical figures. On the right side of the base the emperor promotes commerce by exhorting Mercury to untie the hands of Trade, shown as a young woman in antique drapery seated on created goods near a waiting ship. The relief on the other side of the base illustrates the emperor's concern for the welfare of the peoples of his far-flung domains, including details of architecture and traditional farming.[9] The sea imagery of the former is balanced and completed by the land imagery of the latter, but in both the imperial concern for the general good is the primary and non-controversial message. From

---

[8]Ilsa Barea, *Vienna* (New York, 1967), pp. 122-123.
[9]Hermann Burg, *Der Bildhauer Franz Anton Zauner und Seine Zeit* (Vienna, 1915), pp. 94-119.

Figure 2. Franz Anton Zauner, The *Monument to Emperor Josef II* (1795-1806), Josefsplatz, Hofburg, Vienna.

a safe distance Franz I could honor his liberal uncle, while keeping to a more conservative path himself.[10] Thus, Franz I appropriated Neoclassicism, the style of the Revolution, to reaffirm Habsburg imperial tradition, while giving only the slightest nod to more progressive ideas.

---

[10]For a discussion of the relationship of Franz II and his uncle Josef II, see Walter Consuelo Langsam, *Francis the Good: Education of an Emperor: 1768-1792* (New York, 1949).

Not only portrait sculptures but Neoclassical works with purely antique themes could take on a contemporary significance. Good examples are found in Canova's two treatments of the civic hero, Theseus: *Theseus and the Dead Minotaur* (1781-1782) and *Theseus and the Centaur* (1805-1819) (Figure 3) owned by Franz I. In the earlier version, his first truly Neoclassical work, Canova set the scene at the end of the drama to illustrate not the violence of battle, but the Classical calm of victory. In the latter, his composition is more active, but its Classical balance stops and fixes any sense of movement. Bassi comments that it is too much based on

Figure 3. Antonio Canova, *Theseus and the Centaur* (1805-1819), Kunsthistorisches Museum, Vienna.

Classical sources such as the metopes from the Parthenon.[11] However, the emphatic lines of Canova's figures seem to have more to do with the studied and bookish eighteenth-century engravings after the Parthenon metopes in Stuart and Revett than on the original time-worn reliefs themselves.

The political meaning ascribed to these works developed as did the aesthetic concerns. The *Theseus and the Dead Minotaur* probably illustrated an Italian patriotic theme, specifically the conflict between Venice and the Ottoman Empire involving the Island of Crete.[12] When Canova returned to the Greek hero in *Theseus and the Centaur*, it had significance for Napoleon, who originally commissioned it for one of Milan's public squares, probably on the occasion of his second coronation in Milan in 1805—the same year he first occupied Vienna. From his first occupation of Milan, Napoleon had been a powerful and popular figure there. Canova couched the Napoleonic myth in the late, very Greek, revolutionary symbolism of the Classical hero battling the part-man, part-horse centaur, who personified the basest emotions and social chaos. The same Napoleonic myth lay behind more realistic images, such as David's *Napoleon at St.-Bernard* (1800), in which he was shown astride a horse, controlling it as he did his armies and, supposedly, his own destiny. Napoleon probably equated the battles of Theseus, the Greek civic champion, with his own military struggles.

No doubt because of the shifting currents of Napoleon's successes and failures, *Theseus and the Centaur* remained in the artist's studio until 1819, when it was acquired for Franz I, on the occasion of his fourth marriage.[13] Given the history of this piece there is no little irony in its acquisition by the Habsburg monarch.

Designed to house *Theseus and the Centaur* was a small replica of the Theseum, a Classical temple in Athens. The Viennese Temple of Theseus was begun in 1820 by Peter von Nobile, a court architect. The Habsburg monarch did not intend to install the Temple of Theseus in the summer informality of the Schön-

---

[11]Elena Bassi, *Canova* (Rome, 1943), p. 34.
[12]Boime, *Art in an Age of Revolution*, pp. 140-141.
[13]Bassi, *Canova*, p. 34.

brunn gardens, but rather near the Hofburg in the new Volksgarten, laid out in 1819. (Figure 4) The Volksgarten occupied the site of the Burgbastei, which Napoleon had demolished with great and widely destructive explosions only ten years before.[14]

Figure 4. Peter von Nobile, Temple of Theseus (1820) in Volksgarten (1819) near the Hofburg, Vienna.

As in the *Theseus and the Centaur* itself, there is a good deal of irony in the building of this little Neoclassical temple. Franz I selected this building in the Doric style, the most severe, heroic style associated with the French Revolution. Further, according to Kassal-Mikula, the Neoclassical style itself would come to be associated with the Habsburg court, because of this and other

---

[14]Stella Musulin, *Vienna in the Age of Metternich: from Napoleon to Revolution: 1805-1848* (Boulder, CO, 1975), p. 95.

commissions.[15] Thus the Classical rules that once gave a sense of order to the Revolution were appropriated by a conservative government in order to set strict standards that precluded any revolution in style. Into this Temple of Theseus was installed the sculpture that Napoleon had commissioned to celebrate his victories. All this, while Napoleon lay dying at Elba.

But another point should not be missed. Even while it was being built, the Temple of Theseus was largely irrelevant. Although the all-encompassing Ringstrasse and great additions to the Hofburg—the Neue Hofburg and the Heldenplatz—were not yet built, the small temple was, from the beginning, hardly more than a large garden folly without an important governmental purpose. This is in contrast with Napoleon's La Madeleine in Paris, which was large, centrally located, and desirable enough to be converted to another purpose when the times changed. Even though La Madeleine became a church upon its completion in 1842, its severe and powerful shape is an undeniable reminder of its revolutionary origins.

As the repressive era of Metternich set in after Napoleon's fall, the Habsburg's problem was to create a more humane image. The Neoclassical ideal, illustrated by the Temple of Theseus, was bent to serve the domestic needs of the middle- and upper-classes, who were denied a political voice in the highly controlled government. In buildings such as Josef Kornhäusel's rebuilt Schottenhof (1826-1828), Neoclassical severity became modesty and Neoclassical regularity lost many of its Classical roots. The proportions remain, but the forms are self-effacing, not noisy revolutionary statements.

Theseus and his temple were more properly Neo-Greek, not just Neoclassical. The refinement of Neo-Greek sculpture and the strictness of Neo-Greek architecture were selected for monuments that were associated with cultural matters and democratic thought.[16] This was the proper understanding of the style that was advanced by the scholar, Johann Winckelmann, who had made

---

[15]Renata Kassal-Mikula, "Architecture from 1815 to 1848," in Robert Waissenberger, ed., *Vienna in the Biedermeier Era: 1815-1858*, anon. trans. (New York, 1986), p. 142.

[16]Geoffrey Broadbent, *Neo-Classicism* (London: Profile 23 A.D. special issue, *Architectural Design* 49 no. 8/9 [n.d]), p. 6.

systematic studies of the arts of Greek and Rome. Famous in his own time, he was awarded a gold medal by Maria Theresa.[17] In selecting the Neo-Greek *Theseus* and the copy of the *Theseum* for his new park, Franz I knew his Classical symbolism on many levels.

On the other hand, Neo-Roman grandeur was associated with empire and republican virtue.[18] As the nineteenth century progressed, the Neo-Greek diminished and the Neo-Roman took more territory, especially along the Ringstrasse. With Karl Kundmann's *Pallas Athena* (1902) in front, Theophil von Hansen's Parliament (1873-1883) supposedly referred to Greek democratic ideals. However, Parliament's broad practical facade is definitely Roman. Not only does Parliament differ in style from the earlier, pure Neo-Greek Temple of Theseus, it differs in function: Parliament is a true center of power. Its temple forms were freely modified to suit the needs of a modern parliamentary government in a central European climate. In contrast, the Temple of Theseus, across the Ringstrasse, has little useful interior space. It is a park ornament, hardly noticed by the passing tourists.

Finally, Canova's *Theseus* itself was removed from the temple and placed in the new Art History Museum (1881) built by Gottfried Semper and Karl von Hasenauer. As the Temple of Theseus became an ornament for the Volksgarten, the *Theseus* became part of the ornamentation of the art museum. The sculpture sits on the landing of the grand stair to the main galleries. It is so much a part of the decor that this large, dramatic work is rarely mentioned in the guidebooks that describe the works of art at this great museum. We are not invited to contemplate *Theseus and the Centaur* as an example of a Classical hero overcoming the beast. We cannot; we are on the stairs going someplace. Thus Canova's *Theseus* and Beyer's mild figures in the Schönbrunn gardens share the same fate at the hands of those with imperial power. Good and not-so-good, all the art became part of the overall decor, the furniture, of the imperial city.

At Schönbrunn the eagles were kept because they did not change the undeniable meaning of the palace. Indeed, the eagles

---

[17] Praz, *On Neoclassicism*, p. 63.
[18] Broadbent, *Neo-Classicism*, p. 6.

now seem merely a quote from the grand, but never-built, designs for Schönbrunn made in the 1690s by Johann Bernhard Fischer von Erlach, who flanked the main gate with a pair of columns capped by the imperial emblems. As Napoleon's son, the Duke of Reichstadt, was kept with respect and affection until his early, but apparently quite natural, death at Schönbrunn, so too the eagles were kept. Neither son nor eagles had any power as Napoleon's surrogates. Like imperial family members, imperial symbols had to be respected, whatever their source.

As did the revolutionaries, the Habsburgs made political use of Neoclassicism. The strict style and the ancient symbols were appropriated to justify the stability and the social order established by the monarchy. The Habsburgs had no need to destroy the revolutionary art; they just absorbed it.

ANTONIO CANOVA AND

AUSTRIAN ART POLICY

by

Christopher M.S. Johns

When the political aspects of Antonio Canova's sculpture come under scholarly scrutiny, it is often his work for Napoleon and other members of the Bonaparte family that receives the most attention. This phenomenon is partly attributable to the spectacular nature of Napoleonic art patronage as an expression of cultural power and to the competitive proclivities of many members of the family. For instance, Napoleon, long aware of Canova's fame, only sought to possess a Canova sculpture after his brother-in-law, Joachim Murat, purchased *Cupid and Psyche*, a masterpiece that elicited universal praise.[1] Similarly, Pauline Borghese commissioned her portrait as Venus Victrix after Canova had been commanded by her brother to carve the colossal *Napoleon as Mars*.[2]

---

[1] Fred Licht and David Finn, *Canova* (New York, 1983), pp. 164-171 and Mario Praz and Giuseppe Pavanello, *L'opera completa del Canova* (Milan, 1976), p. 98, illustrated as plate 17.

[2] For the Borghese portrait, see especially Licht and Finn, *Canova*, pp. 130-143. The Apsley House *Napoleon* has been studied by Hugh Honour, "Canova's 'Napoleon'," *Apollo*, 98 (1973), 180-184; and by Licht and Finn, pp. 97-103. See also my forthcoming article "Antonio Canova's 'Napoleon as Mars': Nudity and Mixed Genre in Neoclassical Portraiture," *Proceedings of the Consortium on Revolutionary Europe* (in press).

As a usurping dynasty, the Bonapartes sought to use the arts for their glorification and as a means of legitimizing their rule in the time-honored realm of art politics. Although much can be learned about the role of art in revolutionary era politics by study of Canova's Napoleonic commissions, the sculptor's Habsburg patronage rewards study equally, for it sheds much light on the

Figure 1. Antonio Canova, *Hercules and Lichas*, 1795-1812. Rome, Galleria Nazionale d'Arte Moderna. Photo: Art Resource.

Figure 2. Antonio Canova, Tomb of the Archduchess Maria Christina of Austria, 1798-1805. Vienna, Augustinerkirche. Photo: Author.

legitimist art policies of an established dynasty and reveals the sculptor's attempts to remain politically neutral. This essay will examine two important Canova monuments with links to Imperial Austria: *Hercules and Lichas* (Figure 1) and the renowned Tomb of the Archduchess Maria Christina (Figure 2). In analyzing the reasons why the former was rejected by the Emperor Francis II and the latter work accepted, emphasis is placed on the theme of ambiguity within an allegorical or mythological context, a flexible definition of meaning deemed essential by Canova at a time when he was under tremendous political pressure from the French. Moreover, these two group sculptures examined in the context of their creation, patronage and installation provide essential clues to the sculptor's own political convictions and his attempted separation of political specificity from the universal, enduring aesthetic he was trying to achieve.

Hercules and Lichas was originally commissioned from Canova in March 1795 by Don Onorato Gaetani, a member of the Neapolitan nobility, and the sculptor had completed the full-scale *modello* by April of the following year.[3] Unfortunately, the fall of the Bourbon monarchy in Naples forced the patron into exile and he defaulted on the contract. For three years Canova attempted in vain to attract a patron for a marble version of the *modello*. In May 1799, the artist was approached by Count Tiberio Roberti, a functionary of the Austrian government at Verona, to create a monument to celebrate the Imperial victory over the French at the battle of Magnano.[4]

Due to numerous commissions and political uncertainties, Canova declined to create a new sculpture, but instead offered *Hercules and Lichas* to Verona as a victory monument. His letter to Roberti proposing the sculpture is of great interest and directly addresses the issue of art and politics:

> Voi già sapete che a Roma io stavo lavorando per certo signore di Napoli un gruppo rappresentante 'Ercole furioso che getta Lica nel mare', e questo della grandezza del celebre 'Ercole Farnese'. Non so poi se io v'abbia mai raccontata la storiella di certi Francesi sopra di quel gruppo. Questi dicevano che tal'opera avrebbesi dovuto collocarla a Parigi; che l'Ercole sarebbe stato 'l'Ercole francese', che gettava la Monarchia al

---

[3]Licht and Finn, *Canova*, pp. 188-191; Praz and Pavanello, *L'opera del Canova*, pp. 106-107. See also Christopher M.S. Johns, "Antonio Canova's Drawings for 'Hercules and Lichas,'" *Master Drawings*, 27 (1990), in press.

[4]The Canova-Roberti correspondence has been published by Giuseppe Consolo, *Ercole e Lica di Antonio Canova che Verona acquistava per eternare la memoria della battaglia dei 5 Aprile 1799* (Padua, 1839). The author thanks Edgar Peters Bowron for supplying a photocopy of this rare book. See also Giampaolo Marchini, "La battaglia di Magnano e un mancato monumento del Canova a Verona," *Vita Veronese*, XXVIII (1975), 329-335.

vento. Voi ben sapete ancora se io per tutto l'oro del mondo avessi mai aderito a tale idea. Ma ora questo 'Ercole' non potrebb'egli forse inverso della proposizione dei Francesi? Non potrebb' essere Lica la licenziosa libertà.

(You already know that in Rome I was working for a certain Neapolitan gentleman on a group representing the furious Hercules throwing Lichas into the sea, and this of the dimensions of the celebrated 'Hercules Farnese'. I do not know if I have ever recounted to you the little story of some Frenchmen concerning that group. They said that such a work must be set up in Paris; that Hercules would have been the "French Hercules," who was throwing Monarchy to the winds. You know well whether I would ever have adhered to such an idea for all the world's gold. But now this 'Hercules', perhaps would he not be able [to be] the inverse of the proposition of the French? Could not Lichas be licentious liberty?)[5]

Canova's absolute rejection of the French interpretation of the marble group and his corresponding eagerness to sell the idea to Verona as an Austrian monument must indicate pro-Austrian sympathies on the part of the sculptor, even if it was also in his financial interest to express himself thusly to Count Roberti. Canova, from his youth in the Veneto, had felt great attachment to his homeland and was outraged by Napoleon's cynical betrayal of the Serene Republic to Austria in the Treaty of Tolentino. And even though he resented the loss of the independence of Venice, the artist viewed Austria as a conservative, Catholic, and stabilizing influence, while he had good reason to associate France with anti-clericalism, violence to works of art, and social revolution.

Initially, Roberti and the Verona governors accepted Canova's offer for the *Hercules and Lichas* as a monument to Magnano but in a letter of 22 June 1799, the Imperial minister, Baron Thugut, forbade the Veronesi to purchase Canova's sculpture, expressing the Emperor's absolute veto of the project. Thugut cited Francis II's paternalistic concern for his new Italian subjects and the Imperial desire not to overburden the citizens of Verona with the

---

[5]The letter is quoted in Consolo, *Ercole e Lica di Canova*, pp. 16-17.

expense of the sculpture and its erection in the Piazza Brà.⁶ This decision must have been made with much reluctance, since Francis admired Canova greatly and had even attempted to persuade his celebrated Venetian subject to move his studio to Vienna. The Imperial ban on *Hercules and Lichas* was probably pronounced because of the ambiguity of the theme. Perhaps Francis was aware of the French response to the sculpture recorded in Canova's letter to Roberti, and he certainly knew of the traditional symbolic association of France and the demi-god Hercules. Such a work was open to varying interpretations, and for that reason was not suitable as a political monument. Francis II, long accustomed to the traditional Habsburg utilization of the arts for cultural and political aggrandizement, understood that Canova's group sculpture simply would not do. As a matter of art policy, an ambiguous monument must be rejected.

Even though Canova was disappointed with his failure to "place" *Hercules and Lichas* in Verona,⁷ he was still obliged to Francis for the continuation of his pension that had previously been granted by the Republic of Venice. In 1798, Canova had actually journeyed to Vienna to petition for the pension, and he not only achieved his primary purpose but also received a major commission from the Habsburgs for a tomb of the Archduchess Maria Christina, the recently deceased daughter of the late Empress Maria Theresa.⁸ This tomb, Canova's masterpiece in funerary sculpture, is profoundly different from traditional Christian tombs. The use of the pyramidal architectural setting and the presence of a funeral cortège consisting of figures representing the various stages of life (significantly, they are neither portraits nor personifications) underscore the tomb's central conceit: the universality of death. The absence of identifiable entities troubled the patron, Maria Christina's widower Prince Albert of Saxe-Teschen, who simply

---

⁶*Ibid.*, pp. 29-31. Thugut dated the letter from Vienna.
⁷*Ibid.*, pp. 31-32, 20 July 1799, a letter in which he responded graciously to the Provedditori of Verona after learning of the Imperial veto.
⁸For the Habsburg tomb, see Licht and Finn, *Canova*, pp. 66-75; and Fred Licht, "Canovas Monumentalplastik," in *Ideal und Wirklichkeit in der bildenden Kunst in späten 18. Jahrhundert*, ed. Herbert Beck, Peter C. Bol and Eva Maek-Gérard (Berlin, 1984), pp. 170-172. My account of the monument is greatly indebted to Licht's eloquent description and incisive analysis.

supplied his own *dramatis personae*.⁹ For an Imperial tomb in the Augustinerkirche celebrating an archduchess noted for piety, the monument is decidedly reticent about the individuality of the deceased, who is relegated to a bust profile portrait accompanied by a flying genius of death and a cherub at the apex of the pyramid. Only the setting of the tomb suggests a traditional Christian and Habsburg context.

The underplaying of individualism and dynastic symbolism with its accompanying funerary allegory are central components of Canova's tomb and are crucial for its interpretation. In an uncertain political climate and with the artist's desire to assert the superiority of aesthetic choice over subject matter, Canova's monument is self-consciously unpolitical and unpropagandistic. That his Austrian patron was a bit perplexed by the tomb's ambiguity and radical departure from tradition, seen in Albert's wish to invent a cast of characters for the cortège, is in some ways only a response of surprise at an unpolitical public sculpture in an era dominated by politically engaged public monuments. The Habsburgs, like Napoleon and many of Canova's other patrons, little understood the sculptor's goal of declaring art politically neutral. They wished merely to glorify themselves and their ideologies through art and to accrue the immense cultural prestige possession of Canova's sculptures conveyed. The artist's strategy of detachment was largely successful, due to the protection afforded him by his fame, but the impact of his artistic agenda was only an adumbration of the notion of art for art's sake that was to have such a decisive impact on later nineteenth-century art.

The rejection of *Hercules and Lichas* by the Habsburgs and the slightly modified acceptance of the Maria Christina tomb reveal an intelligent and consistent Imperial arts policy during the Napoleonic era. In refusing a public position for a work whose theme was, in their eyes, compromised by ambiguity, Francis II demonstrated his traditional concern with subject matter. The Emperor recognized the unacceptability of the marble group because he understood that public art must be unambiguous if it

---

⁹Canova's opposition to allegorical interpretation for the figures in the cortège and his ultimate acquiescence on the issue is recorded in Licht and Finn, *Canova*, p. 72, in English translation.

is to fulfil its primary function of political propaganda.[10] Canova's Imperial tomb shares the interpretive relativity of *Hercules and Lichas* but its emphatically Imperial setting and the dynastic associations of the church rendered the work acceptable. In short, the Habsburgs knew what they wanted and how far they were willing to compromise their political agenda, even to accommodate the age's most celebrated artist.

---

[10]This idea as a general feature of revolutionary public art has been observed by Hugh Honour, *Neoclassicism* (Harmondsworth, Middlesex, 1968), p. 78.

THE CALL TO REVOLUTION IN THE BOUDOIR:

A NEW LOOK AT MOZART'S SUSANNA IN

THE MARRIAGE OF FIGARO

by

Doris P. Tishkoff

In this exciting bicentennial year of the French Revolution, one thinks immediately of Mozart's opera *The Marriage of Figaro* in respect to the importation of revolutionary ideas from France to Austria in the decade of the eighties. Here was a theater piece that provoked a riot in 1784 when it finally opened at the *Théatre Français* after a protracted battle with the royal censors. Here was a piece in which a sharp-tongued, sharp-witted servant usurped stage-center from his noble master, a thinly veiled projection of what was to come. Here, it would seem, was a daring maneuver by Mozart and his librettist, Da Ponte, to circumvent the censors and expose Viennese opera-goers to a work that Napoleon later proclaimed to be "The revolution in action."[1]

In actual fact, although thoroughly a man of the German Enlightenment, Mozart was neither a francophile nor a fellow-traveller with political radicalism. Indeed, both Mozart and his father harbored a thinly-veiled contempt for the French, their

---

[1] Pierre Augustin Caron de Beaumarchais, *The Barber of Seville and the Marriage of Figaro* (New York, 1983), p. 30. See also Frederick Brown, *Theater and Revolution: The Culture of the French Stage* (New York, 1980), Chapters 1 and 2 for a general discussion of the interconnections between the theater and ideas that might "contaminate the mind of France" (p. xi).

godless ways, and their loose morality. When Voltaire died in 1778, Mozart wrote to his father "that godless arch-rascal, Voltaire, has died like a dog, like a beast."[2] And when Mozart returned to Paris as a young man of twenty-two, it was only because his father ignored his pleas to remain in Mannheim, where he had fallen madly in love with Aloysia Weber. His father insisted that he try to recapture his earlier fame as a *wunderkind* in the French capital. His mother, Anna Maria, was sent along as chaperone, although she was hardly necessary, given the dire warnings about the perfumed and rouged French beauties whom Leopold considered little better than whores, and whom Wolfgang avoided for fear of venereal infection.[3]

Nonetheless, after a fruitless search for another promising comic libretto, following the success of *Abduction from the Seraglio*, when Mozart read the Beaumarchais play he knew at once that it was precisely the piece for which he had been waiting. Undoubtedly, the notion of a lackey who outwits and even humiliates his royal master appealed to the composer's sensibilities, for the indignities which he had suffered at the hands of Archbishop Colloredo were still fresh in his mind. The problem was that the gifted composer had chafed at being regarded as merely another household servant. In May of 1781, Mozart wrote to his father, recalling the final bitter dismissal from Colloredo's service: "I didn't know that I was a *valet de chambre*, and that broke my neck."[4]

Certainly, Mozart was shrewd enough to appreciate the sensation the comedy caused not only at the *Theatre Français*, but everywhere in Europe where it was excitedly received as a daring exposé of the decadence and ineffectuality of the aristocracy. In Paris, it had run for sixty-eight nights, and had taken in some 347,000 livres at the *Theatre Français*; Mozart hoped that with such a libretto, he might achieve the success that had eluded him thus far as an operatic composer, his reputation resting on his fame as a keyboard virtuoso and composer.[5] Yet despite these

---

[2]Emily Anderson, ed., *The Letters of Mozart and His Family* (3rd ed., New York, 1985), 8 July 1778.
[3]*Ibid.*, February 1778.
[4]*Ibid.*, 12 May 1781.
[5]Beaumarchais, *Barber of Seville*, p. 23.

practical considerations, Beaumarchais' comedy attracted him because he recognized in it a radically new theatrical style and language. Above all, Mozart the dramatist responded to the underlying revolution in human relationships that lies beneath Beaumarchais' scathing wit.

For although Mozart was an idealist, profoundly immersed in Enlightenment concepts of brotherhood, progress, equality, and a place in the sun for individuals of talent and merit, he was not a political radical.[6] indeed, his experience at the court of Joseph II, Europe's most radical enlightened despot, was hardly the equivalent of Beaumarchais, whose variegated career was inextricably linked to ideas and events that became the pathway to revolution. In Austria, however, the realization of Enlightenment programs such as the abolition of torture, religious tolerance, and an assault on the hegemony of the Church were implemented from above.[7]

If anything, Mozart must have felt the climate of Joseph's court to be a breath of freedom from the stifling atmosphere in Salzburg and Colloredo's contempt for his genius. Ironically, however, Joseph's determination to break the stranglehold of the conservative aristocracy, and his plans for the modernization of Austria, made him stingy in matters of the arts, especially in the case of the young composer who was not even Italian! On the other hand, Joseph had a cultivated and progressive taste in music, favoring the new Italian *buffa* style in opera rather than the older *seria* style that reflected the tastes, the life-style and values of the aristocracy, an important factor in his commissioning Mozart to do *Figaro*.

Even in the matter of Da Ponte's claim to have circumvented Joseph's initial objection to the transmutation of the Beaumarchais play, one should keep in mind Joseph's liberal policies in the matter of censorship. Some claim that he confiscated plates of contraband works, only to print them himself in order to reap the

---

[6]For more on this see H.C. Robbins-Landon, *Mozart and the Masons: New Light on the Lodge "Crowned Hope"* (London, 1982), and Katherin Thomson, *The Masonic Thread in Mozart* (London, 1977).

[7]T.C.W. Blanning, *Joseph II and Enlightened Despotism* (New York, 1970), see pp. 64-72, "The Tolerant and Humane State." See also Derek Beales, *Joseph II* (2 vols., Cambridge, 1988).

profits. However, in the case of pornography he was not so liberal. As to the theater, although not prudish himself, he subscribed to the Enlightenment notion of its didactic and moral function. Joseph's real objection to *Figaro* was not its political ramifications, but the question of propriety, in that the plot opens in the bedroom, hinges upon seduction, and draws an uncomfortably realistic portrait of the endemic libertinism of the aristocratic classes. The question he put to his advisors was, "Is it decent?"

Consequently, revision of the libretto was no problem for Mozart, for his music was in a realm far above crude sensuality, and carried the day with Joseph. Moreover, it is in the nature of opera to focus on and intensify the essential human drama. And in so doing, many of Beaumarchais' direct shots at the legal and political abuses of the old order were deflected. Instinctively Mozart shifted from a concern for the fetters of political servitude to the chains that bound both privileged and common classes to loveless marriages or to the disembodied sex of the hardened libertine. In Mozart's *Figaro* the deeper levels of reform are to be found in the region of the human heart, and their goals accomplished through the sublimity of lover rather than the tragedy of bloodshed.

In this respect, Mozart's treatment of Susanna, parallels and even extends that of Beaumarchais, for of all *Figaro*'s various characters, it is Susanna who embodies the eighteenth-century principle of love in respect to its natural power. Yet Susanna's centrality in this respect, as well as to *Figaro*'s powerful social and political dynamics, has been under-appreciated.[8] For the most part, attention has focused on Figaro as a proto-revolutionary figure who will see his master "dance to my tune," deflecting from the seemingly less radical relationship between maid and mistress in Almaviva's castle.[9] Since it is men who, in the great stream of history, have been seen as the movers and doers of things, Figaro's stance has seemed to be a trumpet-call to revolution, and his

---

[8]Not so Michael Levey who wrote in *The Life and Death of Mozart* (New York, 1972), p. 179: "The ultimate outwitting of the Count comes not from Figaro but from and Countess and Susanna. Reason, wit and ingenuity are enshrined in the women, who are none the less intensely loving."

[9]R. Pack and M. Lelash, eds., *Mozart's Librettos* (New York, 1965), p. 105.

maneuvers to defend his conjugal rights interpreted by a host of writers as symbolic of those natural rights for which the common man was ready to lay down his life in pre-revolutionary France.

Thus, scant attention has been paid to the revolutionary import of a lady's maid whose exuberance and strength throws her mistress's weaknesses into sharp relief or, for that matter, to the centrality of women of all classes on the pathway to the French Revolution and the events of that upheaval. It was, after all, in the salon over which cultivated and privileged women reigned that enlightenment ideas proliferated, and the nobility's progressive notions were fertilized by the genius of the *philosophes*. And in a more immediate sense, one forgets that the fish-wives and other common women of Paris bore arms alongside their men when ideology became action. It was a siege of women-wives, mothers, working women, vendors, prostitutes, and even a few privileged women, who led the assault on Versailles in October 1789 and brought the royal family back to Paris.[10] Similarly until the recent consciousness-raising by feminist and revisionist historians, the rumblings of revolution in the boudoirs of Almaviva's castle have seemed too low-key to be taken seriously.

Not so, however, in *Figaro*'s own century. Something was happening in the world of maids and mistresses that concerned numerous contemporary writers, alarmed by the threat to social order by the fact that it was becoming increasingly difficult to tell the difference between the lady's maid and her mistress. In England, Samuel Johnson complained that he might find himself addressing a mere maid with the same deference he would pay to her mistress, not knowing the difference. And Daniel Defoe found himself mortified and put

> very much to the blush, being at a friend's house and required of him to salute the ladies. I Kis'd the Chamber-Jade into the

---

[10]For more on this subject, see Vera Lee, *The Reign of Women in Eighteenth-Century France* (Cambridge, MA, 1975) for a lively overview of women of all classes, and more recently, Joan Landes, *Women in the Public Sphere During the French Revolution* (Ithaca, 1989). Outdated, but interesting for his biased account of the women's march on Versailles is Thomas Carlyle, *The French Revolution* (1837; repr. 3 vols., Philadelphia, [1891]), I: Book VII, Chap. VI, "To Versailles," and Chap. VII, "At Versailles."

bargain, for she was well dressed as the best. Things of this kind would be avoided if our Servant Maids were to wear livery as our Footmen do, or if they were obliged to go in a Dress suitably to their station.[11]

Others feared the effects on the imagination of common women of a new kind of heroine emerging in novels, the theater and in opera. Unlike the witty maids of earlier writers such as Molière and Lesage who, for all their audacity, understood their place in a rigidly stratified society, this new servingmaid-heroine had a more profound psychological dimension. Indeed, she was emblematic of a new kind of woman, emerging for the first time as a full human being, conscious of her natural rights in a more universal sense than her earlier prototypes.

In the case of *Figaro*, especially Beaumarchais' play, one might even say that it is Susanna, not Figaro, who figuratively speaking "begins the revolution." Initially, Almaviva's real intention in giving the newlyweds a magnificent conjugal bed and "the most convenient room in the castle" eludes Figaro. Only when Susanna tells him that the room is convenient in more ways than one— "My Lord, the Count, tired of cultivating rustic beauties, has a mind to return to the castle, but not to his wife; it's yours he has cast his eye on"—does the wily Figaro catch on to the ruse. And only then does he mobilize himself for the intrigues that he loves so well. As the bell rings and Susanna leaves to answer her mistress' call, her words "Que le gens d'esprit sont bêtes," (How stupid clever men can be!) are still ringing in his ears. And significantly, although Mozart begins his opera by giving each of them independent melodic lines in the opening duet, by the close of the scene it is Figaro who sings Susanna's tune—that is, her melodic line—as if to underscore her teasing question: "Sei tu mio

---

[11]Daniel Defoe, *Everybody's Business is Nobody's Business* (1725), quoted in Bridget Hill, *Eighteenth Century Women: An Anthology* (London, 1987), p. 238. Also interesting in respect to styles in clothing, *Figaro*, and social change was an exhibit at the Metropolitan Museum, New York, called "Costume and Dress in the Age of Napoleon" (January-April 1990). On exhibit were several women's dresses of the latter part of the eighteenth century that were inspired by Suzanne's costume in the Beaumarchais play, a style popularly referred to as "A la Suzanne."

servo o no?" (Are you my servant or not?)[12]

In fact, the potential for disruption of the order of authority is as explosive in her ladyship's boudoir as in the count's regal chambers or his law court. Like her prototypes in literature and the theater, Susanna blooms with health, vitality, strength and gusty savoir-faire in handling those around her. By contrast we first meet the countess closeted in her bedroom, the cloister of so many aristocratic women, where they spent their days in indolence, cut off from the world, debilitated by ennui and those mysterious maladies called the "vapors"—fainting spells of some vague, hysterical source. If the count is Figaro's dupe in his blind vanity, his obsession with chasing about after rabbits and nubile peasant girls, the countess is Susanna's ward in the passivity that infects even her sexual being. Like her husband, she seems destined by birth to confused immobility, as events she only vaguely understands shape her life. And, although hardly older than her maid, Rosine depends upon Susanna in matters both great and small. The maid dresses her, arranges covert meetings with the adoring Cherubino, defends her from her husband's wrathful jealousy, and cures the root cause of her melancholy, her husband's cold indifference. Susanna's strength derives in part from her mistress's weakness, from knowing too well how helpless Rosine would be without her. The irony of privilege in any caste system is its erosion of strength, the crippling effect on those who are forbidden by their status to do work of any kind.

The recent filming of Laclos' eighteenth-century novel *Les Liaisons Dangereuses* vividly depicts the tedium and artificiality of the life of the average woman of the privileged classes, whose only escape from boredom was card-playing, gossip, the endless, convoluted intricacies of high fashion and high intrigue.[13] And in that world, the lady's-maid played a pivotal role quite unlike that of the ordinary jack-of-all-trades serving-maid who, in a modest household, would be up at the crack of dawn to light the fire that

---

[12]Pack and Lelash, *Mozart's Librettos*, pp. 101 and 103 for the latter, and Beaumarchais, *Le Marriage de Figaro*, XI, p. 11, for the former.

[13]For more on this, see Doris Tishkoff, "I Have Created Myself; Sex, Love and Power in Laclos' *'Les Liaisons Dangereuses'*," *Transactions of the Samuel Johnson Society of the Northwest*, XV (1984), 73-83.

would warm the house, to compete at the marketplace for the best produce, fish, or fowl, and to bring water from the local cistern for the family's needs. The ordinary housemaid had to cook, do laundry, make beds, set and clear the table, clean the dishes, silver and cooking pots, scour the pewter, dress, feed and put the children to bed, wash floors, staircases and entryways, and "when she was done [with] her work sit down to spin."[14] We see these creatures of endless toil in numerous paintings of the period, perhaps bent over a huge sink crowded with cooking pots as in Giuseppe Maria Crespi's *Woman Washing Dishes*, or engaged in endless drudgery as in Chardin's *Woman Peeling Potatoes*. Little wonder that in rare moments of repose their "spirits cried out and [their] hearts were in pain."[15]

But the world of domestic service had its own caste-system, and in the hierarchy from scullery through upstairs and downstairs maids, cooks, housekeepers, and even governesses, it was the mistress' personal lady's-maid that was at the very top.[16] In general, they were among the more educated and cultivated of working women of the eighteenth century, being the most literate, having social graces, even musical and dancing talents, and keeping abreast of the latest fashions. Since their duties included reading to their mistress, gossiping, walking abroad, handling correspondence and accounts, receiving guests, joining them in "conversation and games," and acting as accomplices in their amours, it was difficult, as Johnson notes, to distinguish between maid and mistress.[17]

Thus, in the shifting, unsettled social world of the latter half of the eighteenth century, the position of lady's-maid provided the most advantageous conduit to ascending social mobility. For example, Samuel Richardson's famous lady's maid, Pamela, from the novel published in 1740, acquires first an education (reading,

---

[14]Hill, *Eighteenth-Century Women*, p. 240.

[15]Barbara K. Wheaton, *Savoring the Past* (Philadelphia, 1983), Chapter 5, "Kitchens and Cooks," has interesting material on maids in smaller households.

[16]John Laurence Carr writes in *Life in France Under Louis XIV* (New York, 1970), that the Princesse d'Harcourt was almost knocked over by a maid who refused to accept her blows, and that the daughter of the Duc de la Rochefoucauld married a footman. See pp. 47-49.

[17]Defoe, *Everybody's Business*.

writing, needlework, dancing, music), then her mistress's fine clothes (silks and linens), and, finally, Mr. B, her mistress's son, and a title to boot![18] Although *Pamela* may have been a fiction, even a romance, records show that lady's-maids did, indeed, occupy a privileged place in the family, were better paid, and had fewer menial duties to perform. Consequently, in the waves of social mobility precipitated by the revolution, it was the lady's-maid who stood ready to replace her aristocratic mistress when the revolution gave the final blow to the old order.

Cissie Fairchilds, in her study of servant-master relationships, *Domestic Enemies: Servants and their Masters in Old Regime France*, has suggested that the household was a mini-battlefield wherein the class struggle was most exposed, and "issues of autonomy and control were continually fought out."[19] One pre-revolutionary pamphlet even described lady's-maids and valets as "dressing, waking up, putting to bed, leading around, and indulging [their mistress or master as though they were] a child of three."[20]

But in Almaviva's castle, the household dynamics are of a different order, for here one deals with a work of art, and not real life. *Figaro*'s plot revolves around a typical stylistic device of eighteenth-century comedy: role-reversal through disguise and change of dress. And in that respect, Susanna is not so much in competition with her mistress as she is her accomplice and even role-model. Rosine's single-minded quest is to win back her husband's love. For that, she not only reverses roles with her maid, but comes to understand that what her husband seeks in a

---

[18] Samuel Richardson, *Pamela, or Virtue Rewarded* (London, 1740; repr. New York, 1958). An exhibition at the Wildenstein Gallery, New York, entitled "The Winds of Revolution," (November-December, 1989) featured a painting by J.A. Giroust, *Mlle. d'Orléans Taking a Harp Lesson*. Central to the painting is Mlle. d'Orléans' close companion, a beautiful English woman named Anne Sims, but dubbed Paméla by her patron Mme. de Genlis in honor of Richardson's heroine. Like her namesake, she did marry into the peerage, but unlike the fictional Pamela, she died in poverty. (See Wildenstein Gallery, "Winds of Revolution," exhibition catalogue [New York, 1989], pp. 60-62).

[19] Cissie Fairchilds, *Domestic Enemies: Servants and their Masters in Old Regime France* (Baltimore, 1984), pp. xii, xiii. See also Sarah C. Maza, *Servants and Masters in Eighteenth-Century France* (Princeton, 1983), and Jean Hecht, *The Domestic Servant Class in Eighteenth-Century England* (London, 1956).

[20] *Ibid.*, p. 167.

woman is what Susanna has: "liveliness of manner, some indefinable quality that constitutes charm; and occasional rebuff perhaps?"[21] The fact that Rosine's hopes, not only for revitalizing her marriage, but for love itself, hinge upon exchanging clothing and even reversing roles with Susanna is loaded with meaning. When maids lead the way, as does Susanna, it is clear that the social hierarchy has been seriously weakened by the gathering force of the winds of change.

Thus, Susanna's unerring conviction, her will to self determination is counterpoised against her noble mistress's resignation: she is the antithesis of despair, the feminine counterpart of her radical lover Figaro, "the shining apostle of the man who makes his own destiny."[22] Not only does she display a striking equality in her musical emblems (for example, the strings and clarinet accompaniment in her principle aria "Deh vieni non tardar," an instrumentation conventionally reserved for noble characters), but Mozart has moved her to the foreground in all of her musical numbers. In all six of her duets, Susanna "is at least equal to, if not the better of her partners--not to mention most of her other ensembles, and this is reflected as much in Mozart's music as in the dramatic action."[23]

In respect to the dynamics between Susanna and her master, all her energies are directed to evading the long-standing, albeit unwritten code that extended the lord's rights over his servant to the bedroom as well, having its roots in the quasi-legal feudal notion that a master's property rights implied that he owned his serf's body as well.[24] By the late eighteenth century, the notion of the odious *droit de seigneur* was virtually obsolete. However, as everyone knew, a master took it as his right to have sex with his female servants. The latter were selected as much for their attractiveness as for their working skills. In a society in which marriages amongst the upper classes were matters of economics and social strategy, the maid was not only the most convenient, but the safest—free from venereal disease—and the most willing,

---

[21]Beaumarchais, *Marriage of Figaro*, p. 206.
[22]*Ibid.*, p. 30.
[23]Tim Carter, *W.A. Mozart, Le Nozze di Figaro* (Cambridge, 1987).
[24]Fairchilds, *Domestic Enemies*, p. 168.

since to refuse would be to be unemployed and on the streets. In evading Almaviva's plan of seduction, Susanna makes an important statement about her personal rights, dignity and freedom that would hardly be lost on an eighteenth-century audience for whom the mere idea of a woman of the common classes asserting herself was loaded with revolutionary import. Thus *Figaro*'s essential radicalism coalesces equally in the person of Susanna, as in Figaro, the wily servant who outwits his master. Not only does she resist her lord's sexual advances, but even more so than Figaro, she deftly manipulates him. Perhaps nowhere in the opera is Almaviva quite so vulnerable as in the Act Three duet, that begins "Crudel! Perchè finora/Farmi languir così?" (Cruel one! Why do you prolong my suffering so?)[25] Quite deliberately fanning the flames of his ardor with her teasing sensuality, Susanna has the count in her power, dangling him on a thin string of uncertainty with the ambiguity of her "Sì" and "No."

But Susanna's ultimate goal is not the immediate rewards conferred by seduction, a few gulden or some trinkets of jewelry perhaps, but the freedom of self-determination. Figaro's plot does not hinge upon her conquest of the count, but on his abdication of the odious "right of the first night." When, at the end of Act III, the chorus triumphantly proclaims victory for Figaro and Susanna, singing their praises for such a wise lord, "Si saggio signor," [who] yields an offensive right, "A un dritto cedendo, Che oltraggia, che ofende," they also celebrate the victory of a new conception of natural rights over the despised tyranny of the feudal past.[26]

This patently socio-political statement derives, almost verbatim from Beaumarchais' play:

> Young wife about to sing the glory and the praise
> Of a lord who is renouncing a right of former days
> Foregoing his own pleasure, your honour he prefers
> And on a happy husband a virgin bride confers![27]

---

[25]*Mozart's Librettos*, p. 167.
[26]*Ibid.*, p. 187.
[27]Beaumarchais, *Barber of Seville*, p. 189.

However, in the final act of the opera, Da Ponte and Mozart made a striking alteration in excising Figaro's brilliant monologue, the very heart of Beaumarchais' autobiographical portrait. Instead, it is Susanna who takes stage center. As her lover remains obscured in shadow, she sings the lovely aria, "Deh vieni non tardar," the great popular favorite in the original production. Technically, the shift was necessary for balance—that is, to give each of the principles a show-stopping aria. Yet, Susanna's aria is more—it is the epicenter of the opera in its pervasive sensuality and concern for love as liberating force, and Mozart uses a simple, but richly expressive musical language here.

As if in a painting, Susanna is surrounded by shadows and darkness, her inner nature, as it were, illuminated by the music alone. All action on stage has ceased; there is a breathless hush as Susanna begins the recitative and aria, ostensibly aimed at her jealous lover hidden in the shadows, but more insistently, an intimate soliloquy, the delicious anticipation of a young girl about to know sexual love.

With Figaro's cynicism on the inconstancy of women ("Open your eyes a little") still ringing, Susanna sings that her aria is meant for Figaro, to "Reward him in kind for his own suspicions." Yet, the inward quality of her music belies such a purpose. This is Susanna's great monologue, delivered in a flexible, flowing, simple musical language more appropriate to the theater in its spoken style, its accents dictated by the sensibilities of the actress-singer. Clearly, Susanna is not merely acting out a charade here. Her trembling anticipation is that of a young girl about to enter into the great mystery of mature love. Nature envelopes her, intimating at the rapture so heady in her thoughts and imagination:

> Now at last the moment when I yield unresisting to joy in his embraces. Why need I tremble? Away with silly scruples—everything breathes of rapture. I feel it all around me—no more delaying—Night winds whisper and set my pulses throbbing—sweetest of all is the flower that love encloses.[28]

---

[28]Pack and Lelash, *Mozart's Librettos*, p. 197.

As her aria begins, the very pulse of love is suggested by the plucked pizzicati of the strings in a sustained continuo. Subdued orchestral color comes from the delicate melodic line of the clarinet which serves only to punctuate the vocal line. A serene 6/8 time gives a gentle lilt to its rhythm, while the vocal line gently undulates with F above C as its highest reach. Mozart uses the greatest musical economy, excepting a slight surge in the violins that connotes a rush of feeling just before the phrase, "Vieni" (Come my love), and the gentle concluding flourishes. For the eighteenth century, the human voice was the primary musical instrument and Mozart allows the voice of love its fullest expression throughout. As a butterfly emerging from its cocoon, the full woman emerges in the garden, sweet with the sound and smells of nature. Susanna sings:

> Then come, do not be late, my darling! Come where love calls you to enjoy yourself, while there's no moon in the sky, while the air remains dark and the world is silent. Here the brook is murmuring and the breeze is playing, refreshing the heart with its sweet whisper. Here the flowers are smiling, the grass is fresh, and everything favors the pleasures of love. Join me, my darling, among these secluded trees! Come, Come! I want to crown your forehead with Roses![29]

Many writers have suggested that the tender, sensual quality of Susanna's music throughout, but most especially in "Deh vieni non tardar," had a special personal meaning for Mozart—that he was, in fact, in love with Nancy Storace, the charming young English-born, Italian-trained soprano who created the role of Susanna in the original production. Storace's story and her role, not only in *Figaro*, but in Mozart's life, can only be touched upon briefly here. However, there is no question that Susanna's wit, psychological nuances, and the natural, heartfelt quality of her principle numbers reflect the singer's voice, character and stage persona. Even more, Susanna's independence of mind, her insistence on self-determination, were characteristic of Storace herself. Both in her personal life and in the numerous roles she took in the theater of maids and women of the common classes, she imparted

---

[29]*Ibid.*, p. 199.

a dignity, strength and independence that are strikingly modern and reflect the changing status of women in a society pervaded by notions about liberation.

Storace, in fact, was called by some, "that perverse Storace" because of a stubborn streak and a disregard for the social hierarchy that marked her career and life.[30] As a fledgling singer of fifteen in Venice she had the audacity to compete with the great castrato Marchesi at the Pergola Theater in Florence. Marchesi was famous for a trick that drove audiences wild—his famous "bomba," a vocal display in which he would build a spiral of brilliant roulades to a breathtaking climax. In secret, Storace practiced her own "bomba," and performed it one evening to the delight of the audience and the fury of Marchesi. When told by the manager to desist, she responded that "she had a right to her own bomba," and was summarily dismissed.[31] On another occasion in 1794, during her tenure as England's first female *buffa* singer, Storace is reported to have snubbed the royal family, responding to an invitation to sing at Buckingham palace for a paltry fee with the curt remark: "My compliments to your Master and Mistress— tell them I am better engaged."[32]

The latter anecdote reflects a long-standing negativism about Storace's person and career. When one clears away the murky clouds of legend, taking into account the special problems facing the first professional female singers, one cannot help but admire the intelligence, courage, wit and professional dedication of this remarkable woman. She was exceptionally well trained not only as a singer but as a musician, having studied with the famous Rauzzini as a girl in Bath, England, and with Sachini at the famous *conservatorio* for female musicians in Venice. According to her close friends, she had a sparkling wit, was a lively conversationalist, and had a warmth and charm in the theater that was likened to a bright light that illuminated the stage. She counted

---

[30] This is from a forthcoming entry on Nancy Storace by Kalman Birnam in Birnam, ed., *A Biographical Dictionary of Actors, Actresses, Musicians, Dancers, and other Stage Personnel in London, 1660-1800* (Carbondale, IL., in press).

[31] Michael Kelly, *Reminiscences*, ed. Roger Fiske (1826; repr. New York, 1975), p. 111.

[32] Birnam entry on Storace, *Biographical Dictionary*.

among her close friends many great figures of the musical and operatic scene, the greatest of them being Mozart, who, legend suggests, may have been her lover. Together with her brother Stephen, a talented composer, and Michael Kelly, the famous tenor, she was instrumental in modernizing and raising the vocal standards of the English musical theater. Her career as principle female *buffa* in Europe and England lasted some twenty-nine years, eighteen of which were spent with the equally famous English tenor, John Braham, without the legitimacy of marriage. She supported herself and her family comfortably, leaving a sizeable estate at a time when the greatest female singers, especially those who were unmarried, died in penury.[33]

Like Mozart, Storace represents a transitional artist in the period between the stylized, commedia dell' arte inspired *opera buffa* of the early period and the modern genre. One need only compare the maid Serpinna in Pergolesi's short *opera buffa, La serva padrona*, one of Storace's popular roles, and a piece that Mozart virtually raided wholesale when he composed *Figaro*, with Susanna to appreciate the modernity of the latter. Serpinna is a sharp-tongued, bossy maid who tricks her master into making her his bride and mistress of the house, thereby leaving the degradation of the servant's life behind. Susanna, however, has no desire whatsoever to trade places with her mistress—if anything, the opposite would be the case. Unlike Serpinna, she seeks love in marriage, not social mobility. Most important, Mozart's Susanna is multidimensional and real: a complex, ambivalent woman on the brink of knowing the ecstasy of mature love, who contemplates love's paradox and the inevitable loss of innocence that accompanies the rite of passage to full womanhood.

The Hungarian poet Gábor Kazinczy, on attending a performance of *Figaro* wrote that

---

[33]See Tishkoff, "Mozart, Nancy Storace, and the Language of the Heart," in progress, for Storace biography.

Storace, the beautiful songstress, bewitches eye, ear and soul. Mozart directed the orchestra, playing his fortepiano; but the joy which this music causes is so far removed from sensuality that one cannot speak of it. Where would words be found that are worthy to describe such joy?"[34]

Clearly, the collaboration with the sensitive young singer was fortunate for Mozart at this watershed period in opera. Despite the fact that she was *prima buffa* in Joseph's company, he composed her music in a natural, speechlike, heartfelt style, rather than the flashy virtuoso style that most prima donnas demanded to display their vocal technique. Her lovely aria in the last act, "Deh vieni non tardar" is one of the clearest examples of what writers of the day called a "language of the heart" in that it touches the deep and timeless regions of human feelings.[35]

In conclusion, then, if *Figaro* begins with a revolution in the boudoir, that is, a maid who is clearly stronger and more resourceful than her mistress and even her master, it concludes with a revolution in matters of the human heart. In the tonal equality of the culminating chorale-like figure of the finale, Mozart suggests, for one sublime moment, a suspension of class distinction altogether, a world in which there are no valets and masters, maids and mistresses, but four human beings, united by love, who have transcended the degradation of a caste system.

Mozart was all too aware of the inequities of that system in his own brief lifetime. But in his music, he anticipates the society which the Enlightenment believed was around the corner. As he wrote to his father in a letter of 1791: "It is the heart [alone] that confers the patent of nobility on man—although I am no count, I surely have more honor within me than many a count."[36] Sadly, Mozart was buried in a humble grave without the honors accorded his contemporaries, Haydn and Beethoven. But, surely, history has validated his noble conviction.

---

[34] Otto Deutsch, *A Documentary Biography of Mozart*, trans. E. Blom *et al.* (Stanford, 1965), p. 111.
[35] This will be treated in depth in Tishkoff, "Mozart, Storace, and Language of the Heart."
[36] Anderson, *Letters of Mozart*, 20 June 1781.

BEETHOVEN, THE REVOLUTION IN MUSIC AND THE FRENCH REVOLUTION: MUSIC AND POLITICS IN AUSTRIA, 1790-1815

by

John J. Haag

Beethoven! The very name of this man conjures up powerful images for most of us. Triumph over adversity, the creation of imperishable works of art in the midst of personal crisis and immense historical upheaval, the unique genius of an individual utterly determined to create a new vocabulary in music—these are but a few of the themes that inevitably come up when the life and work of Ludwig van Beethoven is scrutinized. But while the musical legacy and human drama linked to Beethoven are in many ways immortal and transcendental, our commemoration of the effects of the French revolution that started in 1789 provides us with an opportunity to examine Beethoven's life, works and impact in their historical context. Beethoven's music belongs to all time, but Beethoven the man was profoundly rooted in the world of the late Enlightenment and the age of the French Revolution.

Born in 1770 in Bonn on the Rhine, Beethoven became a subject in 1784 of the Habsburg Archduke Maximilian Franz, when control of the ecclesiastical Electoral Principality of Cologne passed to Vienna as part of Emperor Joseph II's reforms. Maximilian Franz was a younger brother of Joseph II and fully shared his liberal ideals. Starting in the early 1770s, Bonn began to enjoy the benefits of major cultural reforms including the creation of a first-class national theater. These reforms were, if anything, accelerated under the new regime of Elector Maximilian Franz. Many of the young Beethoven's friends were associated with the Scientific Academy that was raised to the status of a university in 1786. Unlike much of the rest of Europe, Enlightenment in Bonn did not take on an anti-clerical coloration. The young Beethoven, although of humble status, grew up in a society whose aristocratic and inegalitarian nature had been tempered sufficiently by the spirit of reform to permit young men of talent to mingle freely with the community's cultural elite. The generally positive experiences Beethoven had during his Bonn years helps to explain his lifelong belief in reform from above, instituted by a powerful and wise sovereign like Maximilian Franz or Joseph II.

By late eighteenth-century standards, Bonn was a place of remarkable intellectual freedom. The bookstores sold the latest editions of Plato, Plutarch, Rousseau and Montesquieu as well as the newly emerging German classic authors Herder, Klopstock, Schiller and Goethe.[1] It was in such an environment of *Gedankenfreiheit* that Beethoven registered as a student at the University of Bonn in the fateful year 1789. Although his personal life was by no means idyllic—his mother had died in 1787 and his father was in the last stages of alcoholism—Beethoven's future looked promising. Although not a Mozartian prodigy, Bonn's civic leaders thought highly of the young organist and violist, who had also been composing for a number of years.

It was at Bonn University that Beethoven first was introduced to the advanced ideas of the day. One of his professors, the philologist Eulogius Schneider, was a noted scholar and a Franciscan monk whose political beliefs motivated him to resign from his order. In 1790 Schneider published a volume of poetry that included one piece in praise of the fall of the Bastille. Among the names of subscribers to the book we find that of "L. van Beethoven, *Hofmusiker*, Bonn"—a significant gesture of support from a struggling young musician whose income was at best modest. Schneider's enthusiasm for the political changes in France was boundless:

---

[1]Martin Cooper, *Beethoven: The Last Decade 1817-1827* (London and New York, 1970), pp. 86-87.

Think not this a mere stroke of the pen—
This is more, this is our will,
The fate of each French citizen
Shattered, in fragments, the Bastille—
Now France is free, and free her men!²

Ideas that would recur decades later in Beethoven's letters and conversations can be detected in lectures delivered by Eulogius Schneider in the first year of the French Revolution, when all seemed possible and bloodshed had not yet opened the door to fear and pessimism.

Artistically, Beethoven had shown more promise than achievement as he stood on the threshold of his third decade of life. But a political event served as the catalyst for him to create the first musical work with clear fingerprints of his own unique style. The occasion was the death in February 1790 of Emperor Joseph II. Perhaps Eulogius Schneider suggested that Beethoven compose a cantata for the Bonn Literary Society's memorial services for the late ruler. The Society was a stronghold of advanced thinking on the Rhine, and the dismay of its members at the great reformer's demise was genuine. Beethoven composed a large-scale work for chorus and orchestra, but it was received too late for performance (it would not receive its premiere until 1884, when Brahms praised it).

The text for the *Cantata on the Death of Emperor Joseph II, WoO 87* by the local Bonn poet Severin Anton Averdonk reveals little literary distinction, whereas Beethoven's music is the most powerful written up to that point in his life. A number of passages reveal an epic character that will not be seen again in his works for another decade or more.³ Several of the themes in this work, which clearly was more than a chore for a nineteen-year-old strongly under the influence of Josephinian reformist idealism, reappear in Beethoven's only opera *Fidelio*. The opening four bars to the orchestral introduction to Florestan's monologue are all but

---

 ²Quoted in Frida Knight, *Beethoven and the Age of Revolution* (London, 1973), p. 18.
 ³Elsie Codd, "Beethoven in Uniform," *Dublin Review*, CCI (September 1937), 155-156.

identical to the beginning of the *Cantata*. One of the supreme moments in *Fidelio*, the F Major sostenuto in which Leonore unlocks Florestan's chains and he sinks into her arms, and all—soloists, prisoners and people—stand transfigured in their contemplation of the workings of divine and human justice is also derived from the *Joseph II Cantata* of 1790, in this case a chorus. The 1790 composition was a "glorification of one of the most humane and progressive" rulers of modern times, and the mature Beethoven of 1805 may well have incorporated the theme from the earlier work into an emotionally crucial section of his only opera because he saw a parallel between Joseph II and the liberal sovereign of whom the opera character Don Fernando is the ambassador.[4]

Two more compositions from the very end of Beethoven's Bonn period are worthy of note. The first is a companion-piece to the *Joseph Cantata*, the *Cantata on the Coronation of Emperor Leopold II, WoO 88*. This composition, which was also never performed in its day, is musically less distinctive but nonetheless contains strong indications of where its composer was situated on the ideological spectrum. The *Joseph Cantata* had praised the deceased ruler for his achievements ("Then all mankind rose up into daylight"), while the coronation-piece is full of hope for the future: "Peoples, weep no more—He will do as Joseph did." The energy of the final chorus, "Heil! Heil! Stürzet nieder, Millionen" is found decades later magnified immensely as almost identical phrases, this time from Schiller's "An die Freude," are found in the *Ninth Symphony*. The final chorus of the *Leopold Cantata*, youthfully energetic as well as monumental, points ahead to the *Credo* of the *Missa Solemnis*.[5]

Another glimpse at the young Beethoven's thinking about what constitutes the good society is afforded by a song written in 1791-1792 to a text by G.C. Pfeffel, "Der freie Mann." This ringing assertion of man's social equality deserves to be quoted:

---

[4]Mosco Carner, *Major and Minor* (New York, 1980), pp. 237-238.
[5]Elliot Forbes, "Stürzet nieder, Millionen," in *Studies in Music History: Essays for Oliver Strunk* (Princeton, 1968), pp. 449-457.

Who is a free man?
He from whom neither birth nor title,
Peasant smock, nor uniform, hides his brother man;
Who, enclosed within himself, can set at nought
The venal favor of great and small alike—
he is a free man.[6]

It is perhaps worthy of note that the late Bonn works of 1790-1792, of which the three just mentioned are the most distinguished from the perspective of both music and intellectual history, represent a renewal of Beethoven's urge to compose. After a significant beginning in the early and mid-1780's, his compositional energies had lain fallow for almost half a decade. Starting in 1790, a burst of creative energy was unleashed. Is it too unreasonable to suppose that Beethoven, inspired by Eulogius Schneider and other supporters of the inspiring events in France, now had a theme on which to focus his immense talents?[7]

Beethoven left Bonn for Vienna in October 1792. He had visited Vienna five years before and had very likely met Mozart, but had to depart for home owing to his mother's fatal illness. Now he was returning to study with none other than the great Haydn, who had examined the score of the *Joseph Cantata* and been favorably impressed. Passing through Koblenz on the way to Vienna, Beethoven encountered the Hessian troops sent there to defend the city against an anticipated French assault. In his diary he noted "*Trinkgeld* at Koblenz because the fellow drove like the devil right through the Hessian army, at the risk of a cudgeling—one small Thaler."[8] The young Rhinelander quickly made his mark on Vienna, at first not as a composer but as a brilliant virtuoso pianist. He was assertive and irreverent, quickly detecting indifference on the part of his teacher Haydn when some of his lessons were not properly graded; Haydn reciprocated by dubbing the proud young man a "grand mogul" and a "Turkish pasha."[9]

---

[6]Knight, *Beethoven*, pp. 19-20; Georg Kinsky and Hans Halm, *Das Werk Beethovens* (Munich, 1955), pp. 577-579.

[7]Maynard Solomon, "Beethoven's Productivity at Bonn," *Music and Letters*, LIII (April 1972), 165-172.

[8]John N. Burk, *The Life and Works of Beethoven* (New York, 1943), p. 35.

[9]Hugo Leichentritt, *Music, History, and Ideas* (Cambridge, MA, 1938) p. 183.

More important than Beethoven's projection of personal assertiveness was the fact that within a few years of his arrival in Vienna he was able to live a life of considerable independence. When his friend F.G. Wegeler visited Vienna in 1794, he discovered that Beethoven had become well-known in the aristocratic salons of the metropolis; he was not a threadbare newcomer but a young man with money in his pocket whose future appeared limitless. Unlike Haydn and Mozart, Beethoven in no way played the servant's role; he considered himself socially to be his noble patrons' equal and spiritually, by virtue of his gift of musical genius, to be their superior.[10] Both Haydn and Mozart had achieved fame and some degree of financial success (although Mozart mismanaged his income), but both men were in truth little more than well-treated servants.[11] Beethoven revolutionized this relationship, accelerating the social emancipation of European musicians. In accepting patronage, he in no way became a servant. Invited to dine with Prince Louis Ferdinand, Beethoven sat next to his host at the table.[12] Indeed, his relationship with his pupil Archduke Rudolph evolved into a deep friendship of almost total equality.[13]

By the time the young Beethoven's career was taking firm hold in Vienna, that city, and indeed the entire Habsburg state, was in the grips of a growing fear of revolution. The accession of Emperor Franz I in 1792 turned these anxieties into institutionalized paranoia. The Emperor detected conspiracy everywhere, and is reported as having stated that "There is something revolutionary in [Beethoven's] music."[14] Not only the emperor but virtually his entire court was convinced that Beethoven was republican in his sympathies.[15] Not surprisingly, even at the height of his public

---

[10]*Ibid.*, pp. 183-184.

[11]Maurice Bouvier-Ajam, "Beethoven et l'emancipation sociale du musicien," *L'Europe*, XLVIII, no. 498 (October 1970), 37-45.

[12]Franz Gerhard Wegeler and Ferdinand Ries, *Biographische Notizien über Ludwig van Beethoven*, ed. Alfred Christlieb Kalischer (Berlin, 1906), p. 111.

[13]Donald W. MacArdle, "Beethoven and the Archduke Rudolph," *Beethoven-Jahrbuch*, ser. 2, IV (1962), 36-58.

[14]Quoted in Friedrich Kerst, ed., *Die Erinnerungen an Beethoven* (2 vols., Stuttgart, 1913), I, 192.

[15]*Ibid.*, p. 139.

fame, during the period of the Congress of Vienna, Franz asked for and received reports on Beethoven from his secret police.[16] As early as 1793, Beethoven could scarcely fail to notice that the repression was affecting his own freedom to read. That year Schiller's *Die Räuber* was banned on grounds of being immoral and dangerous. By the summer of 1794, opponents of the regime, "Jacobins" to the police, found themselves under arrest.[17] These were mainly critics of the reactionary aristocratic society whose principal activity was to engage in endless discussions of the benefits of the French Revolution, and who often concluded their meetings with the *Marseillaise*, *Ça ira* and other revolutionary songs.[18] Despite the government's hysteria, the twenty-three-year-old Beethoven assessed the situation in a remarkably cool and realistic manner. Writing to his Bonn friend Nikolaus Simrock on 2 August 1794 he summed up his thoughts on the Austrian situation:

> Here it is very hot; the Viennese are afraid that soon they will have no more ice cream; as the winter was so rarely cold, ice is scarce now. Here they have been arresting several persons of importance; they say that a revolution was about to break out—but I believe that as long as the Austrians have brown beer and sausages, they'll never revolt. They say that the gates to the suburbs are to be locked at ten o'clock each night. The soldiers keep their arms well loaded. One must not talk too loudly, or the police give him lodgings for the night.[19]

The letter of 1794 is virtually the only political commentary we have from Beethoven for almost a decade. It is to his music that we must look to see what he was thinking. The private Beethoven

---

[16]Theodore von Frimmel, *Beethoven-Handbuch* (2 vols., Leipzig, 1926), I, 147.

[17]Ernst Wangermann, *From Joseph II to the Jacobin Trials. Government Policy and Public Opinion in the Habsburg Dominions in the Period of the French Revolution* (London, 1959), pp. 133-187; Denis Silagi, *Jakobiner in der Habsburger Monarchie. Ein Beitrag zur Geschichte des aufgeklärten Absolutismus in Österreich* (Vienna, 1962), pp. 177-183.

[18]Donald E. Emerson, *Metternich and the Political Police: Security and Subversion in the Habsburg Monarchy (1815-1830)* (The Hague, 1968), p. 24.

[19]Quoted in Michael Hamburger, ed., *Beethoven: Letters, Journals and Conversations* (Garden City, NY, 1960), pp. 7-8.

of these years may forever remain a mystery, but the public Beethoven was clearly trying to be accepted by the dominant society. An indication of this impulse to be part of the social order is to be found in the two patriotic songs from the years 1796-1797. In November 1796 he published a martial air with a text by *Unterleutnant* Friedelberg, "Abschiedsgesang an Wiens Bürger," followed the following April by another anti-Napoleonic song, "Kriegslied der Österreicher," intended for use by the Vienna Volunteer Corps. Friedelberg himself died in combat in 1800.[20] In 1798 Beethoven is believed to have frequented the French embassy for a number of months and become acquainted with Ambassador Bernadotte, but not all Beethoven scholars believe these contacts actually took place. What did in fact happen during these years— among other things, the dedication of his *Septet, Op. 20* to the Empress Maria Theresa and by the improvisations on "God Save Emperor Franz"—suggests that the composer was more interested in his music and his career than in the world of politics.[21]

By 1802, in a letter to the music publisher Franz Anton Hoffmeister, Beethoven was once again venturing significant political commentary. The composer turned down the suggestion that he write a program sonata in praise of the leaders or ideals of the French Revolution, arguing that the "time of revolutionary fever" had already passed, one indication of this being Napoleon's negotiations with the papacy.[22] Hoffmeister, a close friend of Mozart's, was a noted Viennese Freemason, and it is significant that Beethoven's letters to him all begin with the salutation "Dear Brother," an indisputably Masonic form of address. While no concrete evidence has ever surfaced linking Beethoven directly to a Masonic lodge, scholars continue to build a fairly strong case of circumstantial evidence linking him to Freemasonry.[23]

Another sign that Beethoven was emerging from a period of "ideological quiescence" in the first years of the new century were

---

[20]Kinsky-Halm, *Das Werk Beethovens*, pp. 582-584.
[21]Maynard Solomon, *Beethoven* (New York, 1977), p. 136.
[22]Maynard Solomon, *Beethoven Essays* (Cambridge, MA, 1988), pp. 193-195.
[23]Roger Cotte, "Beethoven et la Franc-Maçonnerie," *Guide Musical* (October 1972), 12-13.

the dedications he placed on some important compositions.[24] Dedications to patrons were a source of income, but these appear to have been expressions of gratitude, friendship and admiration. The dedication of the *Piano Sonata in D Major, Op. 28* to Joseph von Sonnenfels, close advisor to Joseph II, a man who was born a Jew and whose Freemasonic affiliations were well known, could not be viewed as anything but a political statement. Another honorary and unpaid dedication was that of the *Three Sonatas for Violin and Piano, Op. 30*. In this case the dedicatee was the young reformer and enlightened ruler, Czar Alexander I of Russia.

Around the year 1803, Beethoven seriously considered moving to Paris. During these years he was profoundly influenced by musical developments in France. While virtually all of the French music inspired by the revolution proved in the long run to be ephemeral, it provided a transcendental genius like Beethoven with germs of ideas that could be transformed—like carbon into diamonds—through the crucible of his unique mind.[25] Beethoven transformed and integrated the crude trumpet and drum signals and marches of French revolutionary music into his ever-expanding conception of symphonic music and sonata form. The trumpet as used in the *Egmont* incidental music of 1810 is explained by the composer in unmistakably political terms: "The entry of the trumpet points to the freedom obtained for the Fatherland."[26] There is a stylistic similarity between the funeral march composed by Gossec for Mirabeau's funeral and the "Funeral March for the Death of a Hero" found in Beethoven's *Piano Sonata No. 12 in A-Flat Major, Op. 26*.[27] The compositions of other composers active in revolutionary France, Cherubini and Méhul, stimulated Beethoven's stylistic evolution immeasurably—many contemporaries heard echoes of Cherubini in the three *Leonore* overtures, and of Méhul

---

[24]Solomon, *Beethoven*, p. 138.
[25]Arnold Schmitz, *Das romantische Beethovenbild: Darstellung und Kritik* (Berlin and Bonn, 1927), p. 176; Georg Knepler, *Musikgeschichte des 19. Jahrhunderts* (2 vols., Berlin, 1961), II, 554-556.
[26]Schmitz, *Beethovenbild*, p. 176.
[27]Karl Nef, "Beethovens Beziehungen zur Politik," in *Aufsätze* (Basel, 1936), p. 38.

in the *Fifth Symphony*.[28]

During the years 1802-1804 Beethoven composed his *Third Symphony in E-Flat Major ("Eroica"), Op. 55*. As a work of symphonic music the *Eroica* is one of the landmarks of Western art. Equally important is the fact that this work represents the agonized attempts of Beethoven to clarify his own thinking not only about Napoleon Bonaparte but about his own clouded future. The symphony was written as a "Bonaparte symphony" but upon hearing the news that Napoleon had proclaimed himself Emperor of the French in May 1804, Beethoven tore up the dedication-page and changed the name of the work to "*Sinfonia eroica.*" This part of the story is traditional and well known. Recent research by Maynard Solomon and others now indicates that, between late May and late August 1804, Beethoven decided to restore the dedication to Napoleon. By the time of its first performance, a private one at the Lobkowitz palace in December 1804, all references to Napoleon had been dropped. But the title page of Beethoven's own score of the symphony, now in the Archives of the Gesellschaft der Musikfreunde in Vienna, clearly has written on it in Beethoven's handwriting the phrase "Geschrieben auf Bonaparte." It is in pencil and is barely legible because of the passage of time, but the words have never been erased.[29] This symphony doubtless began as an apotheosis of Napoleon the conqueror, but while it was being composed Beethoven was forced to come to terms with the grim facts of his own incurable deafness. He seriously considered suicide, but decided to continue to live for his art. Thus the *Third Symphony* became as much "a transcription of personal experience," of Beethoven's own heroism, as a document of political hero-worship and disillusionment.[30]

Fidelio, Beethoven's only opera, is very much a product of the Age of Revolution. The libretto, adapted by Joseph Ferdinand von

---

[28]Solomon, *Beethoven*, p. 138; Uwe Martin, "'... den Lümmel muß man henken': Französische Revolution und deutsche Musik," *Neue Zeitschrift für Musik*, CL (July-August 1989), 12-17.

[29]Maynard Solomon, "Beethoven and Bonaparte," *The Music Review*, XXIX (1968), 97-98.

[30]J.W.N. Sullivan, *Beethoven: His Spiritual Development* (New York, 1944), p. 135.

Sonnleithner, is based on the original French text *Léonore, ou L'Amour conjugal* by Jean Nicolas Bouilly. The plot is largely imaginary but is based on situations he had known and individuals he had met while attached to the Criminal Tribunal in Tours during the revolution.[31] Beethoven was attracted to the libretto because of the seriousness of its themes and worked for almost two years on the score. Two weeks before opening night, scheduled for 15 October 1805, the Imperial censor banned the performance on the ground the libretto contained subversive ideas. Sonnleithner wrote two letters to the censor arguing that while the character Pizarro had abused his powers, this had been done in a private manner and that Pizarro was in fact punished for his crimes—by his king. The censor quickly relented, but the date for the premiere had to be postponed to 20 November. Unfortunately, on 13 November Vienna was occupied by Napoleon's army. The opening night took place as scheduled, but the conditions were highly unusual. The majority of the audience were French officers—the Viennese aristocracy, Beethoven's usual supporters, having fled in the days before the city's surrender. The press reviews were almost universally critical. After a revision and another unsuccessful run of the opera in 1806, *Fidelio* would remain unperformed until 1814.[32]

Fidelio is the greatest example of the type of opera known as a "Terror" or "Rescue" opera—a genre that appeared during the French Revolution and enjoyed a short-lived popularity in France and German-speaking central Europe. Most of these operas were based on actual events of the revolution, when particularly during the Terror individual aristocrats and entire noble families sometimes escaped persecution at the hands of their Jacobin captors in highly dramatic incidents that were perfect vehicles for the stage. The dramatically powerful trumpet calls that play such a major role in *Fidelio* and in the three *Leonore* overtures composed for the opera are derived from a number of contemporary French

---

[31] David Galliver, "Fidelio—Fact or Fiction?," *Studies in Music*, XV (1981), 82-92.

[32] Carner, *Major and Minor*, pp. 187-189; Willy Hess, *Beethovens Oper Fidelio und ihre drei Fassungen* (Zurich, 1953), pp. 17-20.

operas including those of Méhul, Cherubini and Dalayrac.³³

The libretto of *Fidelio* appealed strongly to the moralistic and puritanical aspects of Beethoven's personality. The piece had none of the "frivolity" that disturbed Beethoven in Mozart's *Don Giovanni*. It is in many ways an opera of ideals, not individuals. Whereas the first version contained characters with significant individual traits, but the time the third version of 1814 had been crafted, what remained was a monumental work of art that stressed ethical conceptions rather than the fates of individual men and women. The deeply moving music makes *Fidelio* a conductor's not a singer's opera. It is scarcely surprising that many of the great conductors of our century (Toscanini, Furtwängler, Klemperer, and others) have been champions of this work. The opera can be made to voice new and important ideas; in 1955, for example, the Wieland Wagner production startled Paris when the opera's prisoners were clad in uniforms obviously based on those of Nazi concentration camp inmates.³⁴ And the jailkeeper Rocco, a colorless functionary who doubtless would not protest if he had to witness a prisoner's murder, is as much a human type found in the late twentieth century as in the early nineteenth. Significantly, Beethoven failed to provide Rocco with a *leitmotiv*.³⁵

The contemporary significance of *Fidelio* appears in countless statements of affection for the piece by musicians and non-musicians alike. The British conductor Sir Colin Davis recently admitted to his own enthusiasm for the work, praising it for its idealism and arguing that it was "a supremely important work because it stands for a vision of life that has little or nothing to do with the acquisition of power and material goods."³⁶ While the theme of conjugal love and loyalty is doubtless a major part of *Fidelio*, the question of justice also looms large. Thus Leonore's

---

³³Winton Dean, "German Opera," in Gerald Abraham, ed., *The Age of Beethoven, 1790-1830* [The New Oxford History of Music], Vol. VIII (London, 1982), p. 472n.

³⁴"New 'Fidelio' in Paris," *New York Times*, 11 March 1955.

³⁵Manfred Wagner, "Rocco, Beethovens Zeichnung eines Funktionärs," *Österreichische Musikzeitschrift*, XXXVII (July-August 1982), 369-379.

³⁶Richard Osborne, "Sir Colin Davis: Notes from a Conversation," *Gramophone*, LXV, no. 768 (May 1987), 1540.

rescue of Florestan is but part of the liberation of political prisoners from a state prison. The German philosopher Ernst Bloch has pointed out Leonore's determination as part of a universal imperative for justice: "Whoever you are, I will rescue you."[37]

War returned to Vienna in May 1809 with the second French occupation of the city. Beethoven himself took refuge in the home of an acquaintance, covering his head with pillows to protect his ears from the sound of bursting shells.[38] The flight from Vienna of Archduke Rudolph and the entire imperial court inspired Beethoven to compose his *Piano Sonata No. 26 in E-Flat Major, Op. 81A*, often known as the *Les Adieux* sonata although Beethoven preferred that it be given a German designation, *Das Lebewohl, die Abwesenheit, das Wiedersehen*. With the French occupation still a fresh memory, Beethoven composed, between October 1809 and June 1810, his most substantial dramatic score after *Fidelio*, incidental music to Goethe's play *Egmont*. The overture and nine sections of dramatic music that constitute Beethoven's Opus 84 were inspired by one of Goethe's most heroic works. Completed in 1788, the Goethe play uses much poetic license to depict the life of Count Egmont of Lamoral (1522-1568), whose execution by order of the infamous Duke of Alva marked a turning point in the Dutch struggle against their Spanish oppressors.[39]

In Beethoven's incidental music to *Egmont*, the well-known overture is virtually a tone poem summing up the drama's emotional peaks and valleys; it concludes in a "Symphony of Victory" that ends the play as Egmont ascends the scaffold. In her song "Die Trommel gerühret," Klärchen, Egmont's secret lover,

---

[37]Ernst Bloch, *Literarische Aufsätze* (Frankfurt am Main, 1965) [Ernst Bloch Gesamtausgabe. Bd. 9], p. 579, quoted in Hans Joachim Marx, "Beethoven as a Political Person," in *Ludwig van Beethoven, 1770-1970* (Bonn-Bad Godesberg, 1970), p. 32.

[38]George R. Marek, *Beethoven: Biography of a Genius* (New York, 1969), p. 397.

[39]Renato Saviane, "Egmont, ein politischer Held," *Goethe Jahrbuch*, CIV (1987), 47-71; Adolf Fecker, *Die Entstehung von Beethovens Musik zu Goethes Trauerspiel Egmont. Eine Abhandlung über die Skizzen* [Hamburger Beiträge zur Musikwissenschaft. Bd. 18] (Hamburg, 1978), pp. 16-17.

describes vividly how thrilling it is for her to see the soldiers march by, with fifes and drums adding to the patriotic fervor; how fine it would be, she sings, if she could be a man and join them in defense of the nation. In the "Melodrama" section of the music the condemned Egmont, asleep in his cell, sees a vision in the form of the Goddess of Freedom, and her face is that of his beloved Klärchen. Very likely Beethoven and his contemporaries saw a close parallel between events in the Spanish Netherlands in the 1560s and the contemporary situation of a humiliated Central Europe under the yoke of Napoleon. Egmont was the embodiment of the idea of national liberation, and Beethoven's music did much to increase the confidence of nationalists who felt that even the French could one day be defeated.

When Napoleon's empire finally began to crumble, Beethoven and other composers were ready to add their talents to the general outpouring of nationalistic enthusiasm. Both Franz Schubert and Carl Maria von Weber composed patriotic works glorifying the warriors who had liberated the fatherland. Weber's cantata *Kampf und Sieg* was filled with rousing male choruses, Prussian horn calls and a rout of the French *Ça ira* by tunes associated with the victorious Allies including *God Save the King*. At the first performance of *Kampf und Sieg* in 1815, General Nostitz, a veteran of the Battle of Leipzig, remarked to Weber: "In your music I hear the voice of the Nations, in Beethoven's big boys playing with rattles."[40]

Beethoven's musical reputation reached a popular high-point during the years of the *Befreiungskrieg* against Napoleon. His fame increased largely as a result of the sort of music that General Nostitz criticized, namely occasional pieces written to commemorate the current military and political situation. The Beethoven composition disparaged by the musically discriminating General was *Wellington's Victory or the Battle of Vittoria, Op. 91*, a battle piece to honor the great victory over Napoleon in Spain by British forces in June 1813. Originally intended for the

---

[40]Otto Erich Deutsch and Donald R. Wakeling, *Schubert: Thematic Catalogue of all His Works in Chronological Order* (New York, 1951), pp. 41, 48, 83-84 and 97; John Warrack, *Carl Maria von Weber* (2nd ed., Cambridge, Eng., 1976), pp. 169-170.

"Panharmonikon," a mechanical brass band devised by the inventor and entrepreneur Johann Nepomuk Mälzel, Beethoven orchestrated his score for a standard symphony orchestra when Mälzel's scheme to take the contraption to England fell through. The piece was immensely popular, a contemporary newspaper noting that the "applause rose to the point of ecstasy."[41] Not only was Beethoven emotionally encouraged by this newly discovered popularity, the box office take was handsome indeed and represented more income than he had ever earned from concerts—or would ever again earn.

The year 1814 marked feverish composing activity on the part of Beethoven, almost all of it focused on topical works related to the immediate political scene. The capitulation of Paris in March 1814 was marked by a piece for bass, chorus and orchestra, *Germania, WoO 94*.[42] A chorus in honor of the Allied rulers assembled for the Congress of Vienna, *Ihr weisen Gründer glücklicher Staaten, WoO 95* was apparently never performed, and an *Overture in C Major, Op. 115*, "For Our Emperor's Name Day," was completed too late for performance on the intended day of 4 October 1814.[43] Performed with great success was the *Cantata for Four Soloists, Chorus and Orchestra, "Der glorreiche Augenblick," Op. 136*, which deeply impressed the rulers who were busy in Vienna trying to restore Europe to its pre-Napoleonic state.[44] Beethoven was invited to many of the festivities associated with the Congress of Vienna; he received much praise and benefitted financially as well. In his entire lifetime he gave only eleven public concerts in Vienna for his own benefit; of these, five took place in the year 1814!

But the fame and prosperity ended almost as quickly as it began. Beethoven's assertion that he had long "cherished the desire to place some important work of mine on the altar of our

---

[41]Solomon, *Beethoven*, p. 222; Matthias Wendt, "Die Zeit der großen äußeren Erfolge. Die Auseinandersetzung um Beethovens Opus 91, Wellingtons Sieg oder die Schlacht bei Vittoria," in Siegfried Kross, ed., *Beethoven: Mensch seiner Zeit* (Bonn, 1980), pp. 73-95.
[42]Kinsky-Halm, *Das Werk Beethovens*, pp. 550-551.
[43]*Ibid.*, pp. 331-333 and 552.
[44]*Ibid.*, pp. 411-417.

Fatherland"[45] was doubtless sincere, but the Fatherland (or at least its leading citizens) had fickle taste. From 1815 to his death in 1827, Beethoven's name was in eclipse in Vienna. The heroic style of his music no longer suited an epoch that became increasingly limited and bourgeois in its ideals. Abandoned by virtually all of his aristocratic patrons except for the always-loyal Archduke Rudolph (Kinsky, Lichnowsky and Lobkowitz had died in 1812, 1814 and 1816, and Rasumovsky returned to Russia in 1815), Beethoven presented to the outside world the appearance of an eccentric, sometimes unkempt misanthrope. Despite all, a small circle of friends remained intensely loyal to the deaf genius, whose powerful intellect was as curious as ever not only about musical developments but the political landscape and such newfangled inventions as flying machines.[46] The period of Restoration that began in 1815 influenced Beethoven profoundly; up to that time he had produced works in a great variety of genres. Now as public interest in music declined, he concentrated on far fewer genres.[47] Perhaps we should be grateful to Wellington and Metternich for creating the stable anti-revolutionary era that fostered the atmosphere of artistic neglect that compelled Beethoven to turn inward and compose such towering masterpieces as the *Ninth Symphony*, the *Missa Solemnis*, and the late Piano Sonatas and String Quartets.

The years after 1815 were most distressing for Austrians who, like Beethoven, believed passionately in *Gedankenfreiheit*. The rigid police state of Metternich and his police chief Count Sedlnitzky spied on one and all, and it was probably only the influence of Archduke Rudolph that provided Beethoven with a significant measure of immunity from official harassment. Others were less fortunate. Even the mild-mannered Franz Schubert found himself briefly in police custody in 1820, when the repression was at its height; a friend, Johann Senn, was less fortunate—he was deported to his native Tirol after languishing in jail for fourteen months

---

[45]Solomon, *Beethoven*, p. 223.
[46]Harry Goldschmidt, *Die Erscheinung Beethoven* (Leipzig, 1974), p. 23.
[47]Georg Knepler, "Zu Beethovens Wahl von Werkgattungen," *Beiträge zur Musikwissenschaft*, XII (1970), 308-321.

without trial.[48] Beethoven was physically safe but among his circle of friends he lashed out against a government he regarded as a "paralytic regime."[49] In the words of a visitor of 1816, "He defies everything and is dissatisfied with everything, blaspheming against Austria and especially Vienna." On another occasion Beethoven characterized the Viennese as being "worthless from the Emperor downwards," skewering them with a pun: "Österreicher, Eselreicher" (Austrians, Ass-trians).[50]

After his death, the Beethoven mystique quickly took on a life of its own. His protean personality and immense artistic legacy enabled his admirers to attribute to him divine powers; Berlioz described the Vienna master as an eagle "athirst for the infinite." By the 1880s French intellectuals discovered in Beethoven a man of the people, a socialist leader and "the dispenser of salvation and creator of a new moral universe."[51]

Throughout the twentieth century Beethoven has continued to be rethought, reexamined and redefined. Doubtless new interpretations of his life and impact will appear in the future. Perhaps even some new documentation will surface (although this is unlikely if not impossible). Psychohistory may possibly add significantly to our understanding of Beethoven the man. But none of this will likely displace Ludwig van Beethoven from his central position in the pantheon of modern culture. His restless, unsettled spirit and the music it created—music that often ends in triumph after immense struggles—will remain an expression of those elemental, titanic forces in Western civilization that have made the world since 1789 uniquely creative and at times explosively unstable.

---

[48]John Reed, *Schubert* (London, 1987), pp. 21, 79 and 81; Hans J. Frölich, *Schubert* (Munich, 1978), pp. 220-221. See also the stimulating study by Frieder Reininghaus, *Schubert und das Wirtshaus. Musik unter Metternich* (Berlin, n.d. [1979]).
[49]Karl-Heinz Köhler, Grita Herre and Dagmar Beck, eds., *Ludwig van Beethovens Konversationshefte* (8 vols., Leipzig, 1968-1983), I, 300.
[50]Cooper, *Beethoven: The Last Decade*, pp. 20 and 89.
[51]William S. Newman, "The Beethoven Mystique in Romantic Art, Literature and Music," *Musical Quarterly*, XLIX (1983), 354-365; Alessandra Comini, *The Changing Image of Beethoven: A Study in Mythmaking* (New York, 1987).

POLITICAL THEATER IN THE AGE OF REVOLUTION: MOZART'S *LA CLEMENZA DI TITO*

by

John A. Rice

The eighteenth century saw theater as a potent shaper of opinion and behavior. The views of the Italian playwright and librettist Giovanni De Gamerra, in a treatise called "Osservazioni sullo spettacolo," published in 1790, are typical: "True and wholesome theater reforms the heart, refreshes the spirit, and teaches us to live with circumspection. That is how theatrical spectacle becomes a school for the nation, where youth finishes its education with less danger than in social gatherings and clubs."[1] De Gamerra saw theater as an effective means for the sovereign to exercise his authority:

---

[1] "La vera e sana Commedia riforma il core, rischiara lo spirito, e c'insegna a vivere circospetti. Ecco come lo spettacolo teatrale diviene una scuola per la Nazione, dove la gioventù termina la propria educazione con minor pericolo, che fra le conversazioni ed i circoli." Giovanni De Gamerra, "Osservazioni sullo spettacolo in generale, sulla tragedia, sulla tragedia domestica-pantomima, sulla commedia, sugli attori, sull'abito scenico, sulle decorazioni, e sugli autori per servire allo stabilimento del novo Teatro Nazionale," in *Nuovo teatro del Sig. Gio. De Gamerra tenente nelle armate di S.M.I.* (Venice, 1790), I, iii.

Theatrical spectacle, established on the basis of wise laws and of careful reform, can be regarded as a means always available to the sovereign power, to be used to inculcate in his subjects the most useful and important beliefs. In time of war it can increase patriotic heroism. In peace it can increase useful contacts among the people, and can enhance their taste for the arts of commerce and for useful work.[2]

The theater is a school not only for the people, but for the ruler as well, according to De Gamerra, who cited one work in particular, Metastasio's libretto *La clemenza di Tito*: "Has our century not seen an emperor at a performance of *La clemenza di Tito* listening to the voices of humanity and of forgiveness?."[3]

Many eighteenth-century operas carried political messages. The political allegory of opera around the time of the French Revolution offers us a particularly vivid example of the interconnections between politics and theater in the eighteenth century. Consider some of the operas that reached the stage for the first time in the year 1791, as revolution continued to transform the political landscape of France and the rest of Europe looked on in alarm or admiration. In Paris, audiences saw Grétry's *Guillaume Tell*, in which proud, virtuous Swiss citizens overthrew despotism (the opera was banned under Napoleon). Also in Paris, Cherubini's *Lodoiska* depicted the rescue of a virtuous woman from the clutches of a wicked tyrant. When Méhul's *Adrien* (libretto based on Metastasio's *Adriano in Siria*) was in rehearsal in Paris near the end of 1791, it caused a storm of protest from revolutionaries, who saw in the triumphal procession of Emperor Hadrian a favorable allusion to the Habsburg Emperor Leopold II. "The people of Paris would rather burn down the Opéra than see kings enjoy their triumph here." With these words the painter David is

---

[2]"Lo spettacolo teatrale stabilito sulla base di leggi savie, e d'una sensata riforma può riguardarsi come un mezzo sempre pronto per la sovrana potestà, onde farne uso per inculcare ai popoli soggetti le massime credute utili ed importanti. In tempo di guerra può destare l'eroismo patriottico. In pace poi somentare le vantaggiose associazioni, il gusto dell'arti del commercio delle fatiche giovevoli alla popolazione, e simili." De Gamerra, "Osservazioni," I, vii.

[3]"Questo nostro secolo non vide forse un Cesare alla rappresentazione della *Clemenza di Tito* ascoltar le voci dell'umanità e del perdono?" De Gamerra, "Osservazioni," I, xxxvi.

said to have joined others in keeping *Adrien* off the stage.[4]

The French saw their revolution mirrored and glorified on the stage; but another opera, first performed in 1791 in a different part of Europe, showed revolution in a very different light. Mozart's last opera, *La clemenza di Tito*, also carries political messages, some of them in direct confrontation with the ideals of the French Revolution. As is often the case with theatrical allegory, the political content of *La clemenza di Tito* is complex, with more than one layer of meaning; the opera must have meant different things to different members of the audience.

When Leopold II came to the throne of the Habsburg monarchy in February 1790, he faced dangerous crises both inside and outside the monarchy. An unpopular war against the Turks had dragged on much longer than anyone had expected; war taxes and forced conscription increased discontent. The powerful nobility of Bohemia and Hungary, frustrated by the constant efforts by Leopold's predecessor, Joseph II, to increase the central government's authority at their expense, and alarmed by his attempts to better the peasants' lot, threatened to rebel. The Hungarian nobility had succeeded in convincing Joseph, on his death-bed, to revoke some of his most important reforms. But even with these concessions in hand, some Hungarians continued to prepare for armed resistance; and the Prussians, old enemies of the Habsburg monarchy, threatened to come to the aid of the Hungarian nobility. Already the Austrian Netherlands were in a state of revolution, having declared themselves an independent republic, the United States of Belgium, on 20 January 1790. The outbreak of the French Revolution in the previous year represented a dangerous and ultimately fatal challenge not only to the French monarchy, closely allied to the Habsburgs by marriage, but also to

---

[4]According to M. Elizabeth C. Bartlet (personal communication) the earliest version of this anecdote is in André René Polydore Alissan de Chazet, *Mémoires, souvenirs, oeuvres et portraits* (Paris, 1837). Bartlet suspects the veracity of Chazet's account; but there is no doubt that politics played a leading role in the debate over Méhul's *Adrien*. See Bartlet, "On the Freedom of the Theatre and Censorship: The *Adrien* Controversy (1792)," forthcoming in the proceedings of the conference "Musique, Histoire, Démocratie" (Paris, 1989).

the tradition of absolute monarchy in general.[5]

Leopold, who had reigned in Florence as Grand Duke of Tuscany since 1765, had become an experienced and skillful ruler during his twenty-five years in Italy. Now forty-three years old, he arrived in Vienna eager to attack the problems facing the monarchy and capable of doing so. An important element in his response to the crises was the use of carefully chosen concessions to appease and to win over various groups adversely affected by Joseph's reforms. By means of these concessions, Leopold was able to divide and thus to weaken the opposition. At the same time, his government began an ideological offensive against the French Revolution and its supporters within the Habsburg monarchy. He mounted a vigorous campaign to portray the revolution as wicked and destructive and to justify the assumptions underlying enlightened absolutism.

Leopold consolidated power slowly, a process manifested in a series of coronations: as Emperor of the Holy Roman Empire (October 1790); as King of Hungary (November 1790); and as King of Bohemia (September 1791). These coronations were affirmations of the strength and resilience of enlightened absolutism. They were opportunities for Leopold to bask in the warmth of pomp and applause, to celebrate and to renew the traditions of the political system that kept him in power. Coronations were also opportunities for those over whom Leopold ruled to display their own traditions, to demonstrate that they were consenting freely to be ruled by Leopold and that such consent came in exchange for Leopold's recognition that his subjects had certain rights and privileges.

Theatrical productions were an essential part of most eighteenth-century coronations. At Leopold's coronation in Frankfurt there were performances of plays and operas, including Salieri's *Axur, Re d'Ormus* and Wranitzky's *Oberon*. In Prague, Haydn's *Orlando Paladino*, Paisiello's *Pirro* and Mozart's *Don Giovanni*

---

[5]The crisis of 1789-1790 is discussed in detail by Ernst Wangermann, *From Joseph II to the Jacobin Trials* (2nd ed., London, 1969), pp. 5-55; see also Robert J. Kerner, *Bohemia in the Eighteenth Century: A Study in Political, Economic, and Social History with Special Reference to the Reign of Leopold II, 1790-1792* (New York, 1932), pp. 82-95, and Adam Wandruszka, *Leopold II* (2 vols., Vienna, 1963-1965), II, 249-261.

were performed in the days before the coronation of Leopold as King of Bohemia.[6] But the main theatrical event in Prague was the première of a new *opera seria* on the evening of coronation day, 6 September 1791: *La clemenza di Tito*, with text by Pietro Metastasio, as revised by Caterino Mazzolà, and music by Wolfgang Amadeus Mozart.

The opera had been conceived and organized in haste. Representatives of the Bohemian Estates (which meant, for all practical purposes, representatives of the Bohemian nobility and of the Catholic Church in Bohemia) had been called into session by Leopold during the summer of 1790.[7] The so-called "Big Bohemian Diet" of 1790-1791 was an extraordinary event, paralleling in some respects the pre-revolutionary conventions of the French Estates called together by Louis XVI. The representatives assembled in Prague worked through the second half of 1790 and the first month of 1791 preparing "Desideria" addressed to Leopold as King of Bohemia; requests for legislation and other actions by Leopold—most of them, in effect, concessions—concerning taxation, serfdom, the Bohemian constitution, and other issues related to the kingdom of Bohemia. The Diet of the Estates met again several times later in 1791; the last of their meetings that year took place in June, and it was presumably during that meeting that the Estates decided to celebrate Leopold's upcoming coronation with a sumptuous and expensive *opera seria*.

On 8 July 1791, a little less than two months before the coronation, Domenico Guardasoni, impresario of the Italian opera in Prague, concluded an agreement with the Estates of Bohemia in which he promised to provide an *opera seria* as part of the coronation festivities.[8] The contract, preserved in the State Archives in Prague, is signed by Guardasoni, by Count Heinrich Rottenhan, Governor of Bohemia, and by four members of the Diet. Governor Rottenhan presided over the Diet and represented

---

[6]On theatrical events in Frankfurt see *Theater-Kalender auf das Jahr 1790* (Gotha, [1790]), p. 276; on theatrical events in Prague see H.C. Robbins Landon, *1791: Mozart's Last Year* (London, 1988), pp. 102-121.

[7]On political life in Bohemia during Leopold's reign the best study is Kerner, *Bohemia in the Eighteenth Century*, to which the following remarks are indebted.

[8]The contract is published in Tomislav Volek, "Über den Ursprung von Mozarts Oper *La clemenza di Tito*," *Mozart-Jahrbuch*, 1959, pp. 274-286.

the interests not of the Bohemian Estates, but of the central government in Vienna; he was, in other words, Leopold's principal agent in Prague. Rottenhan was a skillful politician, adept at the difficult task of representing Leopold before the Diet diplomatically and yet convincingly.[9] He may well have played a crucial role in the negotiations that led to the operatic commission, for it was in his interest especially that Leopold's coronation be as brilliant and impressive as possible. When the opera was performed on coronation-day, Rottenhan sat with Leopold and his family in the royal box.

Guardasoni's contract tells us much about how the opera was organized. It specifies Guardasoni's fee as 6000 florins, or 6500, "if the *musico* should be Marchesi." *Musico* was the normal eighteenth-century term for a castrated male soprano or contralto. (The term *castrato*, common today, usually had derogatory implications when applied to singers in the eighteenth century.) Luigi Marchesi was one of the greatest *musici* of the day. From this and other stipulations of the contract we can concluded that Guardasoni was to pay all expenses, singers' fees as well as those of the librettist, composer, designer and painter of the scenery, out of the sum that he was to receive.

Guardasoni was free, according to his contract, to choose whatever composer he wished for the coronation opera, as long as the composer was "un cellebre maestro." Clearly the composer was not the most pressing concern either for the commissioners of the opera or for its organizer. Guardasoni made every effort to engage "a distinguished composer" to compose the music. After failing with his first choice, Antonio Salieri, he succeeded with his second.[10]

Guardasoni's contract required that the coronation opera be a setting of a newly written libretto, or, if such a libretto could not be attained, that the opera be a setting of Pietro Metastasio's libretto *La clemenza di Tito*. Since time was so obviously short, this stipulation amounted to a requirement that Metastasio's libretto be set.

Metastasio, Habsburg court poet during the period of more

---

[9] Kerner, pp. 111-112.
[10] Landon, *Mozart's Last Year*, pp. 84-87.

than half a century from 1730 to his death in 1782, took as the subject of *La clemenza di Tito* the Roman emperor Titus, who ruled from 79 to 81 A.D. The episode out of which he wove his drama in mentioned briefly by Suetonius in his account, written around 120 A.D., of the first twelve emperors of Rome:

> [Titus] had promised before his accession to accept the office of Chief Pontiff as a safeguard against committing any crime, and kept his word. Thereafter he was never directly or indirectly responsible for a murder; and, although often given abundant excuse for revenge, swore that he would rather die than take a life. Titus dismissed with a caution two patricians convicted of aspiring to the Empire; he told them that since this was a gift of Destiny they would be well advised to renounce their hopes. He also promised them whatever else they wanted, within reason, and hastily sent messengers to reassure the mother of one of the pair, who lived some distance away, that her son was safe. Then he invited them to dine among his friends; and, the next day, to sit close by him during the gladiatorial show, where he asked them to test the blades of the contestants' swords brought to him for inspection.[11]

Metastasio developed his libretto from Suetonius's narrative, deriving the character of Tito primarily from Suetonius's depiction. He built the dramatic action around the aborted coup to which Suetonius refers. But beyond that, *La clemenza di Tito*, like most eighteenth-century librettos purporting to be based on historical events and characters, is mostly fictional. Metastasio gave Suetonius's two patricians names, Sesto and Lentulo (the former being one of the main characters in the drama, the latter appearing on stage only briefly near the end of the opera). As for the rebellion's motivating force, Vitellia, and the characterization of Sesto, its leader, Metastasio found these and much more, as Vernon Lee and others have pointed out, in two of the most admired of French seventeenth-century tragedies, Corneille's *Cinna, ou la clémence d'Auguste* (1642) and Racine's *Andromaque* (1667). These dramas helped Metastasio not only with his title, but also with the

---

[11]Gaius Suetonius Tranquillus, *The Twelve Caesars*, trans. Robert Graves (Baltimore, 1957), p. 292.

general conduct of the plot, with the delineation of characters, and with individual turns of phrase.[12]

Metastasio's *La clemenza di Tito* was first performed in 1734, with music by the Habsburg court composer Antonio Caldara. During the period of thirty-eight years following the performance of Caldara's setting, many of Europe's leading composers, including Hasse, Gluck, Wagenseil, Jommelli, Sarti, and Anfossi, set *La clemenza di Tito* to music. But between 1774 and 1791 not a single major composer is known with certainty to have set this libretto.[13] During the same period some of Metastasio's other librettos were set many times. (*L'Olimpiade* and *Antigono* received at least nine settings each; *Didone abbandonata* and *Alessandro nell'Indie* at least eight.) Although highly respected as a work of literature, *La clemenza di Tito* was apparently not considered by leading composers to be suitable for the operatic stage during the two decades preceding Mozart's setting. Why then did Guardasoni and the Bohemian Estates single out *La clemenza di Tito* in 1791?

La clemenza di Tito was chosen because of the likelihood that audiences would identify Tito with Emperor Leopold, and because of the libretto's multi-faceted political allegory, allegory that would appeal to the sovereign as well as to his subjects. The allegory is anti-revolutionary, pro-monarchist; it must have been interpreted as a warning to Leopold's subjects of the dangers of revolution. At the same time it could be interpreted as a lesson for the sovereign in the advantages of generosity and forgiveness.

Metastasio conceived *La clemenza di Tito* as a political libretto. Adam Wandruszka, biographer of Leopold II, has pointed out that the drama glorifies the idea of *clementia austriaca*, a tradition, long associated with the Habsburg dynasty, of enlightened rule,

---

[12]Vernon Lee (pseudonym of Violet Paget), *Studies of the Eighteenth Century in Italy* (2nd ed., London, 1907), p. 298; see also R.B. Moberly, "The Influence of French Classical Drama on Mozart's *La clemenza di Tito*," in *Music and Letters*, LV (1974), 286-293.

[13]Helga Lühning, "*Titus*-Vertonungen im 18. Jahrhundert: Untersuchungen zur Tradition der Opera seria von Hasse bis Mozart," *Analecta musicologica*, XX (1983), 521.

generous and lenient.[14] Metastasio's libretto was first performed to celebrate the birthday of Emperor Charles VI, and the title character was plainly meant to represent an idealized portrait of the Habsburg ruler. In a *licenza*, or epilogue, that Metastasio addressed to Charles and attached to the first edition of the libretto, the poet coyly pretended that he did not intend the character of Tito to be a portrait of Charles. But his denial, embellished with playful puns, makes clear that the parallel was indeed intended:

> Non crederlo Signor: Te non pretesi
> Ritrarre in Tito. Il rispettoso ingegno
> Sa le sue forze a pieno,
> Nè a questo segno io gli rallento il freno.
> Veggo ben, che ciascuno
> Ti riconobbe in Lui: So che tu stesso
> Quegli affetti clementi
> Che in sen Tito sentiva in sen ti senti:
> Ma CESARE è mia colpa
> La conoscenza altrui?
> E' colpa mia che Tu somigli a lui?
> Ah vieta Invitto AUGUSTO,
> Se le immagini tue mirar non vuoi,
> Vieta alle Muse il rammentar gli Eroi.

(Do not believe it, Sire. I did not try to portray you in Titus. The respectful mind knows well its own strength, and I do not allow myself free rein when I reach my limit. I see well that everyone recognizes you in him; I know that you feel in your heart those generous emotions that Titus felt in his. But is it my fault, CAESAR, that others know this? Is it my fault that you resemble him? Ah, invincible AUGUSTUS, if you do not wish to admire images of yourself, forbid the muses to remember heroes.)[15]

---

[14] Adam Wandruszka, "Die 'Clementia Austriaca' und der aufgeklärte Absolutismus: Zum politischen und ideelen Hintergrund von 'La clemenza di Tito,'" *Österreichische Musikzeitschrift*, XXXI (1976), 186-193.

[15] This and the following quotations from Metastasio's *La clemenza di Tito* are cited from the edition of Fausto Nicolini: Pietro Metastasio, *Opere*, III (Bari, 1914).

The allegory of Metastasio's libretto is so general in its allusions that *La clemenza di Tito* could be, and was, performed in many parts of Europe during the eighteenth century, and in the presence of many different rulers. Yet there are several reasons why *La clemenza di Tito* could have been considered particularly fitting for Leopold's coronation, and particularly relevant to the times in which that coronation took place. At the height of the French Revolution Metastasio's drama showed the enlightened monarch being confronted with a violent rebellion and successfully suppressing it. At a time when revolutionary pamphlets were circulating scandalous stories about the incompetence and immorality of the crowned heads of Europe, the opera showed a ruler who was wise and virtuous and it depicted the coup attempted against him as both unnecessary and futile. Finally, and perhaps most important, an already established association between the Roman emperor Titus and the Habsburg monarch Leopold meant that the political allegory of *La clemenza di Tito* would be obvious both to the sovereign and to his subjects.

Titus, remembered already in antiquity as a model of the benevolent ruler, was compared with many modern rulers during the age of enlightened absolutism. But an unusually strong association between Leopold and Titus had developed even before 1791. Leopold's grand-ducal reign in Tuscany was hailed by many as particularly enlightened, and as early as 1783 comparisons were made between Titus and Grand Duke Pietro Leopoldo, as Leopold was called in Florence. In a guide to the collections of the Uffizi, published in 1783, the author stops in front of a bust of Titus and thinks, almost automatically, of Grand Duke Pietro Leopoldo, although he does not mention him by name: "Fortunate Tuscany," he writes, "we have no need to envy Rome for the happy days of Titus."[16] Poems published in the *Gazzetta toscana*, an official newsletter of the Tuscan court, made a habit of comparing the Grand Duke with Titus. One poem praised Pietro Leopoldo as follows:

---

[16]Francesco Zacchiroli, *Description de la Galerie Royale de Florence* (3 vols., Florence, 1783) I, 59.

E giusto, e pio solo Tu vinci appieno
D'Antonino, e di Tito i fasti egregi.

(Both just and pious, only you can outdo
the memorable deeds of Antoninus and of Titus.)[17]

After Joseph's death and Pietro Leopoldo's departure for Vienna, a poem expressed the Florentines' distress at having lost their ruler:

E se non sei, TITO NOVELLO, accanto
Chi nel cammin darà norma, e consiglio?

(And if you, modern-day Titus, are not near,
who will give us instruction and advice?)[18]

The same imagery was taken up in Germany. A Latin inscription erected by the Elector of Bohemia at Frankfurt during Leopold's imperial coronation imputed to Leopold various specific attributes of the Roman emperors. The attribute that Leopold shared with Titus, a year before Mozart's *La clemenza di Tito* was first performed, was clemency:

Plaude Germania felix
Imperatorem tenes bonitate Traianum,
Clementia Titum, sapientia Aurelium
Jam redeunt Saturnia regna!

(Celebrate, fortunate Germany. You have an emperor who is Trajan in goodness, Titus in clemency, and [Marcus] Aurelius in wisdom. Now the golden age returns!)[19]

But it was left to one Joseph Sartori systematically to lay out the parallels between Leopold and Titus. Sartori's *Leopoldinische*

---

[17]*Gazzetta toscana*, 1789, p. 176 (article dated Livorno, 28 October).

[18]*Gazzetta toscana* 1790, p. 38 (article dated 6 March).

[19]Quoted by Erna Berger and Konrad Bund, eds. *Wahl und Krönung Leopolds II. 1790. Brieftagebuch des Feldschers der kursächsischen Schweizergarde* (Frankfurt, 1981), p. 84.

Annalen is a two-volume account, unremittingly favorable, of Leopold's reign. The second volume appeared in 1793, after Leopold's death; towards the end of this volume Sartori compared Titus to Leopold, whom he called "the German Titus."[20]

Sartori began his parallel by pointing out that the reigns of Titus and Leopold were about the same length, both just a little over two years. The two emperors were about the same age when they died. They shared the same virtues: "Fairness, benevolence, justice, charity." Rebellions marred both reigns. Titus's reign was interrupted by "rebellions of nature, in the form of earthquakes followed by plague and other natural disasters." (Sartori did not mention the most famous natural disaster of Titus's reign, the eruption of Mount Vesuvius in 79 A.D. that destroyed Pompeii.) "Rebellions of man" disturbed Leopold's reign, according to Sartori, who referred specifically to the revolution in the Austrian Netherlands: "He had to lead the rebellious Netherlands back by force of arms. Immediately after peace was restored Leopold's exalted clemency declared a general amnesty for all those seduced and deluded [into rebellion], just as Titus granted to patrician conspirators life and forgiveness." Here Sartori referred to the episode recorded by Suetonius that served Metastasio as the point of departure for *La clemenza di Tito*. He went on to compare the reactions of those forgiven by Titus to the reactions of those forgiven by Leopold: "The patricians appreciated the clemency of Titus; a great part of the Netherlands did not appreciate the clemency granted to them by Leopold, and caused new anxiety for his kind, paternal heart. The Romans were far more grateful than the Christians of the enlightened eighteenth century." Sartori then concluded his parallel by pointing out some important differences between Titus's character and Leopold's. Because this passage is crucial to one's understanding of the allegorical content of *La clemenza di Tito*, and because it has not previously been cited by students of Mozart's opera, it is reproduced in its entirety as an appendix to this article.

Sartori's exposition of the parallels between "the Roman Titus" and "the German Titus" leaves no doubt that the first audience of

---

[20][Joseph Sartori], *Leopoldinische Annalen* (2 vols., Augsburg, 1792-1793), II, 216-219.

Mozart's opera, including the emperor himself, made the same connection, even without being able to draw some of the parallels that Sartori did; they could not know, for example, that Leopold would soon die and that his reign and his life were to be as short as those of Titus.

Having identified Leopold with the protagonist of the drama played out before them, the audience could have easily recognized, in the violent and frightening rebellion with which Act I of *La clemenza di Tito* ends, the revolutionary movements that faced Leopold in 1791, just as Sartori drew a parallel between the patrician conspirators who threatened Titus and "the rebellious Netherlands" who threatened the peace of Leopold's reign.

Two important tasks were involved in turning Metastasio's old libretto into a modern opera rich in contemporary political implications. First it had to be revised. Then, of course, it had to be set to music. The way in which both of these tasks were accomplished in 1791 had the effect of enhancing the libretto's allegorical content. Both revision and composition focussed the audience's attention on three of Metastasio's original six characters, and simplified the plot so that it revolved around the interactions of these three characters, thus making it easier to draw allegorical interpretations from the character and actions of the principals; they downplayed the more positive and inspiring aspects of the opera's revolutionary rhetoric; they emphasized the horror and violence, the senselessness and shame of revolution.

It was normal practice in the eighteenth century, when setting an old libretto to music, to make many changes in the libretto in order to adapt it to the tastes of contemporary musicians and audiences. In preparation for the coronation of Leopold in Prague, Metastasio's *La clemenza di Tito* underwent extensive revision at the hands of the theatrical poet Caterino Mazzolà, who was at the time serving on a temporary basis as librettist for the Viennese court theater. Whether Mazzolà worked in concert with Mozart in this revision is not known, but very likely he did, since both were in Vienna during the summer of 1791 when the opera was being prepared.[21]

The revisions were extensive. Mazzolà cut much dialogue, including a big part of Metastasio's Act II; he compressed Metastasio's three acts into two. He replaced or omitted most of Metastasio's aria texts; he inserted several ensembles, most of them incorporating parts of Metastasio's arias and dialogues.[22]

Metastasio wrote his libretto at a time when there was little threat of revolution within the Habsburg realms. He was able to enliven his opera with some moving talk in favor of revolution without evidently fearing that it would attract the unwelcome attention of censors. Vitellia's rousing speech in Act I, Scene 11 of Metastasio's libretto (Act I, Scene 9 in Mazzolà's revision) has some particularly strong language. Encouraging Sesto to undertake the rebellion, Vitellia refers to Brutus; whether her reference is to Lucius Junius Brutus, who led a rebellion against the last King of Rome in 509 B.C., or to Marcus Junius Brutus, who took part in the plot to assassinate Julius Caesar in 44 B.C. in the hope of restoring the Roman republic, is not clear:

> Io ti propongo
> La patria a liberar. Frangi i suoi ceppi;
> La tua memoria onora;
> Abbia il suo Bruto il secol nostra ancora.
>
> (I propose to you that you liberate the fatherland. Brake its shackles; honor your own memory: let our century have its own Brutus.)

These last words would have sounded ambiguous and threatening to a late eighteenth-century audience in the Habsburg monarchy. Is "our century" the first century A.D., or the eighteenth? The elder Brutus was one of the heroes of the French Revolution.

---

[21] Mazzolà's service to the Burgtheater is recorded in the theatrical records of payment in Vienna's Haus-, Hof- und Staatsarchiv, Generalintendanz der Hoftheater, Rechnungsbücher, 1791, p. 36.

[22] Mazzolà's revisions have been the subject of several studies: Franz Giegling, "Metastasios Oper *La clemenza di Tito* in der Bearbeitung durch Mazzolà," in *Mozart-Jahrbuch*, 1968/1969, pp. 88-94; Don J. Neville, "*La clemenza di Tito*: Metastasio, Mazzolà and Mozart," *Studies in Music from the University of Western Ontario*, I (1976), 124-148; Lühning, "*Titus*-Vertonungen," 79-108.

Voltaire's tragedy *Brutus*, performed in Paris in 1790, inflamed revolutionary passions; David's painting of Brutus (1789) was also appreciated for its revolutionary implications.[23] It is not surprising that Mazzolà cut most of this passage (everything after "liberar"), which must have sounded uncomfortably close to French revolutionary rhetoric. He also cut the promise that Vitellia makes a few lines later, probably borrowed by Metastasio from a speech in Racine's *Andromaque*, that if Sesto should return to her soaked in Tito's blood he will receive from her both love and pleasure:

> Ritorna asperso
> Di quel perfido sangue; e tu sarai
> La delizia, l'amore,
> La tenerezza mia.
>
> (Return soaked in that perfidious blood; and you will be my delight, my love, my tenderness.)

Even if Metastasio modelled this passage on Racine, it is still remarkable for its vivid imagery, its memorable juxtaposition of violence and the pleasant reward for committing such violence; Mazzolà may well have regarded it as unsuitable for a coronation opera.

One of the parts of Mozart's *La clemenza di Tito* in which the concerns of political allegory seem to have played a crucial role in shaping both text and music is the rebellion itself (Act II, Scenes 1-6 in Metastasio; Act I, Scenes 11-14 in Mazzolà's revision). Metastasio referred to the rebellion only briefly; it takes place completely off-stage, with apparently little violence, and it is suppressed with little trouble by troops loyal to the emperor. In Mozart's opera the coup-attempt is much more real, more violent *and terrible. As such, it could have been understood, by a Habsburg monarch and his subjects seeing the opera performed in 1791, as a reference to the terrible events that had recently taken place in the Austrian Netherlands and that were continuing to take place in France, events that would lead, within less than

---

[23]For a fine study of Brutus as a political symbol see Robert L. Herbert, *David, Voltaire,* Brutus *and the French Revolution: An Essay in Art and Politics* (London, 1972).

three years, to the execution of King Louis XVI of France and of his wife—Emperor Leopold's sister—Marie Antoinette (Figure 1).

Metastasio's coup-attempt takes place near the beginning of Act II. Mazzolà, in reducing Metastasio's opera from three acts to two, moved the rebellion to the end of the first act, thus shifting it from a relatively inconspicuous part of the original libretto to a place of prominence. Mozart increased the prominence of the rebellion still further by setting the entire episode as a finale, that is a continuous, coherent musical structure, accompanied by orchestra, in which all the characters except Tito take part, and in which the developing dramatic situation is vividly reflected in the music. (In Metastasio's original the whole episode is treated with the normal alternation of recitatives and exit-arias.) Adding weight and pathos to this finale is the use of an off-stage chorus, through

Figure 1. The finale of Act I as illustrated on the title page of a piano-vocal score of Mozart's *La clemenza di Tito*, Leipzig, 1795. By permission, Stadtarchiv Augsburg.

which the Roman people are heard. (Metastasio made no use of the chorus in this part of his libretto.) In Metastasio's libretto one does not experience the coup-attempt; in Mozart's one feels its terror and violence, and one hears the shock and grief of the Roman people as they react to it.

Metastasio's rebellion is preceded by Sesto's monologue in which he expresses his agony over the step he is about to take. After much indecision he resolves finally not to carry out his treacherous plan, but at that very moment the burning Capitol signals that the rebellion has begun. Yet Sesto is still not certain that it is too late to change his mind, even after seeing the fire. He still hopes to save Tito's life, and goes off to try to do so:

> Forse già tardi
> Sono i rimorsi miei.
> Defendetemi Tito, eterni dei!

> (Perhaps my remorse has come too late.
> Eternal gods, defend Titus for me!)

The rebellion in Mazzolà's revision is preceded by this same monologue for Sesto. But once the revolution begins, for Mazzolà's Sesto there is no *forse*, no "perhaps." He not only sees the fire but also hears the sound of clashing arms; Mazzolà added the lines

> Un gran tumulto io sento
> D'armi e d'armati

> (I hear a great tumult
> of arms and soldiers.)

and Sesto ends the recitative with an unambiguous and painful cry, likewise added by Mazzolà:

> Ahi! tardo è il pentimento.

> (Ah! my repentance is too late.)

In Metastasio's original, the rebellion itself is described very briefly, by Publio, the praetorian praefect and Tito's confidant:

> Roma tutta è in tumulto: il Campidoglio
> Vasto incendio divora...
>
> (Rome is in tumult; a vast fire
> devours the Capitol.)

But the fire, however vast, still leaves room for doubt that it was set on purpose, as Publio says:

> Ah voglia il cielo
> Che un'opra sia del caso, e che non abbia
> Forse più reo disegno
> Chi destò quelle fiamme!
>
> (Ah, would to heaven that this be the result of an accident and that whoever set these flames had no criminal intent!)

In Mazzolà's revision Publio has no doubt that the fire was started on purpose, and that a rebellion is in progress; his words are more menacing than those given him by Metastasio:

> V'e in Roma una congiura,
> Per Tito, ahimè, pavento;
> Di questo tradimento
> Chi mai sarà l'autor?
>
> (There is a conspiracy in Rome, and fear for Tito's life. Who could be the instigator of this betrayal?)

The uprising is real: we hear it terrifyingly evoked by Mozart's music. A sudden plunge to the minor mode coincides with the entrance of trumpets and drums. A fast tempo, frequent syncopations, rapid shifts in dynamics, and tonal instability reflect the confusion, fear and violence of the rebellion. Suddenly, off-stage the people of Rome cry out on a diminished chord: "Ah! Ah!" Surely there is no more vivid evocation of political turmoil than this finale in all of eighteenth-century opera, and surely it is no coincidence that this music was written at the height of the French Revolution.

In Metastasio's drama Sesto announces to Vitellia that Tito has been killed: he did not commit the crime, but he saw one of the conspirators stab the emperor, in spite of his efforts to stop the deed:

SESTO
Già Tito . . . Oh Dio! già dal trafitto seno
Versa l'anima grande.

VITELLIA
        Ah, che facesti!

SESTO
No, nol fec'io, che, dell'error pentito,
A salvarlo correa; ma giunsi appunto
Che un traditor del congiurato stuolo
Da tergo lo feria.—Ferma!—gridai;
Ma il colpo era vibrato. Il ferro indegno
Lascia colui nella ferita e fugge.
A ritrarlo io m'affretto;
Ma con l'acciaro il sangue
N'esce, il manto m'asperge, e Tito, oh Dio!
Manca, vacilla, e cade.

(SESTO
Already Tito . . . oh God! already his great soul is flowing from his wounded breast.

VITELLIA
Ah, what have you done?

SESTO
No, I did not do it. Having repented of my mistake I ran to save him: but I arrived just as a treacherous member of the conspiracy attacked him from behind. "Stop" I cried, but the blow was struck. He left the shameful sword in the wound and fled. I hurried to withdraw it; but with the sword came blood that stained my cloak, and Tito—oh God!—fainted, staggered and fell.)

Since Sesto makes this declaration when he and Vitellia are alone on stage, only they believe that Tito is dead; and even they have some reason to doubt that he is dead: Sesto uses the present tense in referring to Tito's death: "already his great soul is flowing from his wounded breast." Sesto apparently did not wait for Tito to die;

he only saw a man who he thought was Tito fall; later it turns out that the man he saw being attacked was not in fact Tito.

Mazzolà made Sesto's actions more violent. Sesto's account is completely in the past tense; he seems to have no doubt that Tito is dead. Furthermore, his announcement is more public: not only Vitellia but Annio, Servilia and Publio hear and react to the news that the emperor is dead. Sesto says nothing about having tried to save Tito's life; indeed he implies that he himself killed the emperor. He seems to be about to confess his crime before Vitellia hushes him:

VITELLIA
Tito?

SESTO
                      La nobil alma
Versò dal sen trafitto.

SERVILIA, ANNIO, PUBLIO
Qual destra rea macchiarsi
Potè d'un tal delitto?

SESTO
Fu l'uom più scellerato,
L'orror della natura,
fu . . .

VITELLIA
                      Taci, forsennato,
Deh non ti palesar.

(VITELLIA
Tito?

SESTO
His noble soul flowed from his wounded breast.

SERVILIA, ANNIO, PUBLIO
What wicked hand could have stained itself with such a crime?

SESTO
It was the wickedest of men, the horror of nature; it was . . .

VITELLIA
Silence, madman; do not give yourself away.)

Thus Mazzolà implicated Sesto much more deeply in the rebellion than Metastasio did; his crime is greater, his shame more painful. Mazzolà had the soloists and the people of Rome express their shock and grief at the news of Tito's death, and their outrage at his betrayal:

VITELLIA, SERVILIA, SESTO, ANNIO, PUBLIO
Ah! dunque l'astro è spento,
Di pace apportator.

TUTTI e CORO
Oh nero tradimento!
Oh giorno di dolor!

(VITELLIA, SERVILIA, SESTO, ANNIO, PUBLIO
Ah, then the star is extinguished, the bringer of peace.

TUTTI and CHORUS
Oh black betrayal! Oh day of grief!)

Inspired by these words, Mozart slowed the tempo to *Andante*. Duple meter, dotted rhythms, *piano* dynamics punctuated by sudden *forte* outbursts on dissonant chords, an accompaniment that includes trumpets and drums: all these together give Mozart's music the effect of a lugubrious funeral march, an effect all the more powerful because it is placed at the very end of the act.

In Metastasio's libretto, only a few moments after Sesto announces to Vitellia Tito's supposed death, Sesto's friend Annio enters with news that Tito is alive and firmly in control of the government. Thus the threat of revolution and assassination, a threat of which most of the characters in the drama were never even aware, has quickly passed. In Mazzolà's revision, on the other hand, those on stage and in the audience are allowed to believe for quite some time that Tito has been killed. Mazzolà, in transforming the rebellion into the finale of his first act, delayed the outcome of the rebellion and gave Mozart the opportunity to end the act with the funereal *Andante* for soloists and chorus; it is not until after the intermission that the singers and the audience learn that Tito is alive and that the rebellion has failed.

Having suppressed the rebellion, Tito forgives the participants, and the opera ends with a chorus of praise for the virtuous, generous emperor. If in the finale to Act I Mozart evoked the horror and the tragedy of revolution, in the finale to Act II he evoked, with equal power, the grandeur, stability and strength of enlightened absolutism. The choices facing the Habsburg monarchy in 1791 could not have been more simply and clearly formulated than in these two finales. As the triumphant final chorus of *La clemenza di Tito* echoed through Prague's National Theater at the height of the French Revolution, the meaning of the opera was clear, thanks to Mazzolà's skillful reworking of Metastasio's libretto and to the vividness of Mozart's music. To Leopold it said that through *clemenza*, through generosity and forgiveness he, like Tito, could win and keep the love of his subjects; to his subjects it warned that revolution would bring only destruction and shame, that allegiance to the virtuous Emperor-King Leopold, and to the system of government from which he derived his power, would bring an end to the crisis facing the Habsburg monarchy and its subjects and a return to peace and prosperity.

Appendix

Parallel between Leopold II and Titus, from Joseph Sartori, *Leopoldinische Annalen* (2 vols., Augsburg, 1792-1793), II, 216-219.

Nicht bald war eine Paralelle [*sic*] so treffend, als jene zwischen dem Bild Leopolds und dem des römischen Titus. Beide starben im 45 Jahre ihres Lebens. Beide regierten wenig über zwey Jahr. Der römische Titus 2 Jahre, 2 Monate, 2 Tage, der deutsche Titus 2 Jahre und 9 Tage als Regent der österreichischen Erbstaaten, und 1 Jahr 5 Monate als römischer Kaiser. Beide wurden von 50 Millonen Menschen, die ihre Ruhe and Glück durch sie vermehr sahen, bedaurt; Beide waren die Liebe und Lust des tugendhaften Menschen-Geschlechts. Beider Tage waren jeder mit Wohlthaten bezeichnet. Ihre kurze Regierungen sind die längsten in dem Angedenken der Zeitfolge.

Alle die Tugenden, mit welchen die Geschichte das Bild des römischen Titus gemahlt hat, zeichnen uns das von dem deutschen Titus aus. Billigkeit, Menschenliebe, Gerechtigkeit, Wohlthätigkeit waren die Grundzüge des Charakters von Beiden. Der warme Wunsch des Titus, seine Unterthanen alle glücklich zu sehen, ward durch Empörungen der Natur, durch Erdbeben, worauf die Pest folgte, und andere physische Uebel gestöret; Empörungen der Menschen störten Leopolds gleich warmen Wünsche. Er mußte die aufrührerischen Niederländer mit der Macht der Waffen zurückführen. Gleich nach der Herstellung der Ruhe machte Leopolds erhabene Großmuth eine allgemeine Verzeihung der Verführten und Verblendeten bekannt; so schenkte Titus den verschwornen Patriziern Leben und Gnade. Die Patrizier erkannten die Gnade des Titus; ein großer Theil der Niederländer aber jene nicht, die ihnen Leopold gab, sie machten dem gütigen Vaterherzen neue Unruhen. Die Römer waren weit dankbarer, als die Christen des erleuchteten 18ten Jahrhunderts.

Wenn man hier zwischen einigen Unterthanen (denn die ganze Menge der andern guten betete die fürstlichen Tugenden in Wien wie in Rom an), einen großen Abstand bemerkt, so war auch ein vielfacher Abstand in den Eigenschaften und Thaten des Römers und des Deutschen. Titus zerstörte Jerusalem und eroberte Judäa; Leopold schloß Frieden mit den Türken, und gab eroberte Länder zurück. Er gab sie zurück, weil seiner Menschen-Liebe die Opfer, die ein fortzusetzender, und ein neuer dazukommender Krieg erfordert hätte, werther waren, als der oft eitle Ruhm, seine Beherrschungen erweiteret zu haben. Einem Großen, der über diesen Gegenstand mit Ihm sprach, antwortete Er: Nicht in der größern Menge, sondern in dem größern Glücke der Unterthanen liegt der wahre Ruhm der Fürsten. Leopold wog das Recht des Kriegs in der Wage der Menschlichkeit ab, und wenn Er Krieg geführt hätte, so wäre es der gerechteste gewesen, der je geführt worden.

Die Paralelle zwischen Leopold und Titus hört auf, und verwandelt sich in einen unermeßlichen Abstand, wenn die Betrachtung von den Eigenschaften des Herzens zu denen des Verstandes übergeht. Die Geschichte zeigt in dem Titus den liebevollen und gutherzigen, in die Leopold den philosophischen Menschenfreund. Jener ist der Gute aus wallender Empfindung; dieser ist der Gute von Natur und aus durchgedachten Grundsätzen. Jenen lobt man, dieser wird verehrt: denn Titus brachte die Tugend zur Mitgabe; seine vorherige Lebenszeit hatte ihn in üblen Ruf gebracht. Man beschuldigte den Prinzen der Ungerechtigkeit, des Stolzes, des Geizes. Hier hört die Vergleichung auf, die Paralelle schließet sich. Denn were kennt Leopolds gerechte und weise Regierung von Toskana nicht?

Translation

Rarely has a parallel been so appropriate as that between the character of Leopold and that of the Roman Titus. Both died in their forty-fifth year. Both ruled a little over two years: the Roman Titus two years, two months and two days, the German Titus two years and nine days as ruler of the Austrian hereditary lands, and one year and five months as Roman Emperor. Both were mourned by fifty million people who saw their peace and prosperity increased through them. Both were the heart's delight of the virtuous part of mankind. For both rulers every day was marked with good deeds. Their short reigns are the longest in the memory of posterity.

All the virtues with which history has painted the portrait of the Roman Titus distinguished for us that of the German Titus. Fairness, benevolence, justice, charity were the characteristic features of both rulers. The warm wish of Titus to see all his subjects happy was disturbed by the rebellions of nature, in the form of earthquakes followed by plague and other natural disasters; rebellions of man disturbed Leopold's equally warm wishes. He had to lead the rebellious Netherlands back by force of arms. Immediately after peace was restored Leopold's exalted clemency declared a general amnesty for all those seduced and deluded [into rebellion]; just as Titus granted to patrician conspirators life and forgiveness. The patricians appreciated the clemency of Titus; a great part of the Netherlands did not appreciate the clemency granted to them by Leopold, and caused new anxiety for his kind, paternal heart. The Romans were far more grateful than the Christians of the enlightened eighteenth century.

If one notices here a big difference between some [of Leopold's] subjects (for the vast majority in Vienna as in Rome admired the virtues of their prince) [and those of Titus], so too was there a manifold difference between the characteristics and deeds of the Roman and those of the German. Titus destroyed Jerusalem and plundered Judea; Leopold made peace with the Turks and gave back plundered lands. He gave them back because his benevolence, which war, continued and newly declared, would have demanded that he sacrifice, was worth more than the often empty fame of having widened his territory. To a great man who asked him about this matter he answered: "The true reputation of princes consists not in the greater quantity [of their territory] but in the greater happiness of their subjects." Leopold weighed the right to wage war in the scales of humanity; and if he had waged war, it would have been the most just war ever fought.

The parallel between Leopold and Titus ends, and becomes an enormous difference, when characteristics of the intellect are considered instead of those of the heart. History shows in Titus a loving and good-hearted benevolence, in Leopold a philosophical benevolence. The former is goodness that results from spontaneous feeling; the latter goodness that results from nature and from carefully considered principles. One praises the former; one venerates the latter. For Titus brought virtue as a parting gift: his behavior before coming to the throne earned him an evil reputation. The prince was accused of injustices of arrogance, of avarice. Here the comparison ends; the parallel is finished. For who does not know Leopold's just and wise reign in Tuscany?

FEMALE SELF-DETERMINATION IN

THE EARLY DRAMAS OF

FRANUL VON WEISSENTHURN

by

George W. Reinhardt

The story of Johanna Grünberg's arrival in Vienna in 1788 is so charming and characteristic as to merit recounting at the outset. Not quite fifteen and already a successful veteran trouper in Munich, the young actress bound her belongings into a small bundle and floated alone on a raft down the Isar and the Danube to seek her fortune in the Austrian capital. In the following year she became a member of the imperial court theater, and in 1791 she married a nobleman from Fiume with the resounding family name of Franul von Weissenthurn. Born in Koblenz in the Rhineland, the offspring of itinerant thespians, this female Huckleberry Finn had in just three years risen to the pinnacle of her profession and secured an escutcheon for her descendants. For her, as for Johann Pezzl's Faustin, Vienna proved to be the citadel of European enlightenment.[1]

Weissenthurn's career in the court theater spanned the reigns of four emperors, starting with Joseph II. Its climax came in 1809

---

[1] Biographical information derives from Constant von Wurzbach, *Bibliographisches Lexikon des Kaiserthums Österreich, enthaltend die Lebensskizzen der denkwürdigen Personen, welche 1750 bis 1850 im Kaiserstaate und in seinen Kronländern gelebt haben* (60 vols., Vienna, 1856-1891), IV, 341-342.

when she dazzled Napoleon with her performance of Phèdre at the Schönbrunn court theater. With the passage of the years she ceased playing heroines to specialize in the role of mother, a part she had been performing for some years in real life. By 1809 she had been writing dramas for slightly more than a decade. In 1798, at the age of twenty-five, she produced her first literary effort. With characteristic intrepidity she wrote it within a week in order to win a bet. By her death in 1847 she had written sixty comedies and family dramas, including adaptations from French sources and romantic *Lesedramen*. Never a success with critics, Weissenthurn nevertheless enjoyed wide popularity, and her works were frequently staged. They have fallen into almost total oblivion, although Friedrich Sengle, our era's leading authority on the Biedermeier period, predicts that a scholarly connoisseur of grace and playfulness will rediscover the family dramas of Franul von Weissenthurn, Charlotte Birch-Pfeiffer and Princess Amalie of Saxony.[2]

This presentation marks a first step towards rediscovery. Here concentration is on Weissenthurn's earliest works in order to demonstrate how a conservative in a conservative society dared to alter certain conventions of the comic theater of her day to assign a more prominent role to her own sex. Whether her motives were rooted in a post-revolutionary, romantic craving for greater freedom cannot be determined in the absence of biographical data. Surely, however, Weissenthurn's own meteoric rise from marginality to aristocracy must have influenced her zestful trespassing into male terrain; and her humble origins provided a different perspective from which to judge the courtly society of which she had become a part. Her plays demonstrate that despite the stern censorship of the government of Francis II, enlightened views could be enunciated openly as long as they did not challenge economic and political institutions.

Weissenthurn gives some inkling of her combative state of mind in the preface to the first volume of her *Schauspiele*, published in

---

[2]Friedrich Sengle, *Biedermeierzeit. Deutsche Literatur im Spannungsfeld zwischen Restauration u. Revolution, 1815-1848* (3 vols., Stuttgart, 1971-1980), II, 377.

Vienna in 1804.[3] She opens by stating that a woman who, like her, treads a path closed to "sanfte Weiblichkeit" (gentle femininity) is declaring war. She cleverly weakens the attacks of future male critics by conceding that a writing woman seems to overstep the boundaries society has assigned to her: the career of writer "liegt nun ein Mahl außer dem uns angezeigten engen Wirkungskreis und wir scheinen uns zu verirren, wenn wir ihn überschreiten" (lies outside the narrow sphere of activity assigned to us women and we seem to be going astray when we overstep it). She admits that a female scholar evokes universal horror, stuck as she is between the two sexes and abhorrent to both.[4]

After these concessions Weissenthurn insists that she is in fact not a scholar, but she considers herself eminently qualified to write dramas because of her ability to capture "das Gefühl des Schicklichen und Wahren" (the sense of decorum and truth) in scenes that are genuinely effective on stage. Male reason is at times inferior to female intuition and male hostility should be disarmed by a woman who can only counterattack through humble and silent suffering.[5] Weissenthurn belittles the typical comic

---

[3]Johanna Franul von Weissenthurn, *Schauspiele* (Wien, 1804). The following plays are considered here: *Kindliche Liebe, Der Reukauß, Liebe und Entsagung* and *Beschämte Eifersucht.* Numbers in parentheses will refer to this book, which contains volume I and volume II. Weissenthurn's ebullient pride of authorship renders questionable the assertion that female authors in the early nineteenth century restricted themselves to writing letters in order not to challenge contemporary prejudice. See, e.g., Gisela Dischner, *Caroline und der Jenaer Kreis* (Berlin, 1979), p. 92. Dale Spender lists more than a hundred female novelists writing in English before Jane Austen in her *Mothers of the Novel* (London and New York, 1986), pp. 119-137. The lack of familiarity with female authors of this period is perhaps owing more to ignorance than to reticence on their part.

[4]Weissenthurn is not only belittling the notion of women as scholars, but scholarship itself. Untainted by institutional learning her romantic sensibility preferred the beauties of nature. She considered them more rewarding than the darkest lucubrations of the philosophers. She makes this point in her novel *Graf Lohrenburg* (Vienna, 1819), p. 40.

[5]This prizing of female emotion over male reason anticipates the Saint-Simonian conviction that only sentiment could provide a solid bond for a peaceful society. See Claire G. Moses, "The Legacy of the Eighteenth Century: A Look at the Future," in *French Women and the Age of the Enlightenment* (Bloomington, Indiana, 1984), ed., Samia Spencer, p. 411. The opening pages of *Graf Lohrenburg*, a product of the Restoration era, are outspokenly anti-military.

situation of the woman who cannot write without staining her fingers, as, for example, Rosina in *Il Barbiere di Siviglia*, to assert that she would rather blunt a few quills writing than spend her time with woman's work like knitting stockings: "Ich kann das Stricken nicht leiden, das muß mich auch für die Zukunft entschuldigen, wenn dieß nicht meine letzte Arbeit ist" (I can't endure knitting. That will have to serve as my excuse should this prove not to be my last literary effort).

Since Weissenthurn's early production of plays fits the time frame of this volume of essays, one can contrast her vision of the social role of her sex with that presented in Mozart's comic libretti of a decade earlier to document the emergence of a new spirit in the last years of the eighteenth century. Emanuel Schikaneder can be a first example.

In *Die Zauberflöte* the contrast between the generations is marked. While Pamina leads young Tamino through the rites of initiation and is destined to share his power once he becomes ruler, the older generation subscribes to a more patriarchal scheme. A comparison of Schikaneder's text with the rococo sources reveals a striking alteration of the roles played by the senior representatives of both sexes. The opening scenes still emphasize Sarastro's villainy and his maltreatment of the Queen of the Night. The course of the opera soon reveals the blackguard abductor to be a sage endowed with the wisdom prerequisite for the attainment of maturity while the seemingly good female fairy is unmasked as a vindictive potential assassin, a fit companion for the evil blackamoor Monastatos.

This strange reversal of roles has puzzled interpreters. Some musicologists relate it to Mozart's desire to introduce an element of *opera seria* into his German *Singspiel*: the dazzling roulades of an enraged and frenzied coloratura. Social considerations, however, may have overridden those of genre. The relations of an aggressive female to Stygian gloom and the simultaneous apotheosis of the dominant male as solar demigod are fully compatible with the morality of the opera. One can easily picture the complacent Viennese bourgeois nodding in approval while Sarastro and his hierophants enlighten the young folks about the facts of life. The old priest urges Tamino to place no store in the libelous babblings (*Zungenspiel*) of a woman: "Ein Weib tut wenig, plaudert viel" (A woman doesn't do much, but she talks a lot.) In a passage of impressive musical solemnity Sarastro himself assures Pamina that she must eschew the advice of that haughty woman, her mother: "Ein Mann muß eure Herzen lenken, denn ohne ihn pflegt jedes Weib aus ihrem Wirkungskreis zu schreiten" (A man must direct you women's hearts because without him you tend to stray from your proper sphere of activity). Behind *Die Zauberflöte*'s facade of harmony and partnership looms the pyramid of male dominance as a social categorical imperative. In the Masonic Temple of Osiris on the banks of the blue Danube, Isis knows her place.

Così fan tutte's Horatian blending of Stoic *nil admirari* with Epicurean hedonism transposes the theme of male superiority to a less somber key. Written in Italian for an aristocratic audience, it modifies the chiaroscuro of *Die Zauberflöte* by presenting more nuanced images of men and women. The women, who have accepted the role of paragons of virtue all too readily, succumb to the seductive moustaches of their new swains, and the men may become as "philosophical" as their mentor after a decade of married life. As naive as their sweethearts, they all must learn to accept both male and female inconstancy as a manifestation of nature's law. This lesson, which will stand them in good stead after they are married, is imparted to them both by a man and a woman: Alfonso and Despina. When one learns of the bet between the shrewd old cynic and the idealistic youths, one already knows from the title that Don Alfonso will win the hundred zecchini. The women hear the same message from Despina. Yet there is here, too, an imbalance in favor of the masculine. With her palm adequately greased, Despina proves a willing and inventive manipulatrix, but it is the Neapolitan Sarastro, Don Alfonso, who maintains tight control over the action almost from the opening measures to the final chord.

Like Titus in *La clemenza di Tito*, Sarastro and Don Alfonso temper their absolute control with benevolence. Mozart's librettists validate absolutism for their public with the crucial proviso that the ruler must above all be clement. Franul von Weissenthurn applies this qualification to matrimony, modifying it further by urging that a truly enlightened couple arrange their life together along republican rather than monarchical lines. When Count Werthen suggests to his sisters in *Beschämte Eifersucht* that they are living in a republic in which each serves alternately as doge, Julie quickly sets him straight: "Ach!—wir regieren hier nicht, wir werden regiert, wir erfreuen uns nicht der liebevollen Regierung eines Titus. . . . Mein Schwager, unser regierender König, führt das Regiment mit etwas Strenge. Seine Hoheit möchte allein geliebt, allein gefürchtet seyn" (Alas. We are not the rulers here. We are the ruled. We do not enjoy the amiable governance of a Titus. My brother-in-law, our ruling monarch, reigns with considerable severity. His Highness wishes to be the only one to be loved, to be feared).[6] In the eyes of Weissenthurn such patriarchal despotism cries out for repudiation.

Weissenthurn presents her refutation of the sexual ideology of the Mozart operas in one of her most enduring and successful works, *Beschämte Eifersucht*. Juxtaposing the old and conventional with a new spirit of freedom and openness, this three-act comedy proclaims female constancy and the right of women to make decisions for themselves, while challenging Alfonso's assertion of inevitable feminine mutability and Sarastro's assertion concerning woman's need for male guidance. The male characters who share such negative attitudes at the beginning of the comedy must learn to think more humanely before the play ends. A summary of the action will make clear this process of enlightenment.

Two sisters, Marie and Julie, are rusticating at the home of Marie's new and unreasonably jealous husband, Count Solm. In Solm's absence they are being chaperoned by the count's uncle, crusty old Baron Sturz, whose favorite pastime is the tracing of noble pedigrees and favorite topic, as his name indicates, the progressive deterioration of humanity, "die Verschlechterung des Menschengeschlechts." Sturz finds evidence of such degeneracy in trifles like the unwillingness of the women to keep him company while he snores through his postprandial naps. Marie has surrendered almost completely to such boorish male tyranny, disobeying her husband only when he forbade her to send her portrait to the brother whom she has not seen since childhood. She takes seriously the other "prohibitions" of her spouse and is even unwilling to defer breakfast until her tardy lord and master returns home.

Julie eats when she is hungry. With a clever pun she sets her elder sister straight concerning husbandly rights: men may "sich

---

[6]Weissenthurn, *Schauspiele*, II, 104.

höchstens etwas *verbitten*, nicht *verbieten*" (urge us to *desist* but not *insist*).[7] Unlike Marie, she refuses to marry until her fiance Baron Walling has cast off his jealous ways: "Ich halte es für eine Krankheit und will ihm nicht eher meine Hand geben, bis er kuriert ist" (I consider it a disease and refuse to give him my hand until he is cured).[8] Her free spirit expresses itself in frequent acts of charity towards the village poor and in her straying out into the fields beyond the confines of the manorial garden to pick a bouquet of forget-me-nots for her recalcitrant bridegroom. Although she has been ordered not to venture so far, she is, like Sophie in Rousseau's *Emile*, irresistibly drawn to nature.[9] During this pastoral outing she encounters a wounded lieutenant who is in actuality her long-lost brother, Fritz. When she recounts this adventure to her sister, Marie is shocked that Julie did not run away from a stranger and even more dismayed to learn of the stranger's imminent arrival, a serious breach of etiquette in her eyes. Julie counters by urging her to act on her own, to be a bit more assertive in her own home.

To brother Fritz, Weissenthurn assigns the role of ultimate mentor. He has already demonstrated his questioning of authority in his poor academic performance—"viel Talent aber wenig Willen" (much talent but little will)—and in his difficulty adjusting to military discipline. His frank speech and lack of ceremony beguile his sisters as much as his handsome face and uniform. When Fritz learns of the despotism of his brother-in-law and of the even more suspicious nature of Julie's betrothed, he resolves to help these German Desdemonas by teaching their Othellos a lesson they will never forget. The Venetian Republic must be transplanted across the Alps. (Weissenthurn clearly expected her audience to be sufficiently cultivated to recognize the allusion to Shakespeare.) The specific reference to "deutsch" is extremely rare in contemporary Austrian texts, owing to the government's desire to underplay nationalism. It is probably attributable to Weissenthurn's own

---

[7]*Ibid.*, II, 92.
[8]*Ibid.*, II, 105.
[9]Weissenthurn's Julies (here and in *Liebe und Entsagung*) echo the initiative, enterprise and determination to control their own destinies of the Julie of Rousseau's *La nouvelle Héloise*.

German origin. She went so far as to name a brief play *Deutsche Traue*.[10]

Complications ensue when Fritz persuades Marie to grant him a nocturnal *tête-à-tête* in the garden to discuss the fate of her brother. He has learned from a cunning servant that her husband and Baron Walling have already been apprised of his arrival and are hiding in the selfsame garden in order to trap their women *in flagrante*. When the jealous lovers find out about the rendezvous they burst into a paroxysm of rage like Figaro's in "Aprite un po' quegli occhi": "So sind denn die Weiber nur zu unsrem Verderben auf der Welt" (Women exist only to destroy us men).[11] Solm wants to resort to one of the era's punishments for an adulterous wife, banishment to a cloister, and Walling intends to overwhelm Julie with scorn. Both withdraw into a side room to oversee the *liaison dangereuse*. Because the count leaves to summon retribution he hears neither Marie's rejection of her spurious suitor nor her indignant reaction to his lubricious proposition that cuckolds and lovers are destined for friendship since it is male nature to stray: *Così fan tutti*! On his return he peremptorily orders her to her room, but timid Marie has by now acquired sufficient self-confidence to assert that her heart exonerates her from every accusation.

An intense exchange concerning "the iron yoke of matrimony" convinces Count Solm to set aside his threat to sic his flail-wielding peasants on Fritz. He now recognizes the need to temper his jealousy and acknowledge the truth of Fritz's strictures. Only Walling continues to be obtuse. When Fritz deliberately drops Julie's portrait at the baron's feet, Walling instantly renounces his unfaithful "siren." Fritz rushes off in feigned pursuit of Julie's hand while Count Solm fears for his friend's sanity.

The final act brings resolution and insight. Unlike Dorabella and Fiordiligi, Julie proves as impervious to Fritz's false wooing as her sister had been. When he threatens to die at her feet, she scolds him as unbearable. He rewards her by unmasking himself in order to enlist her support. On Walling's arrival Julie reproaches him for being so dishonorable as to spy on her. She

---

[10] Weissenthurn, *Schauspiele*, I, 223-254.
[11] *Ibid.*, II, 132.

explains to him that a married woman will remain faithful to a jealous husband not out of love but for the sake of her own honor while an unwed maiden will simply dismiss a suspicious suitor and find another. With these words she places her hand in her brother's and breaks Walling's heart, momentarily. He bids farewell by kissing her other hand and she bountifully reveals Fritz's identity to him. Without a trace of anger over the benevolent deception, Walling embraces his soon-to-be brother-in-law and grants him permission to assist Julie in punishing any future relapses into his old jealous ways. Solm proves equally tractable. In front of his wife he cooperates in a brief charade of indignation which threatens to explode into a duel. Moved by Marie's concern for his safety, he is at last completely convinced of her innocence. A second revelation on Fritz's part of his fraternal link melds the entire group into a harmonious quintet. To employ the sentimental imagery of the play, the missing blossom of trust has been added to the forget-me-not garland of family life.

Parallels to Mozart texts such as the garden rendezvous, the threat of suicide by the spurned lover and the joking asides of the manipulator, who can scarcely contain his mirth, are obvious. Weissenthurn learned her trade from her immediate predecessors. She, however, rejected Da Ponte's and Schikaneder's view of the relationship between the sexes. For her the imputation of inevitable fickleness is pernicious. Just before the final curtain Fritz assures the public that he has broken a lance for the honor of the fair sex: "Das schöne Geschlecht ist mir heute viel Dank schuldig, denn ich habe mich ritterlich um ihre Ehre herum gestritten" (The fair sex owes me a debt of gratitude since I fought like a knight in defense of its honor).[12]

Fritz is a reverse Don Alfonso—youthful instead of old, idealistic rather than ironic. Although both aim to prepare their pupils for the rigors of matrimony, Fritz urges the men to expect more, and Alfonso urges them to be content with less. What for Alfonso is clearheaded tolerance of the foibles of the weaker sex seems pathological distrust to Fritz. The playfulness and cynicism of the rococo have been supplanted by a sentimental celebration of love and mutual trust. In *Beschämte Eifersucht* Weissenthurn

---

[12]*Ibid.*, II, 167.

has provided an elegant comic counterpart to Beethoven's *Fidelio*. Despite its positive appraisal of woman's nature *Beschämte Eifersucht* relies for its structure on the convention of the male manipulator. In setting up his didactic masquerade, Fritz acts alone until the third act when he initiates Julie into the intrigue. Julie plays a more trifling role than Despina or, to cite a nineteenth-century example, Edritta in Grillparzer's *Weh dem, der lügt*. An alert woman in an age of transition, Weissenthurn here resorts to the traditional device of the chivalric knight's rescuing of damsels in distress to point to the revolutionary and enlightened moral that men must include women in the call for "egalité."[13]

The action of other plays is shaped by more enterprising female characters. In *Liebe und Entsagung* Amalie has gone so far as to marry without her guardian's knowledge or consent. The misunderstandings that shape the plot are based on this secret arrangement.[14] In *Der Reukauf*, a variation on Lessing's *Minna von Barnhelm*, the intrigue is instigated and controlled by another Amalie who succeeds in persuading her cousin Jette's impecunious and timid (*weiberscheu*) tutor to overcome his pride and propose to Jette. In doing so she acts directly counter to the wishes of her guardian, Jette's father, who, another one of Weissenthurn's misguided male parents, has selected an aristocratic fop as his future son-in-law and thus reduced his daughter, in Amalie's eyes, to the level of servitude (*Sklavin*).

Weissenthurn's most salient and reiterated message is that young men and women must be permitted to choose a spouse who will make them happy. Parents who oppose this right are in error, like Jette's foolish father in *Der Reukauf*. When a father tries to force his child to marry for money, as the usurer Wunder does with his son Fritz in *Kindliche Liebe*, the parent will be punished by ostracism, exclusion from the family circle. Since Wunder has, in

---

[13]Fritz represents a variant of the figure which Jane Spencer, in *The Rise of the Woman Novelist, From Aphra Behn to Jane Austen* (Oxford, 1986), pp. 145-163, calls the "lover-mentor." The most significant difference is that other males are the targets of his pedagogical zeal.

[14]Sengle regards the secret marriage as a remarkable combination of boldness with propriety. The daring consists in defiance of paternal authority; the decorum in the acknowledgment at the end of the play of a pre-established harmony between the lovers. Sengle, *Biedermeierzeit*, II, 434.

addition, sent his debtors to prison and scrimped on his son's education, he deserves the harshest of punishments; he is abandoned to a lonely and childless old age. Fritz disowns his father and is adopted by a rich uncle whose bounty will form the economic basis for his future marital happiness.

Even dynastic considerations must yield to the prompting of the heart. Princess Ottilie in *Die fürstlichen Nebenbuhler* yearns to escape from the bondage of diplomacy. She wishes that she were a man in order to be able to determine her own fate ("über meine Bestimmung nachzudenken—sie selbst ordnen zu dürfen").[15] She vigorously protests being "sold" (*verkauft, verhandelt*) in order to restore friendly relations with a neighboring principality and she is convinced that if she were a *Bürgermädchen* she would instantly receive her father's blessing when she presented him with the future husband of her choice. Applying the political model of Schiller's Marquis Posa to the family, Weissenthurn believes that parents should listen to their children, even as the enlightened ruler will heed the advice of his subjects. Absolutism must make way for mutual respect both between spouses and between generations.

Weissenthurn lauds the virtues of honor, loyalty, gratitude, generosity and rural simplicity, as opposed to urban frivolity, materialist greed and courtly pretension. Her female characters incorporate these virtues. They are, in addition, intelligent, enterprising, competent as housekeepers (*Kindliche Liebe*) and concerned with the upbringing of their children. Gael in *Liebe und Entsagung* rejects the assertion that women lack character and vacillate irrationally between laughter and tears.[16] Only when their wishes are respected and their counsel regarded will contentment be attainable for both sexes.

This conception of happiness inclines to the liberal view that the family balanced personal interests, just as commerce balanced those of property, in the direction of the republican theory that marriage formed a society in which people were made moral or

---

[15]Johanna Franul von Weissenthurn, *Die fürstlichen Nebenbuhler*, p. 2. The copy in this writer's possession lacks a title page.

[16]Weissenthurn, *Schauspiele*, II, 17.

virtuous.[17] The latter notion is implicit in Weissenthurn's celebration of domesticity. Yet Weissenthurn appeals primarily to her spectators' self-interest. If parents treat their children worthily, they will be succored by them in old age; if husbands honor and cherish their wives, they will find them even more precious in the "winter of their lives" than in the bloom of youth.[18] *Liebe und Entsagung* concludes with the inculcation of this utilitarian moral: "Der Mensch sollte aus Eigennutz tugendhaft seyn, weil er nur durch Tugenden sich und Andere wahrhaft glücklich machen kann" (Humans should be virtuous out of self-interest. For one can make oneself and others happy only through virtue).[19]

The success of her career indicates that her predominantly aristocratic audience sympathized with Weissenthurn's predominantly bourgeois message. Many of the Austrian noblewomen in the boxes of the Hofburgtheater must have preferred, in theory at least, the life of a good wife occupied solely with her husband, her children and her household to the vanities of a glittering but superficial court. To a considerable degree Weissenthurn contributed to making this "too bourgeois a way of thinking" respectable and attractive.[20]

---

[17] A brief presentation of the difference between liberal and republican views of marriage can be found in Bonnie G. Smith, *Changing Lives. Women in European History Since 1700* (Lexington, MA, and Toronto, 1989), pp. 74-75.
[18] Weissenthurn, *Schauspiele*, II, 43.
[19] *Ibid.*, II, 87.
[20] A quotation from the Marquise de Bombelle's letter to her husband the French ambassador to the Holy Roman Empire (1781), in which she complains of the stifling atmosphere of the court. Cited in Cissie Fairchilds, "Women and Family," in *French Women and the Age of Enlightenment*, p. 98. Fairchilds describes a revolution in the realm of family life in the last decades of the eighteenth century which perfectly fits Weissenthurn's views: "At the heart of this revolution was the emergence of the modern, affectionate nuclear family, in which the spouses married for love, treated each other with dignity and respect, and worked together to raise their children in an atmosphere of security and indulgence," p. 97.

THE ORIGIN OF THE AUSTRIAN NATIONAL ANTHEM AND AUSTRIA'S LITERARY WAR EFFORT

by

Hugo Schmidt

On occasions like the arrival of Chancellor Helmut Kohl in Moscow, we are likely to shake our heads in disbelief upon hearing the Russian army band strike up the German national anthem, a tune most of us cannot help associating with the words "Deutschland, Deutschland über alles." But we might correct our initial reaction after reflecting on the age and the origin of the melody, its original text, and what a role it played in the resistance against an enemy which was, at the time, also Russia's foe. Composed in 1797, it was part of Austria's war effort to inspire the nation in the struggle against the new French republic and the rising star of that invidious artillery officer with the Italian accent.

The idea to have an Austrian national anthem came from the sixty-five-year-old Joseph Haydn, who in turn had been inspired by the English hymn "God Save the King," the first of all national anthems. In this context, the English, as well as the subsequent French anthem, deserve some attention. "God Save the King" was probably written and composed by one Henry Carey, an unsuccessful music teacher who died in 1743, most probably by his own hand. In his posthumous papers, the song "God Save the King" was found. It was published the year after, without Carey's name, by an enterprising London publisher named John Simpson. Apparently Carey had written the song in the year of his death, on the occasion of the campaign of King George II against the French, in the course of the War of Austrian Succession, and his victory in the battle of Dettingen in June 1743, the last time a British king actually appeared on a battlefield. Thus the words "God Save the King" had an immediate meaning in the given situation.

For a while it appeared that the song, which quickly achieved great popularity, would become a kind of generic anthem for all nations, with different texts substituted. August Niemann tried to adapt it for the Holy Roman Empire in 1782, with the opening lines:

> Heil! Kaiser Josef, Heil!
> Dir, Deutschlands Kaiser, Heil!
> Dem Kaiser Heil!
>
> (Hail to Emperor Joseph, Hail
> to you, Emperor of Germany, Hail
> to the emperor!)

The hymn did not become popular. A Danish version followed in 1790, and the famous Prussian one in 1793, "Heil dir im Siegerkranz," with the labored lines, further down,

> Fühl in des Thrones Glanz
> Die hohe Wonne ganz:
> Liebling des Volks zu sein.
>
> (In the splendor of the throne,
> feel the delight of being loved
> by the people.)

The involved syntax proved to be too much for those who sang the hymn faithfully, and soon the words "Wonne ganz" were understood as "Wonnegans" (goose of bliss), and generations of Prussian school children, feeling that the royal consort also rated a place in the anthem, supposedly believed that the line "Die hohe Wonne ganz" was a somewhat disrespectful allusion to the queen. Other German states followed suit in creating their own texts. There are versions of the anthem for Bavaria, Saxony, Württemberg, Mecklenburg-Schwerin, but also for Sweden, Switzerland, and eventually, around 1850, even for Liechtenstein, with the opening lines:

> Oberst am jungen Rhein
> Lehnet sich Liechtenstein
> An Alpenhöhn.
>
> (High up at the headwaters of the Rhine
> Liechtenstein is nestled against
> the Alpine slopes.)[1]

Later, some enthusiasts even wrote versions in Volapük and Esperanto. And of course there is America. In 1832 one Samuel F. Smith wrote "My country! 'tis of thee / Sweet land of liberty," which gained great popularity during the Civil War on the northern side and is still mentioned, at times, as a fine potential replacement for the vocally more demanding "Star-Spangled Banner." One would wish that poor Mr. Carey had lived to witness and enjoy at least part of the fruits of his efforts. As it was, he left his family so destitute that they could not pay for his funeral.

In the meantime France had obtained a national anthem, under most unusual circumstances. The great song of the revolution was written by a royalist army officer, Captain Claude Joseph Rouget de l'Isle, who served in Strasbourg in the early 1790s. When Emperor Leopold II and King Frederick William II of Prussia issued the Declaration of Pillnitz in August 1791, threatening France, and France declared war on the Allies in April 1792, de l'Isle wrote a song, "Chant de guerre pour l'armée du Rhin" ("War song for the Rhine army") and presented it at a party in the house of Mayor Dietrich of Strasbourg. The tyrants against whom the song inveighs are, of course, the Austrians and Prussians, but this was forgotten when it spread quickly throughout France. The volunteer corps from Marseille sang it upon entering Paris in July 1792, and from then on it was referred to as the "Marseillaise." In July 1795 it was declared the official national anthem and was sung at every state affair and especially at executions. The enthusiasm it created was stupendous. When the last stanza was

---

[1]Emil Bohn, *Die Nationalhymnen der europäischen Völker* (Breslau, 1908), p. 9.

sung, the mood of the crowds would change from a state of belligerence to pious introspection at the words "Amour sacré de la patrie" ("Holy love of the fatherland"), and people even knelt down. But during the final chorus, "Marchez, marchez," everyone rose again in renewed ferociousness.

How did de l'Isle fare during all this? When he, after the republic had been proclaimed, like all officers and officials had to answer the question whether or not he would abide by the rules of the National Assembly, he answered "No," was stripped of his rank and thrown into jail. Surely he would have been guillotined, an occasion at which no doubt his song would have been played, but it so happened that Robespierre was executed first, and de l'Isle somehow got away, spending the rest of his life impoverished and in obscurity.

The hymn "Gott erhalte Franz den Kaiser" ("God save Emperor Francis"), although inspired by the English anthem, was clearly an answer to the "Marseillaise." Since the latter had become the battle hymn of the republic, much had happened. Louis XVI and his consort, an Austrian princess, had been executed, and revolutionary France threatened the very existence of Austria. Napoleon had defeated Austrian armies both on Italian and Austrian soil, had invaded Styria and had put Vienna within his reach. And, worst of all, the enemy was not another monarchy with which one could deal on accustomed terms, but an unpredictable throng of radicals with ideas that ran contrary to everything the political system of Habsburg stood for. Probably for the first time in history the national leadership began to realize that in order to handle the situation it needed the support of an enthusiastic, patriotically inspired people. Dynastic interests had to be defended, but the defenders on the battlefields had to be aroused to do this out of love for their country. National leaders quickly learned the use of mass psychology.

However, while the good will of the people was desperately needed, their freedoms continued to be curtailed to a ludicrous degree. The many liberal steps of Joseph II, such as a measure of freedom of the press, were revoked at Joseph's death. A court decree of September 1790 summarily rescinded the liberal legislation concerning the press and reiterated the pre-Josephinian view that the supreme charge of the state is "die Aufrechterhaltung der allgemeinen Ruhe" (the preservation of public peace and order)² and that publications that might disturb this peace must be prohibited. It is easy to see that instilling the people with patriotic frenzy, as the authorities now set out to do, had its dangerous aspects, for enthusiasm, even if it is a patriotic one, was still a disturbance of this "public peace," and the authorities had to learn to walk a thin line. Subsequent years brought additional restrictions. When Francis II ascended the throne in 1792, the Court Chancellery issued a decree that no articles from the foreign press could be reprinted which aimed at an "excitement of feelings" through the spreading of "dangerous opinions."[3] Among the additional laws published thereafter was one specifying that journalists should not only avoid uncensorious remarks about the French Revolution, but that it would be welcomed "wenn solche Zeitungsschreiber als Gelehrte aufgemuntert würden, bei wirksamer Gelegenheit die üblen Folgen der französischen Revolution lebhaft darzustellen und sich dabei besonders einer populären, jedermann leicht faßlichen Schreibart zu bedienen" (if such journalists and scholars were encouraged to compose lively descriptions of the disastrous consequences of the French revolution, and in doing so employ a popular style accessible to all).[4] In 1795 there appeared a revised directive of censorship which served mostly as a guide through the thicket of previous decrees but also outlined the penalties for infringements against any of them. Paragraph nr. 4, for example, stipulated that nothing whatsoever could be printed without express permission of the office of censorship. If it happened nevertheless, the punishment included confiscation and destruction of the edition, loss of printing license, and a fine of fifty guilders for every copy of the publication, or incarceration of one day per unpaid guilder. If a printer produced an announcement or leaflet, for example, concerning a benefit concert in an edition of one thousand copies (the usual number at the time) without securing prior permission, he would be subject to a fine of fifty thousand guilders or to a jail sentence of fifty thousand

---

[2]E.V. Zenker, *Geschichte der Wiener Journalistik von den Anfängen bis zum Jahre 1848* (Vienna and Leipzig, 1892), p. 87.
[3]*Ibid.*, p. 88.
[4]*Ibid.*, p. 90.

days or 137 years. In 1798 four decrees were issued by the Court Chancellery, one of which prohibited coffee houses from subscribing to literary journals because this would make it possible that "eine Art von Lesekabinetten entstehet" (a type of reading circle would appear).[5] It is not surprising that at times reading per se would be considered a controversial activity. In 1803 newspapers were forbidden to make mention of any "domestic institutions" and "government business" unless they received express orders from the government to do so. All pronouncements and judgments of the office of censorship were final, without recourse and appeal.

In such times of repression, one should think, it would take an amount of gall to expect of the people manifestations of their love for the ruling dynasty, and it is symptomatic of the situation that this happened nevertheless. Austrians' patience seemed inexhaustible, and it was not a member of the imperial court, but the most loyal subject, Joseph Haydn, who came up with the idea of a national anthem. Haydn had been to England twice, shortly beforehand, from 1790 to 1792, and again from 1794 to 1795, and had witnessed the impact a patriotic hymn can have when sung by an assembled crowd. In 1797 he mentioned the idea of having an Austrian national anthem to Baron van Swieten, one of the great patrons of the arts, and van Swieten in turn contacted Francis Count Saurau, a high-ranking state official and a most energetic Jacobin-baiter. He had been deputy president of the notorious *Polizeihofstelle* (imperial police department), which was later to be headed by Count Sedlnitzky, and was *Regierungspräsident* (governor) of Vienna and Minister of Finance and of Police. He also headed a commission charged with the investigation of and jurisdiction over all suspected conspiracies against the government. In this capacity he had established an effective net of spies and pursued potential traitors with great zeal. He would resort to using stool pigeons pretending to be malcontents and then have those arrested for treason who would not disagree sufficiently with his informers' disloyal remarks. Saurau attained a certain measure of immortality by his much-quoted lament that the distinguished mineralogist and satirist Ignaz von Born, whom he actually called his friend, "durch den Tod ihm entronnen sei" (escaped him by

---

[5]*Ibid.*, p. 92.

dying)⁶, before he could initiate proceedings against him. During the ruthless Jacobin persecutions of Vienna in 1795, Saurau's commission accused, among many others, another friend of his, Martin Prandstätter, of high treason, claiming that he had knowledge of some alleged treacherous activities. He was sentenced to confiscation of property, to being put into the pillory on three consecutive days with a sign pinned on him proclaiming "Theilnahme am Landesverrath" (taking part in acts of high treason) and subsequently to thirty years in jail, where he probably died. His was one of the lighter sentences. Others on trial along with him were condemned to death by hanging or to sixty-year jail terms.⁷ The widespread belief that political repression in Austria was quaint and not to be taken seriously is unfounded. The tiger was not made of paper, and its claws were dangerous.

This same Count Saurau now took charge of the making of the national anthem. The composer had volunteered his services, and now a poet had to be found to write a text. There was no time for a contest and for submissions of entries; Saurau made his own remarkable choice. He commissioned a man by the name of Lorenz Leopold Haschka to do this patriotic service, and this choice was characteristic of him. Haschka was not only a shameless opportunist, but also a spy and an informer. No doubt he was, at the time, in Saurau's services. As a youth he had joined the Society of Jesus. After the order was abolished in 1773, he managed as a journalist and occasional poet in Vienna. Supposedly the poet Johann von Alxinger once helped him out with a large sum of money which, some claim, Haschka used to buy stock in the lucrative slave trade. During the Josephinian era he discovered his liberal leanings and showed himself to be a raving opponent of the Pope, the clergy and royalty, and made his views known in strings of odes. He even made it into Goethe's and Schiller's *Xenien*, where one muse remarks:

---

⁶Constant von Wurzbach, *Biographisches Lexikon des Kaiserthums Österreich, enthaltend die Lebensskizzen der denkwurdigen Personen, welche 1750 bis 1850 im Kaiserstaate und in seinen Kronlandern gelebt haben* (60 vols., Vienna, 1856-1891), XXVIII, 280.
⁷Wurzbach, XXIII, 195.

> Aber jetzt rat' ich euch, geht, sonst kommt noch gar der Gorgona
> Fratze oder ein Band Oden von Haschka hervor.
>
> (But now I beg you to leave, lest there appear the grimace of Gorgon
> Or a volume of odes by Haschka.)[8]

After Joseph's death Haschka quickly changed colors again, turned into a loyal defender of the reestablished status quo, and joined the staff of the secretary to the Cardinal-Archbishop. He was also in the pay of the police as an informer and was assigned to researching secret connections, a charge which, as one biographer comments, must have been child's play for him, since he had been, in succession, "Jesuit, Freimaurer [freemason], Illuminat, Rosenkreuzer [Rosicrucian] und Kryptojesuit."[9]

Haschka's output of odes was truly prodigious. He wrote them on the occasion of any newsworthy event, with titles such as "On Leopold II's Return from the Coronation in Frankfurt," or "On the Day of Homage 6 April 1790," or "On the Peace of Campo Formio" (actually no cause for celebration in Austria). Haschka himself commented: "Even if my odes had no literary value, they will remain noteworthy historically since my lyre followed conscientiously the great events of its days."[10] Contrary to Schiller's fears, there was never a whole volume of Haschka's odes, but they appeared as leaflets and in various almanacs, especially in one edited by Haschka himself, the *Literarische Monate*, and its successor, the better-known *Wienerischer Musenalmanach* (1777-1796). The latter, in its last years, contained increasing numbers of patriotic poems and demonstrates well the beginnings of this genre in Austria.

In a memoir composed twenty-three years later, Saurau described the circumstances of the writing of the hymn—not very truthfully, for he takes credit for having come up with the idea

---

[8]Johann W. Goethe, *Werke*, ed. Erich Trunz (4 vols., Hamburg, 1948), I, 221.

[9]Wurzbach, VIII, 23.

[10]Johann W. Nagl, Jakob Zeidler and Eduard Castle, *Deutsch-österreichische Literaturgeschichte* (4 vols., Vienna, 1899-1937), II (1914), 332.

and for having chosen Haydn as the composer:

> I often regretted that we had not, like the English, a national air calculated to display to all the world the loyal devotion of our people to the kind and upright ruler of our fatherland, and to awaken in the hearts of all good Austrians that noble national pride so indispensable to the energetic fulfillment of all the beneficial measures of the sovereign. This seemed to me more urgent at a period when the French Revolution was raging most furiously and when the Jacobins cherished the idle hope of finding among the worthy Viennese partisans and participators in their criminal designs. I caused that meretricious poet Haschka to write the words and applied to our immortal countryman Haydn to set them to music, for I considered him alone capable of writing anything approaching in merit to the English "God Save the King." Such was the origin of our national hymn.[11]

And Haschka did write a text, leaning heavily on "God Save the King." The first two lines, repeated at the end, are as simple as they are memorable, but the four lines in between are not any better than the middle part of the English hymn:

> Gott erhalte Franz den Kaiser,
> Unsern guten Kaiser Franz!
> Lange lebe Franz der Kaiser
> In des Glückes hellstem Glanz!
> Ihm erblühen Lorbeerreiser
> Wo er geht, zum Ehrenkranz!
> Gott erhalte Franz den Kaiser,
> Unsern guten Kaiser Franz!

> (God save Francis the Emperor,
> Our good Emperor Francis!
> Long Live Francis the Emperor
> In the brightest splendor of his destiny!
> Where he treads may branches of laurel grow
> Into wreaths of glory!
> God save Francis the emperor
> Our good Emperor Francis!)

---

[11] J. Cuthbert Hadden, *Haydn* (London, 1934), pp. 112-13.

There are four stanzas altogether, but only the first became popular.[12]

Haydn's melody, which has become truly immortal, gives the hymn its distinction and lifts it high above the general limitations of this genre. It became popular immediately and played an important part in creating a wave of patriotic fervor throughout the Austrian lands. Translations into the other languages of the Austrian empire followed very quickly. Saurau made sure personally that the imprimatur was given promptly. This happened on 28 January 1797; and on 12 February, the emperor's birthday, the hymn was sung for the first time in the Hofburgtheater by the entire audience, who had been given copies of the text, as an homage to the emperor, in his presence, before the curtain rose to the main event of the evening, Dittersdorf's comic opera *Der Doctor und der Apotheker*. On the same evening, the hymn was sung during similar celebrations in most other theaters in Vienna and in theaters in Prague, Graz, Innsbruck, Trieste, and others. We have to admire this feat of logistics and coordination. At the event in the Hofburgtheater the emperor was so moved, we are told, that he stood in the rear of his box, and only when the people's ovations continued did he step forward to show his gratitude.[13] Haydn received the standard gift of the times in recognition of his efforts: a golden snuff box adorned with a portrait of His Majesty, sent to him by the emperor through Saurau. Haydn thanked Saurau in humble terms, for writing to the emperor directly would have seemed presumptuous to him:

> Excellency, such a surprise and such grace, especially about the portrait of my kind monarch, I have never experienced in view of my modest talents. I thank your Excellency with all my heart and am ready to serve your Excellency at any time. . . . I am, in deep respect, your most submissive and obedient servant, Jos. Haydn.[14]

---

[12]Nagl, et al., *Deutsch-österreichische Literaturgeschichte*, II, 335.
[13]Paul Nettl, *National Anthems*, trans. Alexander Gode (New York, 1952), p. 54.
[14]*Ibid.*, p. 55.

To his great sorrow, Haydn never received a medal or decoration from the Austrian Empire, after having been feted in England and receiving an honorary doctorate from Oxford University. But this was probably a mere oversight and an example of *Schlamperei*. Haydn's hymn became a lasting symbol of the veneration in which the people held the House of Habsburg, and later on it even did its share in holding the crumbling empire together. One quickly noted that it followed the same rhythm and cadences as the "Tantum ergo," and people indeed looked upon it as a prayer. Grillparzer even wrote a poem about the effect the anthem had upon him. As is common with such success-stories, there were also voices that questioned Haydn's authorship, accusing him of borrowing a Croatian folk song or stealing from an Italian composer, Antonio Zingarelli. But it was shown irrefutably that the Croatian song in question is a far cry from Haydn's, and that Zingarelli stole from Haydn, not vice versa.[15] Two months after writing the hymn Haydn incorporated it into a string quartet, op. 76 nr. 3 in C major, subsequently called the *Emperor Quartet*. Haydn loved the melody dearly and played it often for his private pleasure. It was the last piece of music he played on 26 May 1809, five days before his death at the age of seventy-seven. At that time the French army had occupied Vienna, and it is worth noting that the French treated the composer of their archenemy's hymn much better than they did the creator of their own Marseillaise. They had entered Vienna on 13 May, just one week prior to the battle of Aspern, Napoleon's first defeat. Apparently it was Napoleon personally who placed an honor guard in front of Haydn's house to spare him molestations, and a few days later, when the news came that Haydn was mortally ill, loads of straw were spread in front of his house in order to muffle the noise of wagons and cannon rattling by. Haydn's house (purchased from the proceeds of his English visits) was in Gumpendorf, then a village outside the city walls, and the main approach to the city from the west was via the Gumpendorfer Straße, directly past Haydn's house. Haydn's last visitor was a French officer, Clément Sulemy, captain of hussars and a gifted musician, who called on 17 May to pay his respect. He sang for Haydn, who was confined to bed, the aria "In

---

[15]*Ibid.*, pp. 55-59.

Native Worth" from the *Creation*. Haydn was deeply moved, had himself helped up from his bed and embraced his visitor. It may well have been Sulemy's last song as well, for he was killed in action at Aspern four days later, even before Haydn died.

But back to 1797 and to the likes of Saurau and Haschka, Haydn's unlikely companions in creating his masterpiece. Haschka, with his excellent connections, quickly made his way. He became the custodian of the Imperial and Royal University Library and a professor of aesthetics at the Theresianum Academy. Saurau continued in his efforts to protect Austria from the rebels. This determined suppressor of the slightest flicker of democratic sympathies turned to the people of Vienna in April, two months after the making of the hymn. The military situation had become critical, and Saurau urged the stalwart citizenry of Vienna to prove once again their love for the emperor and prepare for the defense of the capital. He charged the city council and the trade guilds with carrying out the details, and one week after his appeal 37,600 untrained men, the so-called *Wiener Aufgebot* (Viennese contingent) of 1797, were ready and eager to give their lives. Even their upkeep was paid for by the citizenry of Vienna rather than by the national government. Among them there was, for example, a youth of not quite sixteen named Ignaz Castelli, who was to become a playwright and a poet and later wrote a vivid description of his brief adventure at soldiering.[16] It was a kind fate indeed that kept the Viennese volunteer corps from being employed against Napoleon's crack troops. But quite aside from the poignancy of their results, the propagandistic efforts of Saurau and others had borne rich fruit, and the new national anthem no doubt had contributed its share in firing up the sentiments. The gathering of the *Wiener Aufgebot* resulted in a small flood of patriotic poetry, and the authorities were well aware of the value of such contributions in the manipulation of public opinion.

If one chooses to view Austria's patriotic literature of the Napoleonic era as a whole, the efforts of the 1790s, including the hymn, constitute only the beginnings of this movement. The main thrust occurred in the first decade of the new century. In 1804

---

[16]Ignaz F. Castelli, *Memoiren meines Lebens* (4 vols., Vienna and Prague, 1861), I, 69-83.

both Francis and Napoleon assumed the title of emperor, of Austria and France respectively, after very complicated deals of mutual recognition. For a two-year span Francis was emperor both of the Holy Roman Empire and of Austria, still a subdivision of the former, an absurdity about which, for example, Talleyrand, Napoleon's foreign secretary, cracked jokes in public.[17]

The establishment of a new empire called for literary support. One obvious medium, especially in Austria, was the theater. A broad wave of patriotic plays swept across the stages. Its first torchbearer was the historiographer Joseph Hormayr, who held forth on the virtues of historical plays in the salon of Caroline Pichler and initiated the efforts by writing two plays himself, *Friedrich von Österreich* (1805) and *Leopold der Schöne* (1806). Almost all of these plays have been justly forgotten, but some continue to be mentioned in literary histories, for example the tragedy *Zriny*, by an occasional visitor from Germany, Theodor Körner. It was played in Vienna alone over a hundred times. Grillparzer's *Ottokar* (1823) came too late to be part of this wave, but it should be noted that the Ottokar story was popular among playwrights of the time and that there were no less than nine Ottokar plays between 1785 and Grillparzer's.[18]

The literary efforts reached a peak in 1809, and the German-speaking countries were not the only ones where the power of the word had been discovered. A person as sober-minded as Napoleon instructed his minister of the interior in September 1808 to generate rousing songs for his troops and even furnished him with ideas as to the nature and content of songs for troops being sent to Spain.[19] Archduke John was another "highly placed personage" who took great interest in the literary aspect of the war. He collected anti-Napoleonic flyers from England and Spain and passed them on to Hormayr, Friedrich Schlegel and other literati for translation or other methods of utilization. Count Stadion,

---

[17] Eduard Wertheimer, *Geschichte Österreichs und Ungarns im ersten Jahrzehnt des 19. Jahrhunderts* (2 vols., Leipzig, 1884-1890), I, 198.

[18] Josef Wihan, "Matthäus von Collin und die patriotisch-nationalen Kunstbestrebungen in Österreich zu Beginn des 19. Jahrhunderts." *Euphorion*, Ergänzungsheft 5 (1910), 168.

[19] *Achtzehnhundertneun: Die politische Lyrik des Kriegsjahres*, ed. Robert F. Arnold and Karl Wagner (Vienna, 1909), p. 129.

who had replaced Cobenzl as Chancellor in 1805, worked furiously to transport the population to a high degree of patriotic excitement. One observer commented that all moderation had been thrown to the winds and that one could hear language with a "Jacobin flavor."[20] In specially called gatherings, war songs were sung, and theaters presented nothing but occasional plays written with the sole purpose of exciting the audience. In 1808, Heinrich von Collin had received from an unidentified high authority an assignment to write songs for the militia, the *Landwehr*. Collin was eager to respond, and in 1809, before the outbreak of the war, his "Lieder österreichischer Wehrmänner" (Songs of Austrian Militiamen) appeared. In a preface Collin quite superfluously explained that they were to inspire Austria's militia with courage and heroic virtue. The feelings to be aroused were patriotic, but not national. Firing national or ethnic sentiments was a strict taboo in multi-national Austria. The word "deutsch," for example, does not occur a single time in all of Collin's *Wehrmänner* songs. Here lies a crucial difference between the Austrian and the German brand of patriotism of the time. It is of interest that Collin's poems, like the national anthem, were translated quickly into some of the other tongues spoken in the empire, among them Czech, Polish and Slovene.

The contribution to the war effort by another poet of the period, Ignaz Castelli, veteran of the *Wiener Aufgebot* of 1797, deserves mention. Castelli wrote a poem of seventeen stanzas, "Kriegslied für die österreichische Armee" (War Song for the Austrian Army). It was printed in a huge edition (Castelli's own figures vary between 100,000 and 300,000) and distributed among the soldiers by the direct order of Archduke Charles. It begins:

> Hinaus, hinaus mit frohem Muth!
> Hinaus ins Feld der Ehre,
> Damit der Feinde Übermuth
> Nicht unsrer Brüder Hab' und Gut
> Und unser Land verheere!
>
> (Onward with fresh courage!
> To the field of honor,

---

[20]Wertheimer, *Geschichte Österreichs und Ungarns* II, 281.

Lest the enemy's arrogance
Devastate our brothers' goods
and our country!)[21]

Distinctive imagery and rhetorical originality were not among the virtues of this genre. In a later collection of the patriotic poetry of 1809,[22] sixteen of the poems begin with the adverbial imperative "Auf!" But Castelli's poem could have easily become the poet's undoing. When copies of it were found on captured and fallen Austrian soldiers, Castelli's name was proscribed by Napoleon's order (as was Collin's), meaning that the poet would be shot if caught. The fate of another "Literat" (man of letters), the bookseller Johann Palm, three years earlier, had shown that Napoleon was prone to carry out such threats. Since French forces were approaching Vienna, Castelli, who did not have the means to undertake an expensive journey on his own, sought the help of the authorities, certain that it would be given to a persecuted patriot. He managed to obtain an audience with Emperor Francis, the brother of Archduke Charles whose order to distribute the poem had been the cause of Castelli's troubles to begin with. What happened during this audience shows that Austria's literary war effort was not necessarily pursued in all quarters, or that the left hand did not always know what the right hand was doing. Castelli explained the situation to the emperor and asked to be made part of the personnel that accompanied daily shipments of imperial treasures and important papers down the Danube into Hungary—a fair enough request. The emperor demanded to see proof of Castelli's proscription and the poet humbly presented a copy of the French *Moniteur* containing the note. After reading it the emperor demanded harshly: "So you have written a war song? And who ordered you to do so?"[23] Castelli, "as if struck by thunder," considered the audience over and left respectfully. Nevertheless he managed to join the crew of a vessel of the provincial diet and helped transport, by water and land, a shipment of fifteen crates deep into Hungary. They had reached Temesvar, not too far from

---

[21]*Achtzehnhundertneun*, 62.
[22]See note 19.
[23]Castelli, I, 154.

the safety of the border to the Ottoman Empire, when peace was concluded and they could return.

Imperial indifference to war literature notwithstanding, the population of Vienna was unanimous in its enthusiasm for Habsburg before Vienna was taken by Napoleon in May. There is a report about one musical academy of March 1809 by the composer and friend of Goethe's, Johann Friedrich Reichardt, who wrote that the program was arranged only by the dictates of patriotic enthusiasm. Trying to convey the atmosphere of the event, Reichardt describes how the audience often joined in, singing along part of each verse in a state of wild frenzy. Special outbursts of enthusiasm greeted one song by Collin, "Österreich über alles," with the opening lines:

> Wenn es nur will
> Ist immer Österreich über alles
>
> (If it only wants to
> Austria is always above all else)

There were loud screams, clapping, jubilation, and sobs, from the imperial box down to the pit.[24] It turns out that the famous "Deutschland, Deutschland über alles" by Hoffmann von Fallersleben has a colorful history. Adding "über alles" to the name of a country was by no means Hoffmann's invention. The version "Österreich über alles" appeared as the title of an economic treatise by Philip Wilhelm von Hörnigk as far back as 1684, *Österreich Über alles, wann es nur will. Das ist: wohlmeinender Fürschlag, Wie mittelst einer wohlbestellten Landes-Oeconomie, die Kayserl. Erbland in kurzem über alle andere Staat von Europa zu erheben. Durch einen Liebhaber der Kayserl. Erbland Wohlfahrt* (*Austria above all else, if only it wants to. That is, a well-meaning suggestion how the imperial dominions can be raised above all other European countries by means of a sound national economy. By a friend of the imperial dominions.*) The book was widely read, used throughout the eighteenth century, and reprinted some twelve times. Even Emperor Joseph II used it as a guide for his econ-

---

[24]Wihan, p. 129.

omic policy. A variation of the title was used in 1786 in a pamphlet "Frankreich über alles, wenn es nur könnte" (France above all else if only it could). In 1798 one Philip von Gemmingen began issuing a periodical by the name of *Teutschland über alles, wenn es nur will* (*Germany above all else if only it wants to*).[25] In 1801 the phrase "Österreich über alles" reappears as the last line of an anonymous pamphlet, "Es ist Friede" (There is peace) and eight years after that in Collin's above-mentioned poem, which quickly became the most famous in the Wehrmänner cycle. It was sung, for example, at the end of a play, *Unterthanenliebe*, by one Joseph Gleich, performed in Vienna in April 1809.[26] Even Beethoven jotted down the first few lines in a notebook, and it is possible that he had planned to set the poem to music.[27] A musical setting by C.F. Schwenke appeared in Hamburg and Mainz in 1813, with a variation of the opening lines, "Wenn es nur will, ist immer Teutschland über alles!"[28] It is only a small step from here to Hoffmann von Fallersleben (whose name, incidentally, Heinrich Heine could not resist rhyming with "sich übergeben" [to nauseate]). Hoffmann merely used a more than well-established rhetorical topos when writing his poem in 1841, and his one stroke of genius, of course, was making his words go with Haydn's popular tune. But we should note that Austria supplied Germany not only with the melody to its later national anthem, but with the models for its text as well.

Judging from the experiences of the twentieth century, we tend to shrug off the effect of inspiring literature on the soldiers in the trenches. The reality of war has little to do with the elevated rhetoric of war poets, and the genre, as a whole, disappeared at the end of the first world war at the latest. But in the Napoleonic era, if one can believe the reports of eyewitnesses, soldiers were inspired by songs and even sang them in the midst of battle. A bulletin from the Austrian headquarters of 17 April 1809 states: "Die Truppen sind von einem vortrefflichen Geiste beseelt und

---

[25]Robert F. Arnold, "Deutschland, Deutschland über alles," *Zeitschrift für Wortforschung*, IV (1903) and VIII (1906/7), IV, 325.
[26]Arnold, VIII, 4.
[27]*Achtzehnhundertneun*, pp. 342-343.
[28]Arnold, VIII, 4.

singen Kriegslieder unter dem Donner des Geschützes" (The troops are in excellent spirit and are singing war songs amid the thunder of cannon). And the battle of Aspern on 21 May supposedly began with troops singing "jubelnde Kriegslieder" (exultant war songs).[29] But the unfortunate ending of the campaign of 1809 may have contributed to a toning down of the enthusiasm in 1813, when the emperor gave strict orders that all passionate outbreaks were to be avoided.[30]

Two names, so far, have been mentioned in connection with Austria's literary efforts that do not seem to have a place there: Theodor Körner and Friedrich Schlegel. Was there an infiltration of German Romanticists into the Austrian scene? There was indeed an influx in the critical years. After Prussia's defeat in 1806 many patriots, and especially the writers among them, turned their hopes to Austria. In the fall of 1807 August Wilhelm Schlegel appeared in Vienna, accompanied by Madame de Staël, in June 1808 brother Friedrich followed, and in August of the same year Ludwig Tieck. Leo von Seckendorff and Karl August Varnhagen joined the Austrian forces. Varnhagen fought at Aspern and Wagram, where he was critically wounded. Seckendorff, who served as a captain in the *Landwehr*, was wounded at Ebelsberg and died when the house to which he had been taken caught on fire. Heinrich von Kleist was more fortunate. He travelled to Austria on foot with Friedrich Dahlmann, wandered about the battlefield of Aspern two days after the battle, and both men were promptly arrested as French spies by the circumspect Austrian authorities. To prove his innocence and loyalty, Kleist produced a few of his own patriotic poems, with the remarkable result that some Austrian officers reproached him for sticking his nose into things that were of no concern to a loyal subject. It required the personal intervention of Field Marshal Count Hiller to set the two of them free.[31] In August 1811 Theodor Körner arrived in Vienna and joined the circle around Friedrich Schlegel. The imprint left by the Schlegel brothers was surely the most profound. August

---

[29]*Ibid.*
[30]*Achtzehnhundertneun*, p. 285.
[31]Helmut Sembdner, ed., *Heinrich von Kleists Lebensspuren* (2nd ed., Bremen, 1964), pp. 292-93.

Wilhelm held his lectures "Über dramatische Kunst und Literatur" (Concerning dramatic art and literature) early in 1808, pointing to the historical tragedy as the supreme genre of Romantic literature, especially the tragedy with national themes. His advice was eagerly heeded by a generation of playwrights. Friedrich's activities in Austria lie in a different area. Aside from contributing patriotic poetry, he had been working, since the summer of 1808, in the *Staatskanzlei* (state chancellery) in a section which we now would call the press bureau, and after war was declared on France on 15 April 1809, he was a *Hofkriegssekretär* (imperial war secretary) in the *Geheime Kanzlei* (privy chancellery) of the supreme commander, Archduke Charles. In this capacity he authored most of the proclamations that appeared over Charles' signature, some of them composed in very stirring prose. The irreverent Viennese made his presence and activities, and those of another German immigrant in government service, Friedrich Gentz, a butt of their jokes and said, playing on the juxtaposition of the abundance of spiritual food versus the need for the material kind, that the soldiers were really well off now because they had "Gäns-Schlegel" ("goose legs," or what we call drumsticks). Schlegel was not the most popular person in the headquarters. Without the slightest conception of the military aspect of warfare he made a nuisance of himself buttonholing preoccupied staff officers and generals and addressing them with an unmilitary "Hören Sie mal" (hey, listen). When it began to dawn on him that the campaign was not going well and when the archduke no longer needed new proclamations, Schlegel left Charles' headquarters posthaste in a reasonable easterly direction and made it all the way to Budapest.[32]

Finally, the later fortunes of the national anthem are worth mentioning briefly. Haydn's hymn remained Austria's anthem to the end of the empire. Naturally, the text had to be changed when Emperor Francis was out of the picture. Simply replacing "Franz" with "Ferdinand" would not work for rhythmic reasons. A new text had to be found, and the search was accompanied by a good deal of trouble. Chancellor Metternich had a contest arranged and fourteen texts were submitted, some by distinguished authors such as Grillparzer. But Metternich's *Staatskanzleirat* (State Chancellery

---

[32]*Achtzehnhundertneun*, pp. 317-318.

Councillor) Karl Jarcke, a man from North Germany, had included a ringer, a compatriot of his, the poet Carl von Holtei. Holtei's was a feeble concoction with an awkward refrain:

> Ja, den Kaiser Gott erhalte
> Unsern Kaiser Ferdinand
>
> (Indeed, God save the emperor
> our good Emperor Ferdinand)

The stressed "Ja," the Viennese quickly noted, resembled the braying of a donkey. A sardonic countertext sprang up immediately, with the opening line "Auf dem Ballplatz sitzt ein Preuße" (a Prussian is sitting in the chancellery). A different text had to be chosen, this time one by the Austrian Joseph von Zedlitz, which was used until 1848. Then the wise decision was made to omit the emperor's name from the text altogether, since "Franz Joseph" would have been a complete rhythmic disaster. The new text:

> Gott erhalte, Gott beschütze
> Unsern Kaiser, unser Land
>
> (God save and protect
> Our emperor and our country)

by Johann Gabriel Seidl was ready for Francis Joseph's wedding in 1854 and prevailed as long as the monarchy did. What was substituted for it in 1920, a text by Karl Renner with music by Wilhelm Kienzl, did not catch on. In 1929 Haydn's melody was reinstated with a new text by Ottokar Kernstock:

> Sei gesegnet ohne Ende
> Heimaterde wunderhold
>
> (Be blessed forever
> beloved fatherland)

which did not catch on either. In 1938, as we know, an existing and well-known text was substituted, and today Austrians do not quite agree on whether or not that one caught on. After 1945 an entirely new hymn was created, with a text by Paula Preradović and a melody that is perhaps by Mozart. But the old "Kaiserlied" has not been buried altogether in Austria. It was played, for example, during the requiem mass for Empress Zita in Saint Stephen's cathedral in Vienna in April 1989, as a tribute to the consort of the last ruler of the monarchy.

What happened to Haydn's melody in Germany? Hoffmann's poem of 1841 was promptly forbidden in almost all German states because of its anti-dynastic message and its appeal for a united country. It did not even become the anthem after Germany *was* unified in 1871. It was, absurdly, during the Weimar Republic, in August 1922, under the presidency of the Social Democrat Friedrich Ebert, that "Deutschland, Deutschland über alles" was made Germany's official national anthem. After 1933 it was augmented by the "Horst-Wessel-Lied," a combination to which one should have objected if for no other reason than at least on musical grounds. After 1945 West Germany wisely retained Joseph Haydn's tune rather than Horst Wessel's, but not Hoffmann's controversial words. Eventually his uninspired third stanza was found to be acceptable and is the current text. (It is axiomatic of national anthems that the lyrics of subsequent stanzas grow progressively worse.) In the end the anthem is still at its best when played without words, as it was by the organist at Saint Stephen's during Empress Zita's obsequies or by the Russian army band at Helmut Kohl's arrival in Moscow.

THE *WIENER ZEITUNG* REPORTS ON THE FRENCH REVOLUTION

by

Alex Balisch

The general assessment in historical writing is that the Central European newspapers of the period of the French Revolution misunderstood much of what was happening in France. It is held that the press portrayed the beginning stages of the revolution as just a reform movement in the spirit of the Enlightenment, comparable to the reforming activities of the Habsburg emperor Joseph II. Even an article on the history of the *Wiener Zeitung* in the *Festschrift* commemorating the 250th anniversary of the paper presents this view.[1] It is also maintained that only the proclamation of the republic in France and the execution of the royal couple brought about a swing towards anti-French and anti-revolutionary attitudes. That such a change of attitude occurred in the Austrian press under Francis II is correct. The postulation, however, that the press was unaware of the true nature of the events in France and presented only the official viewpoint of the Austrian government, needs revision. Before examining this matter, however, the general conditions of the newspapers in Central Europe during that period shall be examined briefly.

At the time of the French Revolution the press was a relatively new institution. If one disregards the predecessors of regularly appearing newspapers (broadsheets, simple news sheets, trade fair

---

[1]Wilhelm Böhm, "Geschichte der *Wiener Zeitung*" in *Festschrift 250 Jahre Wiener Zeitung* (Vienna, 1953).

news, and the like), newspapers with fairly regular publication could then look back on a history of only about one hundred years. The irregularly appearing news sheets and broadsheets cannot be called true newspapers in our modern sense, as they appeared only when news-worthy events occurred and as they had no fixed name or title.

Partly as a backlash from the Reformation, censorship of all publications became more stringent and newspapers were subjected to a censorship which varied in severity. In the Catholic South the Jesuits acquired near complete control over censorship.

During the seventeenth century, newspapers published on a regular basis appeared in several parts of the Germanies but unfortunately, very little is extant from this period. However, it has been established that in some major centers of Central Europe weekly newspapers existed.[2] The major newspapers secured for themselves the services of correspondents in the larger European centers who transmitted their reports through the *Ordinary Post* and with increasing frequency also through *Extra-ordinary Post* relay messengers.[3] The names of these correspondents are nearly impossible to ascertain as they obviously kept their involvement and connection with newspapers a secret in order to protect themselves. Considering the often very accurate information they supplied, one can presume that these correspondents were themselves influential people or at least were in social contact with people of influence. Frequently, however, newspapers simply reprinted (pirated), reports from other newspapers. These practices lasted well into the nineteenth century with few improvements.

Political and religious restraints upon the inhabitants of the Habsburg lands resulted in the suppression of any freedom of the young press. Newspapers, in order to survive, restricted themselves to the reporting of news without editorializing or offering criticism. Any critics of existing religious or political conditions had to resort to anonymous *Flugschriften* (broadsheets). This condition survived until the late eighteenth century, and it was

---

[2]For a comprehensive treatment of the development of German-language newspapers see: L. Salomon, *Geschichte des deutschen Zeitungswesens* (Aalen, 1973).

[3]Salomon, p. 39.

under these circumstances that the press in Austria emerged.

The paper which during the eighteenth century developed into the most important newspaper in the Habsburg monarchy was the *Wienerisches Diarium*, in 1780 re-named *Wiener Zeitung*. Still published today, it is one of the oldest newspapers of Europe. The newspapers which had appeared during the seventeenth century never reached a high level nor did they last long into the eighteenth century. The *Diarium*, when its first issue appeared on 8 August 1703, thus had little competition. The monopoly its owners held with the privilege to publish official decrees and governmental announcements, gave it the appearance of a government-run paper.[4] However, this was, in fact not so. The *Wiener Zeitung* remained a privately owned paper throughout the eighteenth century, operating under and protected by imperial privilege. (Only in 1857 was its publication taken over by the state[5]). However, during most of the eighteenth century it was the only newspaper of any significance in the imperial capital. (During the eighteenth century the paper appeared every Wednesday and Saturday).

The strict censorship under Charles VI (1711-40) and Maria Theresa (1740-80) had an extremely detrimental influence on the development of critical journalism. The publishers retained their practice of printing news without comment and carefully avoided anything which might arouse the displeasure of the censors. News items were reported as they were received from the correspondents. In the publication of news from within the monarchy, the *Wiener Zeitung* was restricted to using only official releases from the government.

Joseph II in the second year of his reign (1781) issued the new edict on censorship, which brought a nearly complete relaxation of censorship although not a complete freedom of the press.[6] Only little space is devoted in the edict to the periodical press, especially newspapers, and restrictions applied only to internal

---

[4]Salomon, p. 218, also *Festschrift 250 Jahre*. This was public opinion in Europe in the eighteenth century.
[5]Böhm "Geschichte der Wiener Zeitung," p. 29.
[6]Kurt Strasser, *Die Wiener Presse in der Josephinischen Zeit* (Vienna, 1962), pp. 10ff.

affairs of the monarchy and the court. The reporting of foreign news was hardly affected by the provisions of the edict as long as it did not affect or relate to measures or actions by the imperial government. How often the governmental office of censorship (the Court Book Censorship Commission [*Bücherzensur Hofkommission*] actually intervened and censored such articles can no longer be ascertained as most relevant documents were destroyed in the fire in the Palace of Justice in Vienna in 1927. Obviously, the *Wiener Zeitung* preferred to practice caution and, even during Joseph II's reign, refrained from editorializing and printing interpretative reporting. Occasionally, however, editorial opinion seems to reveal itself through the selection of phrasing or tone of the reports. On the other hand, it cannot be proven whether this selection and tone originated with the correspondents of the *Wiener Zeitung*, who were never identified, or with the editor. An attempt was obviously made to print only information from reliable sources, and occasionally one finds a warning that the following report's reliability could not be ascertained.

After the death of Joseph II in 1790, and especially with the beginning of the reign of Francis I (1792), the censorship was again gradually intensified.

The reports in the *Wiener Zeitung* showed that the publishers were well aware of the troubles of the French monarchy in the 1780's, and they recognized as one of the main factors of these troubles the unequal incidence and ineffective collection of taxes. The opposition of clergy and part of the nobility to the proposed tax reforms was duly reported and the tone of the reports suggests that the paper's correspondents were familiar with the demands of the bourgeoisie.

The immediate and widespread opposition to the edicts of 8 May 1788, which restricted the powers of the *parlements*, was reported in detail, and the readers were given a detailed explanation of the organization and traditional powers of the French *parlements*. Several issues during June and July 1788 in fact contained a short course in French constitutional structure.

It was at this point that the *Wiener Zeitung* recognized the imminent danger for the French monarchy and expressed fear of possible civil war. The unrest in the provinces certainly justified these fears. The first news of the king's intention to call the Estates General was reported in the issue of 26 July 1788 and one month later the projected date of the opening was reported as 1 May 1789. The paper at once reported that the constitution of the Estates General on the basis of 1614 would cause great dissatisfaction among the Third Estate. On 10 December 1788 the *Wiener Zeitung* stated that "the vast majority of the nation opposes this arrangement and demands as only just that the middle classes, who up till now . . . have been practically ignored, should be given the rights they deserve in this state which they nearly exclusively support, feed and enrich." Equally, the injustice of the system of taxation is illustrated with figures showing the burden put on the shoulders of the bourgeoisie in comparison to the small contribution made by the nobility. Similar reports appeared in several issues of the *Wiener Zeitung* throughout December 1788.

Considering the accurate reports of the negotiations of the *parlements* and the notables and of official announcements from the government, it is maybe odd that only indirect mention[7] is made off the pamphlet-campaign of the last months of 1788.

On the other hand, from January 1789 on, several reports stressed both the demands of the Third Estate for double representation and voting by head, as well as the violent opposition to these demands by the privileged orders. On 10 January 1789 the *Wiener Zeitung* expressed the fear of the dangerous division developing out of this disagreement and pointed to the indecision of the court.

The drawing up of the *cahiers*, the election of deputies, and the opening of the Estates General was reported in great detail and some of the speeches of king and ministers were reprinted in full in accurate translations. Nearly immediately the *Wiener Zeitung* pointed to the seemingly unbridgeable cleft between the Third Estate and the privileged orders.

From here on the *Wiener Zeitung* identified its sources of information as "letters from Paris" and as the "official diary of the Estates."[8] The most important speeches, topics of debates, and resolutions are reported in great detail and with admirable accuracy and perception.

The proposal by Abbé Sieyès of 10 June 1789 to make a last

---

[7]By reference to "many voices of discontent and criticism."
[8]*Wiener Zeitung*, 24 June 1799, p. 1603.

attempt to persuade the privileged orders to join with the Third Estate and, in case of refusal, to constitute the Third Estate independently was reported on 1 July and on 4 July, the *Wiener Zeitung* reported that the middle classes "had actually constituted themselves as the National Assembly."

Quite correctly the paper recognized the threat of riots as one of the reasons why Louis XVI finally on 27 June (reported on 4 July) ordered the fusion of the three orders. On 22 July the *Wiener Zeitung* reported that this fusion unfortunately did not remove the conflicts between the orders and that the king was still lending his ear to persons who did not have the welfare and unity of the nation at heart. Although the reports did not spell it out, it must have been clear to the readers of the *Wiener Zeitung* that the vacillating attitude of the king was much to blame for the developments.

The news of the storming of the Bastille appeared in the *Wiener Zeitung* on 29 July with further details in the two following numbers. That the mob wanted to confiscate arms and not liberate prisoners, although not explicitly stated, becomes clear from the context which included reports on preceding attempts by the mob to acquire arms.

The *Wiener Zeitung* missed little of the events of the following months and continued to give full coverage of the news from France.

The detailed report on 2 September from France of events from 4 to 11 August signifying the end of the Old Regime pointed out the epoch-making significance of these measures. The "Declaration of the Rights of Man" too, received its deserved recognition by a verbatim translation.

On 21 October 1789 the *Wiener Zeitung* used for the first time the term "Revolution" in reference to the events in France. However, the term was applied specifically to the unrest and riots which had erupted in Paris as a result of the mockery of the National Assembly by the nobility and the royal couple during the royal banquet on 1 October 1789. Only from July 1791 onward was the term "Revolution" applied in our modern sense to the developments as a whole.

The reports from France thus far, had been factual, unemotional, but with editorial approval clearly showing between the lines. Therefore, it is surprising—and there seems to be no explanation for it—that the *Wiener Zeitung* published, as an insert without comment, a private letter from an unnamed Parisian which contained vehement, fanatic accusations against the leading men of the National Assembly, especially the Duke of Orléans and Mirabeau.[9] What prompted the editor to reprint this violently anti-revolutionary letter can no more be ascertained. It is somewhat puzzling as the paper reverted in its next issue to its normal factual and unemotional style of reporting which it maintained until the outbreak of the war in 1792. Even for some time thereafter the *Wiener Zeitung* refrained from such violent tirades against the French authorities. And it is noteworthy that the *Wiener Zeitung* reported the increasing friction between the Austrian and the French governments in an extremely sketchy manner. The declaration of war by France on 20 April 1792 is not reported at all and the late May issues—without preparation—bring occasional reports about the early stage of hostilities. A possible explanation is that the outbreak of hostilities between France and Austria had been made public in Vienna by posters (*Anschlagzettel*) and the *Wiener Zeitung* found it unnecessary to repeat what already was common knowledge. Only in June did official statements by the Austrian government appear, explaining the events leading up to the war and from this time on the *Wiener Zeitung* began to publish official Austrian war reports, a sign of the growing interest of the Austrian government in the press. However, the paper continued to use largely direct reports by correspondents from Paris or reprints from French newspapers.

From the beginning of the war the Austrian government exerted increasing influence on the reporting of foreign news, especially concerning the war. Wilhelm Böhm in his "History of the Wiener Zeitung" points to the growing interest of the government in the press and its power to influence public opinion. But the government would not yet decide to transform the *Wiener Zeitung* into an official governmental organ. Only on 2 January 1805, shortly before the renewal of war against Napoleon, did Emperor Francis take this step.[10]

---

[9]*Ibid.*, 4 November 1789, p. 2800.
[10]*Ibid.*, 2 January 1805.

When the attacks by the French radicals against Louis XVI increased in intensity the *Wiener Zeitung* adopted a hostile attitude toward the Jacobins and also reported, with an obvious feeling of horror, the September massacres. The abolition of the monarchy on 21 September 1792 was characterized as "a perpetuation of anarchy."[11] In this context the paper stressed that "how the intervention by foreign courts becomes even more imperative to save that 'great state'."

The reports from now on included editorializing passages in an emotional style which was in dramatic contrast with the earlier dry, factual and impersonal accounts.

The reports of the 'outrageous' trial of Louis, his execution—referred to as regicide—and the excesses of the Terror are an indication of the changing attitudes toward the French Revolution at court, in the press, *and* in public opinion.[12]

Finally, in 1794 the execution of Robespierre was reported with obvious editorial satisfaction, but clearly the editors did not delude themselves into great expectations for the future attitudes of the French authorities, as the bigotry of the Thermidorian reaction was explicitly discussed.

With the establishment of the Directory, the revolution lost its impetus and changed its character. Therefore, the reporting in the *Wiener Zeitung* of the stormy events of the following decades need not be examined here. The *Wiener Zeitung* had, in spite of its initially important factual reporting, recognized the significance of the developments in France very clearly and changed its attitudes, not so much because of pressure from the Austrian government, but because of the changing style and character of the French Revolution and because of the course it took. The general quality of the reporting, its factual quality and the comprehensive coverage of the developments, would stand up well in a comparison with modern reporting. This becomes more noteworthy when one considers that regular newspapers had made their first tentative appearances less than a century before the French Revolution and were still, in many cases, rather unstable enterprises.

---

[11] *Ibid.*, 6 October 1792.
[12] *Ibid.*, see February issues 1793.